THIS CORNER OF CANAAN

A Book Series of Curriculum Studies

William F. Pinar
General Editor

Vol. 19

PETER LANG
New York • Washington, D.C./Baltimore • Bern
Frankfurt am Main • Berlin • Brussels • Vienna • Oxford

Reta Ugena Whitlock

THIS CORNER OF CANAAN

Curriculum Studies of Place
& the Reconstruction of the South

PETER LANG
New York • Washington, D.C./Baltimore • Bern
Frankfurt am Main • Berlin • Brussels • Vienna • Oxford

Library of Congress Cataloging-in-Publication Data

Whitlock, Reta Ugena.
This corner of Canaan: curriculum studies of place
and the reconstruction of the South / Reta Ugena Whitlock.
p. cm. — (Complicated conversation: a book series of curriculum studies; v. 19)
Includes bibliographical references and index.
1. Southern States—Study and teaching. 2. Education—Curricula—Southern States.
3. Southern States—Civilization. 4. Regionalism—Southern States.
5. Group identity—Southern States. 6. American literature—Southern States—
History and criticism. 7. Southern States—Social conditions.
8. Southern States—Religion. I. Title.
F208.5.W48   975.07—dc22   2006025282
ISBN 978-0-8204-8651-2
ISSN 1534-2816

Bibliographic information published by **Die Deutsche Bibliothek**.
Die Deutsche Bibliothek lists this publication in the "Deutsche
Nationalbibliografie"; detailed bibliographic data is available
on the Internet at http://dnb.ddb.de/.

© 2007 Peter Lang Publishing, Inc., New York
29 Broadway, 18th floor, New York, NY 10006
www.peterlang.com

Printed in the United States of America

For my family...

Table of Contents

Preface:
Reconstruction

William F. Pinar

Don't you see? Rage muted becomes nostalgia for a place that never was.
--Reta Ugena Whitlock

And can never be.

Soon after arriving in Louisiana it became obvious that there was an idea that brought me there. Reassembling it from casual comments made by LSU administrators, I discerned there was an expectation that I was bringing with me advanced concepts of education that would enable the state to surge ahead economically. Quite aside from the simplistic assumption that there is a causal relationship between education and prosperity, the idea seemed to me simultaneously self-hating and saturated with the hatred of others. It was self-hating as it implied local Louisianans couldn't figure things out on their own.[1] The idea seemed politically reactionary as it implied limited local responsibility for three centuries of assault on poor whites and all blacks. In effect, we Yankee experts were to clean up the mess three centuries of white racism and elitism had institutionalized.

As impossible—as obnoxious—was the idea that brought me to Baton Rouge in 1985, it forced upon me a set of considerations I had not before fully faced. Promptly—with help—I started to study southern history and culture, study structured by race.[2] The 1991 collection on "place" (Kincheloe and Pinar, 1991) was the initial report of that study of the South, followed by a 1993 collection in which I theorized curriculum as racial text (Castenell and Pinar, 1993). From that preliminary work I focused on the gender of racial politics and violence (2001), then on the genealogy of whiteness (2006a).

During my twenty years at LSU I encouraged several of my brightest Ph.D. students to undertake studies of the South. Susan Edgerton (1991, 1996) was the first to accept this invitation; Ugena Whitlock was among the last (see also Casemore [in press], Jewett, 2006, Ng-A-Fook, 2006). As an emerging specialization within the academic field of education, Southern curriculum studies holds great significance not only for curriculum studies, but for teacher education, the "foundations" of education, as well as for history, literature, and, of course, Southern Studies. I claim the same for the present volume.

Condemnation and Crucifixion

What I am doing is a Southern reconstruction.

--Reta Ugena Whitlock

The institutionalization of rage, revenge, and resurrection—Whitlock works these concepts in Chapters 3 and 4—typifies the political history of the American South. Political violence has fueled the present political ascendancy of the Confederacy.[3] Not only for the sake of the South, but for the sake of the United States, last century's failed Reconstruction must again be undertaken. This time reconstruction cannot be conducted by the federal (Confederate) government, of course. If it occurs at all, reconstruction will occur through the political, intellectual, and psychological labor of the South's own progressives. Due to the very personalism of Southern culture that Whitlock describes and performs, progressives have tended to suspend their activism for the sake of family and friends.[4] For good reason: when Southern progressives—consider the case of George Washington Cable (see Pinar 2001, 92), for instance—did take unpopular stands, their lives were threatened. While physical death is less likely now than in Cable's time, the price of activism remains high.

Despite the price, Reta Ugena Whitlock remains in love with the South. *Because* she loves the South she confronts its nostalgia. "I will not fight any longer for a Lost Cause," she tells us, "but will continue to look to the South for causes worth fighting for." One cause is the hearts and minds of Southern schoolchildren. One central site of that struggle is the school curriculum, as conservatives have long known.[5] Focused on the curriculum—the meaning of the past for the present and our prospects for the future—Whitlock appreciates that political culture both informs and is informed by what students study. Because it is "culture" white Southerners imagine they are "protecting" when they vote for conservative candidates, culture is one sphere that must be reconstructed. The reconstruction of culture occurs through the education of the public.

Wryly, Whitlock acknowledges that "reconstruction is a volatile word in the context of Southern studies." Not only the word's association with events 140 years ago is in play here, the very construct of reconstruction contests the conservatism to which so many white Southerners cling. Recall that social reconstruction (and not just of the South) was the primary educational aspiration of many progressives 75 years ago, progressives still vilified by conservative politicians and scholars (see, for instance, Ravitch 2001).

Social reconstruction requires the racial restructuring of the South. Whitlock works to unravel the knot that is white racism, its compact and convoluted interconnections with home, family, class, and church. By confronting whites (and in particular, neo-Confederate white men), Whitlock contributes to the dissolution of whiteness and to the racial restructuring of the South and the nation.

For Southerners, the site of confrontation between an unreconstructed past, a reactionary present, and a progressive future is not only the lunch-counter, the bus, the school: it is the home. "Home is not a sanctuary," Whitlock appreciates, no "place of safety and comfort. It is a place of reconstruction, of the working through." Home is where Whitlock asserts both her religious fundamentalism and her queer identity. "Fundamentalism is my native tongue," she tells us, "and I speak it now, but queerly."

No curse of the Covenant, Whitlock's speaking in tongues performs the labor of reparation.[6] It is labor simultaneously intellectual and spiritual:

> I therefore want to reveal the complexities, paradoxes, anomalies of spirit
> and desire that I bear witness to as a queer fundamentalist—not a funda-
> mentalist, not a lesbian woman void of other identity experiences, not a
> critic with an overdetermined attachment to one theoretical discourse, per-
> spective, or ground for thinking—but as a person with truly problematic
> and contradictory identifications and desires.

Demonstrating Aoki's (2005 [1985/1991], 232) crucial concept of
"creative tensionality," Whitlock teaches "ethically from within the
tension of these contradictions." Declining to abandon her faith, her
sexuality or her home, embracing contradiction and tension: Ugena
testifies to the reciprocity of psychic and social reconstruction
through reparation.[7]

It is precisely the complexity of tension that is suppressed in the
literalism many fundamentalists—Christian, Islamic—embrace. In
their insistence on certainty, on a bifurcated world of good and evil,
many fundamentalists vacate the earth in an anti-intellectual, trea-
sonous "rapture" in which the fate of the nation is a casualty of individual "salvation." While the United States has suffered religious
extremists from its genocidal genesis, it was only during the "radical"
racism of the late nineteenth-century South—the apex of—that religious fundamentalism spread throughout the South. Historian Joel
Williamson (1984) argues that the latter was a function of the former.

Not only Southern fundamentalism follows from nineteenth-
century radical racism. I argue that many contemporary white Southerners' "conservative" values—Black and Black (1992, 9) list "traditional family values, the importance of religion, support for capital
punishment, and opposition to gun control" and I would add opposition to abortion and to civil rights for lesbians and gay men—preserve
traces of earlier racist recalcitrance. The reactionary rage that animates some white southerners' engagement with these issues pro-
vides the clue to the presence of the past. While southern
"conservatism" cannot be reduced to residues of racial hatred—it is
broader and more complex than that—it cannot be understood apart
from it either. What Lillian Smith understood to be true in the South
over fifty years ago reverberates still:

Southern tradition, segregation, states' rights have soaked up the fears of our people; little private fantasies of childhood have crept there for hiding, unacknowledged arsenals of hate have been stored there, and a loyalty covering up a lack of self-criticism has glazed the words over with sanctity. No wonder the saying of them aloud can stir anxieties until there are times when it seems we have lost our grasp on reality. (Smith, 1963 [1949], 135).

It is nothing less than the reconstruction of "reality" that is at stake in the curriculum development[8] Whitlock has undertaken.

Communion

[C]onversation is inextricably linked to communion.
--Reta Ugena Whitlock

Speaking the language of Christian fundamentalism, Ugena reminds her fellow fundamentalists that human hatred—whether in the form of homophobia, racism, sexism, classism, or ageism—destroys spirituality. "Celebrating the agency of all people," she admonishes, "strengthens the spirit—both our individual and collective spirits." Appealing for openness, trust and dialogue, Whitlock calls for unity in diversity: "When we begin and end with love, we confront discomfort, fear and rage with openness, not narrowness; peace, not violence." Whitlock is not only sagacious; she is savvy, for in Foucaultian terms, such language constitutes a reverse discourse (see Savran, 1998, 55).

A "reverse" discourse, Didier Eribon (2004, 312) explains, "speak[s] on its own behalf, demand[s] that its legitimacy...be acknowledged, often in the same vocabulary, using the same categories by which it was...disqualified." "What takes place," Eribon (2004, 313) continues, "might be a reappropriation of the meanings power has produced in order to transform their value." In the mouths of conservatives, calls for openness, trust, and dialogue are insincere platitudes in the service of political manipulation. In reclaiming Christianity as a potentially progressive force (as, historically, it was for many African Americans: see Pinar, 2001, 1138), Whitlock "reverses" this insincerity, rendering "communion" no fetishistic displacement of community, but an educational restructuring of privilege and possession. "The language of fundamentalism," Ugena knows, "is a powerful tool."

Unlike the oedipal politics of the enraged straight son, the "misfit" queers the South by haunting it, not in the service of nostalgia, but of reconstruction. In Flannery O'Connor's stories, Ugena tells us, "the Misfit functions to disrupt, and with this rift comes grace." Grace and redemption carry a "price," Whitlock reminds, still using biblical language, and that price is death. "For the South," she asserts, significantly, this means focusing on the death through which grace, and Southern reconstruction, may occur. The South must lay to rest the Lost Cause—through which there will be neither resurrection nor remission of Southern sins.

In the liberation of death—in the "shattering of the white Southern self"—a "new communion of reconstruction" constitutes resurrection, not of the lost cause, but of the democratic cause the South rejected and the North has never realized. By occupying "spaces between sin and redemption," Whitlock continues, the subjectivity of the misfit "troubles truths about good and evil, right and wrong, salvation and damnation."

Concluding the book—it constitutes, I submit, an intellectual breakthrough (see Axelrod, 1979) in Southern Studies—Ugena is reminded of James Macdonald's (1995, 173) "hermeneutic quest" in which curriculum theory is likened to a moment in the meditative hermeneutic cycle. So conceived, Macdonald (1995, 181) explained, "the act of theorizing is an act of faith, a religious act…. What defines [both theory and pedagogy] is the spirit and vision that shines through the surface manifestations."

Inspired by Macdonald, Whitlock writes that "the spirit of curriculum is an *inspirited* curriculum," not only a spiritual and phenomenological concept (see Aoki, 2005 [1987], 359), but a profoundly political one as well. For Whitlock, the inspirited curriculum is one "invigorated with the daily practice of making meaning and transgressing social codes." Adopting Appiah's concept of cosmopolitanism, she suggests, may enable teachers to provide "a curricular forum so that we—strangers all—may, as singular and social citizens of the cosmos, come to the realization that we matter to each other." In such a forum, the study of the South becomes an educational opportunity for communion wherein "Southerners might acknowledge one another and engage one another in conversation about progressive social, cultural, and political movement." It is conversation populated by the past:

> Communion is a common sharing of mourning in the search for hope. In remembrance of bodies lynched, for example, there might be a radicalized communion in which forgiveness is sought, reparation paid. Spiritual and social reparation, ultimately, is the price of Southern restoration, and it is one that some white Southerners are loathe to pay.

Whitlock is one white Southerner ready to pay, one white Southerner who invites other white Southerners to join her in reparation.

Sometimes subtly, sometimes baldly, often humorously, Reta Ugena Whitlock faces her Pharisees and declines both crucifixion and condemnation, offering us instead communion through complicated conversation. In teaching as a misfit, Whitlock disrupts the sacrilegious ceremonies of conservatism and reclaims the—her—South, reconstructing the Confederate States of America as the future home for the progressive United States of America the Declaration of Independence promises us all.

Notes

1   There was little in the scholarly literature in the mid-1980s to articulate a progressive curriculum of place, including for the South. In the collection of essays (Kincheloe and Pinar 1991) introducing the concept of "place" to curriculum studies, I pointed to the educational significance of regional studies generally, as my co-editor—Joe Kincheloe, then teaching in Louisiana, too—emphasized critical theory in understanding curriculum as a form of social psychoanalysis.

2   It was, for me, a return to race. As a senior at Ohio State in 1968, I had enrolled in an experimental urban education program taught by Professor Donald R. Bate-

xviThis Corner of Canaan

man (see Bateman 1974). In that program I was introduced to the work of Paulo Freire, began tutoring in the inner city of Columbus, and prepared to join the pedagogical regiment of the revolution (or so I hoped). As my anxious white mentor teacher watched, I taught black eighth-graders Richard Wright's *Black Boy* and Eldridge Cleaver's *Soul on Ice*. Nixon had been elected president that fall, and soon I realized my role in black liberation was, well, more complicated than I had first appreciated. For a dozen years afterward I focused on the politics and phenomenology of subjectivity, on what later (and through an identity politics prism) would be called whiteness studies. It would take the facticity of Louisiana to force me to confront my own racialization.

3   The denial of basic human rights (presumably guaranteed by the Geneva Accord) to prisoners at Guantanamo, the invasion of Iraq (and its misrepresentation to the American public), the torture at Abu Ghraib: these headline the violence abroad perpetuated by the Republican (read: Confederate) Party. Domestically, the refusal to raise the minimum wage, the anti-gay initiatives (most famously focused on the issue of marriage), exploiting the fear of terrorism and mindless flag-waiving typify the violent tactics of "conservatives" determined to destroy democracy for the sake of God and country (not the USA, I am arguing, the CSA). George W. Bush becomes intelligible as a Confederate—not American—President. Whitlock uses a botanical metaphor to depict the political influence of the South, namely that it "spreads like kudzu through the rest of America." The vine is home-grown, of course, not Asian, and much worse than a nuisance.

4   A character in Lillian Smith's *Strange Fruit* personifies the problem of the Southern progressive. After a lynching,

> Prentiss Reid, editor of *The Maxwell Press*, sat late in his office. Yellow sheets of paper lay in front of him, covered with pencil marks. The town's religious skeptic, the admirer of Tom Paine, the man who fought Prohibition, who had dared raise questions in 1917 about the persecution of aliens, had drawn a blank for tomorrow's editorial. Anything you say now will do more harm than good. That's the trouble. Always the trouble! Say what you think, make a gesture, you stir up a mare's nest. Make things worse than they were before—so they say.
>
> He lit a cigarette; stared at the bookshelf above his desk. *Holy Bible, Common Sense, Age of Reason, Rights of Man*. Four books worn from handling. Pages

marked, words underlined, comments scribbled in the margins. There was
no man in Maxwell who could with so much ease cite Holy Writ in an argument as could the town's infidel; and none who could quote whole pages
from Tom Paine as casually as if from a talk with a friend (Smith, 1972
[1944], 364-365).

What will this progressive Southerner say about the lynching of an innocent
black man? Reid rationalizes his inaction; instead of criticizing his fellow
Southerners, he blames the North.

> Prentiss Reid lit another cigarette; stared into the wall, shrugged, wrote
> rapidly for a few minutes. ".... [B]ut what's done now is done. Bad, yes.
> Lawlessness and violence are always bad. And this particular form smacks
> of the Dark Ages. It hurts business, it hurts the town, it hurts the county, it
> hurts everybody in it. But it's time now to get our minds on our work, get
> back to our jobs, quit this talking. Those who participated in the lynching
> were a lawless bunch of hoodlums. We don't know who they are. They
> ought to be punished. But who are they? No one seems to know.... As for
> northern criticism. There will be plenty. All we can say is: if the damn
> Yankees can handle these folks better than we who've had more than two
> hundred years' practice, let them try it. Lord knows, they're welcome to try
> it. Up there. And we might ask them how about their own gangsters? And
> how about East St. Louis and Chicago? (Smith, 1972 [1944], 367)

These are references to the famous 1917 East St. Louis (see Pinar, 2001, 672) and
1919 Chicago race riots. For Reid, they are excuses to rationalize silence.

5   From evolutionary theory (linked by Southerners to godlessness) to African
     American history and culture (linked by Southerners to the Communism) to re-
     ligious (in)tolerance and now gay and lesbian history and (again, 80 years after
     the Scopes Trial) to evolutionary theory (see Good, 2005), Southerners have led
     the way in denying school children access to the truth (see Zimmerman, 2002).

6   Freud's construction of the primal scene, Ned Lukacher (1986, 44) points out,
     represents an effort to define the "work of reparation in terms of the affirmation
     of the ineluctability of difference and deferral." Supplementing financial pay-
     ments, reparation—in particular, unraveling the knot of whiteness—becomes an
     ongoing "undecidable intertextual event that is situated in the differentiated
     space between historical memory and imaginative construction, between archi-

val verification and interpretative free play" (1986, 24). For me (Pinar 2006a), race is the curse of the Covenant; reparation requires restructuring the relationship between (white, heavenly) father and (sublimated, religious) son.

7   Quoting Fanon (1968, 247)—"the consciousness of the self is not the closing of the door to communication, but guarantees it"—Nigel Gibson (2003, 189) points out that "this 'self which does not close the door to communication develops by undergoing mediation (and therefore self-negation) and only then embraces the other in mutual recognition." In religious and educational (rather than Marxist) terms, Whitlock acknowledges the same reconstructive reciprocity between the subjective and social.

8   After the Reconceptualization, curriculum development is an intellectual—not bureaucratic—labor of study and teaching (Pinar, 2006b).

References

Aoki, Ted T. (2005 [1985/1991]). Signs of vitality in curriculum scholarship. In William F. Pinar and Rita L. Irwin (Eds.), *Curriculum in a new key: The collected works of Ted. T. Aoki* (229-233). Mahwah, NJ: Lawrence Erlbaum.

———. (2005 [1987]). Inspiriting the curriculum. In William F. Pinar and Rita L. Irwin (Eds.), *Curriculum in a new key: The collected works of Ted T. Aoki* (357-365). Mahwah, NJ: Lawrence Erlbaum.

Appiah, Kwane Anthony. (2006). *Cosmopolitanism: Ethics in a world of strangers.* New York: W.W. Norton & Company.

Axelrod, Charles David. (1979). *Studies in intellectual breakthrough.* Amherst: University of Massachusetts Press.

Bateman, Donald R. (1974). The politics of curriculum. In William F. Pinar (Ed.), *Heightened Consciousness, Cultural Revolution, and Curriculum Theory: The Proceedings of the Rochester Conference* (54-68). Berkeley, CA: McCutchan.

Black, Earl and Black, Merle. (1992). *The vital South: How presidents are elected.* Cambridge, MA: Harvard University Press.

Casemore, Brian. (in press). *The Autobiographical Demand of Place: Curriculum Inquiry in the American South.* New York: Peter Lang.

Castenell, Jr., Louis A. and Pinar, William F. (Eds.) (1993). *Understanding curriculum as racial text: Representations of identity and difference in education.* Albany: State University of New York Press.

Edgerton, Susan H. (1991). Particularities of "otherness:" Autobiography, Maya Angelou, and me. In Joe L. Kincheloe and William F. Pinar (Eds.), *Curriculum as Social Psychoanalysis: The Significance of Place* (77-97). Albany, NY: State University of New York Press.

———. (1996). *Translating the curriculum: Multiculturalism into cultural studies.* New York: Routledge.

Eribon, Didier. (2004). *Insult and the making of the gay self.* [Trans. Michael Lucey.] Durham, NC: Duke University Press.

Fanon, Frantz. (1968). *The wretched of the earth.* [Preface by Jean-Paul Sartre. Trans. by Constance Farrington.] New York: Grove Press. [Originally published by François Maspero éditeur, Paris, France, under the title *Les damnés de la terre,* 1961.]

Gibson, Nigel C. (2003). *Fanon: The postcolonial imagination.* Cambridge: Polity.

Good, Ron. (2005). *Scientific and religious habits of mind: Irreconcilable tensions in the curriculum.* New York: Peter Lang.

Jewett, Laura M. (2006). *A delicate dance: Autoethnography, curriculum, and the semblance of intimacy.* Baton Rouge: Louisiana State University, unpublished Ph.D. dissertation.

Kincheloe, Joe L. and Pinar, William F. (Eds.). (1991). *Curriculum as social psychoanalysis: The significance of place.* Albany: State University of New York Press.

Lukacher, Ned. (1986). Primal scenes: Literature, philosophy, psychoanalysis. Ithaca, NY: Cornell University Press.

Macdonald, B. J. (Ed.). (1995). Theory as a prayerful act: The collected essays of James B. Macdonald. New York: Peter Lang.

Ng-A-Fook, Nicholas A. (2006). *Understanding an indigenous curriculum in Louisiana through listening to Houma oral histories.* Baton Rouge: Louisiana State University, unpublished Ph.D. dissertation.

Pinar, William F. (2001). *The gender of racial politics and violence in America.* New York: Peter Lang.

———. (2006a). *Race, religion, and a curriculum of reparation.* New York: Palgrave Macmillan.

———. (2006b). *The synoptic text today: Curriculum development after the reconceptualization.* New York: Peter Lang.

Ravitch, Diane. (2000). *Left back: A century of battles over school reform.* New York: Simon and Schuster.

Savran, David. (1998). *Taking it like a man: White masculinity, masochism, and contemporary American culture*. Princeton, NJ: Princeton University Press.

Smith, Lillian. (1963 [1949]). *Killers of the dream*. [Revised and enlarged edition. First published in 1949 by Norton & Co.] Garden City, NY: Anchor Books.

———. (1972 [1944]). *Strange fruit*. San Diego, CA: Harvest.

Williamson, Joel. (1984). *The crucible of race: Black-white relations in the American South since emancipation*. New York: Oxford University Press.

Zimmerman, Jonathan. (2002). *Whose America? Culture wars in the public schools*. Cambridge, MA: Harvard University Press.

Acknowledgments

I wonder if everybody who has a book published for the first time feels as exhilarated—and tired—as I do. I wonder whether he or she feels proud and pleased and at the same time a bit of an imposter. I wonder if he or she looks back. I do, and I am still pretty amazed at where I've ended up. I'm living a dream I hardly dared to dream, and, like Minnie Pearl, I'm just so proud to be here. But I am not here alone. I would like to acknowledge a few of the people whom I have had the great fortune of encountering along the journey. I heard somewhere that a memory is made when the heart takes a picture. I have been blessed with many vivid heart-pictures of memory to document my trip.

My family has given me great support through their faith in me and my abilities. Know that you are present in this work. Mother and Daddy, thank you for my upbringing and sense of place. I have always wished the same for my own children. I often hear your voices: Just don't forget who you are…, and I try to honor my roots by doing some good. Tracy, my brother, I admire the man you are, and I am glad to know you—glad that you know me. Jessica and Daniel, you teach me daily by reminding me that life does not take place in my head. You are both wonderful people. I love you and believe in you. I thank your father, Robert Hyde, for the wonderful job he does in helping you navigate the rough spots. Layla, I look at you and know joy. You are all home to me.

To Gladys Kopp, precious partner, beautiful woman. Thank you for taking care of the daily life. Without you, this would not have been possible. I can never repay you for your support, kindness, and love. I admire and respect you as a lovely human being and as a teacher and scholar. Your stories captivate my mind, and I envy your narrative voice. You, too, are present in the work.

To my friends and colleagues at the Louisiana Department of Education, I want to express special thanks for support and life-lessons I might have missed were it not for your example and care.

Edeltress Brown and Latikka Magee-Brumfield (members of the unof-
ficial Black Caucus), thank you for making me an honorary member.
It is you who honor me by being my friends. Latikka, beautiful and
assertive, thank you for encouraging me and not letting me get away
with my white-girl whining. Edeltress, I am grateful for the Matthews
cemetery tour of North Louisiana; it helped me talk about my own
sense of place. And Mary Belezaire, everyone should have the opportunity to know someone like you for at least a little while. Without
actually knowing you, I never would have believed you could have
existed. You are talented, resourceful, interesting, and intelligent.

I want to express my appreciation to my fellow graduate students
at LSU. I do not imagine how I could have gotten through the program—the ins and outs of the doctoral process—without your colle-
giality and networking. Sarah Smitherman, Laura Jewett, Nicholas
Ng-A-Fook, thanks for hanging with me at conferences, with and
without the video camera. Donna Truitt is always a thoughtful and
supportive comrade. Brian Casemore and Nichole Guillory, I am so
grateful that you saw all along the journey what I was trying to express and accomplish—and then told me, so that I would also know.
You both raise a pretty high bar, and I'm glad we're friends.

I wish to thank my friends and faculty at KSU, Nita Paris, Lynn
Stallings, Kim Loomis, Kim Gray, Pam Cole, Faith Wallace, Michael
Ross, Binyao Zheng, Guichun Zong, Alice Terry, Beth Marks, Eliza-
beth Johnson, Susan Stockdale, Barbara Salyer, and Marj Econo-
mopoulos, the most extraordinary department chair in the world.
Michelle Cobb, you are a treasure, thank you! To Toni Strieker and
Judy Holzman, who heard me read about homeplace at a KSU conference, of all places, and have offered support each time we pass
each other in the halls; it has meant so much to me.

And to the teachers whom I have loved throughout my student
life—Mrs. Fowler, Mrs. Wimberley, Mrs. Wells, Miss Renwick, Mrs.
Mansell, Dr. Laubenthal—know that you made a difference, continue
to make a difference. Each of you taught by modeling reflection and
caring, a pedagogy I try to embody. At every point along my journey,
I find a teacher who saw the woman I might become. Thank you.

I wish to express my most sincere gratitude to my doctoral committee at LSU: Dr. William Pinar, Dr. Nina Asher, Dr. Mary Aswell Doll, Dr. Katrina Powell, and Dr. Carl Freedman. Thanks also Dr. Petra Munro and Dr. Bill Doll. Thanks to my colleague and friend, Kathryn Benson, also an LSU alum, for the opportunity to collaborate and find spaces of curriculum theory and teacher education. Thank you, Staci Dennis for your painstaking attention to detail and the wealth of technological skills you brought to this project.

I am indebted to Professor Edward Ayers of the University of Virginia for allowing me to steal the Faulkner quote from which the title of this book is taken. He includes it in the chapter, "What We Talk About When We Talk About the South," in his book, *All Over the Map: Rethinking American Regions (1996)*. I appreciate his not pointing out that it took quite a bit of gall for an upstart to lift such a lovely quote after he had done all the legwork.

Finally, thank you, Dr. William Pinar—Bill—for being my mentor, teacher, and friend. You are a kind and gracious scholar. Most of all, I want to thank you for seeing some potential in me that first semester at LSU. I'll end with a story, of course. During my first year as a doctoral student, you had invited all of us in your Sex, Race, and Masculinity class to your and Jeff's annual Holiday Party. I went—nervous, not knowing anybody very well, and feeling extraordinarily "out of place." As you poured me a glass of red wine in that very crowded, very noisy kitchen, I thanked you for the invitation. You looked me right in the eye and said, "I just want you to know where you are." You have helped me find my voice, but more than that, my place. For that, I am grateful.

Introduction:
Re-thinking Southernness

"Don't you see? This whole land, the whole South, is cursed, and all of us who de-rive from it whom it ever suckled, white and black both, lie under the curse?...What corner of Canaan is this?"

--Faulkner (1954, p. 315)

What would a curriculum be like if the curriculum began with the problem of living a life?

--Britzman (2000, p. 49)

I begin this book in ways that Southerners and non-Southerners alike might predict as obligatory: epigram from Faulkner, allusion to *Gone with the Wind* (keep reading). I figure it is best to get them both out of the way and out in the open. Yet it is my desire that my obvious references will be the last predictable element of the work. This is a Southern study. It is also a *Southern* study, but it has to be; it is written by a Southern woman. Wherever else my politics and social consciousness may lie, my accent, as well as that of my work, is Southern. But just as there is no one Southern dialect, there is also no singular Southern sensibility. This study, like the South, Southerners, or any people for that matter, is neither monolithic nor linear: it cuts and backtracks and goes around in circles as much as a blue tick dog tracking a raccoon on a drizzly night in the Colbert County woods.

I love the South—New Yorkers and Los Angeleans have proclaimed their love of place for decades, without being expected to offer up much explanation as to why. Drew Carey opened his show for several years with the anthem *Cleveland Rocks*. Yet Southern love of place, love of Southern place, cannot remain unconfronted; therefore, much of the study is driven by my attempts to figure out why this love, and for what. I contemplate feeling Southern, Southern place, from the perspective of a white, female, lesbian, working-class, liberal, fundamentalist Christian, teacher educator. There is land here, and people, church, music, food—bits of culture that warm and comfort. But then I consider that very warmth and comfort and question them, for there are also things Southern that I cannot love, that I cannot let soothe me. I will not fight any longer for a Lost Cause, but will continue to look to the South for causes worth fighting for.

So, these pages contain a definite sense of Southern place. Till (2001) explains that "Place is the cultural and spatial context within which we construct and locate our individual and collective identities" (p. 275), and I explore the contexts of the context, so to speak. In other words, if place is a context of the development of a sense of self and sense of being in the world, what social and cultural contexts contribute to the sense one has of this context, place? I like to think of this circle/cycle of self, place, society, and culture as a curriculum of place.

Despite my accent and the imagery and metaphor of my language, I make no attempt at justification or explaining away—no classical allusion either. Just a "single-minded attempt to render the highest possible justice" (Conrad in O'Connor, 1969, p. 80) to the South as place. Moonlight and magnolias, the well-worn euphemism for Southern facades of civility and gentility, obscure the landscape of Southern place in clouds of myth and nostalgia. One cannot unpack and classify that which is shadowed by the past. Place unclouded is central to the study, as it interplays with social and cultural politics to inform and be informed by curriculum. Place complicates the already "complicated conversation" (Pinar et al., 1995, p. 848) of curriculum, and I offer several points at which to join in the conversation: place, self, self and other, culture, and society.

Harsh Mercies

Fifty years after Appomattox, H.L. Mencken decried the intellectual, artistic, and cultural sterility of the post—Civil War South by depicting the region as the Sahara Desert of the fine arts (beaux arts: bozart) in America. He wrote,

Down there a poet is now almost as rare as an oboe-player, a dry-point etcher or a metaphysician....It would be impossible in all history to match so complete a drying-up of a civilization....The vast blood-letting of the Civil War half exterminated wholly the old aristocracy, and so left the land to the harsh mercies of the poor white trash, now its masters. (Mencken, 1958, pp. 73–76)

I grew up, then, in the Sahara of the Bozart. But since nobody told me until I was grown, I grew up not knowing. This means that many of the finer points of so-called "desolation" were completely lost to me, including, as Mencken mentions above, that my people, poor white trash, were masters of a remnant civilization—white, affluent, male, patriarchal, straight. Ashley Wilkes mournfully describes the mythic plantation civilization to Scarlett O'Hara as he sums up the more aesthetic nature of the Lost Cause:

It isn't that I mind splitting logs here in the mud, but I do mind what it stands for. I do mind, very much, the loss of beauty of the old life I loved. Scarlet, before the war, life was beautiful. There was a glamour to it, a perfection and a completeness and a symmetry to it like Grecian art. Maybe it wasn't so to everyone. I know that now. But to me, living at Twelve Oaks, there was a real beauty to living. I belonged in that life. I was part of it. And now it is gone and I am out of place in this new life, and I am afraid. Now, I know that in the old days it was a shadow show I watched. I avoided everything which was not shadowy, people and situations which were too real, too vital. I resented their intrusion. I tried to avoid you too, Scarlett. You were too full of living and too real and I was cowardly enough to prefer shadows and dreams. (Mitchell, 1936/1999, p. 528)

No, it was not so to everyone. Ashley, Mencken's culturally refined Southern poet who perished with the destruction of the regional "old aristocracy," mourns his own South, that of beautiful arts— beautiful living in a shadow show. Ironic that the deluded Ashley was unable to see the vibrant Scarlett and speak to their mutual desire, until Twelve Oaks was laid waste.

I saw *Gone with the Wind* when I was 8 years old, at the old Roxy Theater in downtown Russellville, Alabama, back before cable TV

and theater multiplexes. In 1968, season of Tet, Martin King, Jr., and
Bobby Kennedy, GWTW was still being released annually in Southern
theaters. It was the most cinematically beautiful movie I ever saw,
and I remember Ashley's speech. I remember thinking, although that
sounded mighty fine, it sure did not sound like the place where I was
living. Sad that Ashley had lost his beautiful Twelve Oaks South,
mine remained in the woods and creeks of North Alabama. Perhaps
this is the first harsh mercy: the beautiful arts of the South are not exclusive to the shadow show of Old South culture. Beneath the veil of
nostalgia lies an aesthetic of unfitting Southernness.

It is the mythic South that is barren, and the present South that
clings to those myths. The South of which I write is far from physically barren, marked by its lush humidity. There is heat here, and
wetness, and where these exist, life will also be, and where life, spirit.
The South has conditions ripe for growing and greening. Tender
vegetation loves heat and moisture—thrives in them. I marvel, for
example, at my mother's seemingly effortless knack for getting almost
any vegetation to grow in the hard North Alabama red dirt. "Just go
out," she says when I ask her, "and dig you a little hole and stick a
cutting in the ground; it'll root and come up." Regeneration cannot
occur through arid myths—those such as Ashley's or Mencken's—
that the lifeblood of the South is found within any sterile ideal. Neither will cultivation occur, though, from under the mastery by poor
whites, as Mencken feared, for privileging dries the marrow from
within the branches. The verdant South is of its own wetness; it is as
pungent as the woods after a June rain.

Mencken described a Southern culture anemic from the loss of its
gentrified blood:

> As for…this curious and almost pathological estrangement from everything
> that makes for a civilized culture, I have hinted at it already, and now state
> it again. The South has simply been drained of all its best blood…The war,
> of course, was not a complete massacre. It spared a decent number of first-
> rate southerners—perhaps some of the very best…. (p. 76)

But, blood-letting and healing are harsh mercies. The blood flow of Old South sterility—its "best blood," from marble columns back onto the land—was a sloughing off of the black, dead blood of infertile debris; whereas, the blood (let) of renewal nurtures life. Blood lets the spongy organ of nutrient supply the land and people from whom it flows; we breathe what blood lets.

The Old South aristocracy was not exterminated, as Mencken perceived, delivering the deathblow to Southern beaux art. Rather, the beautiful art that is of the South—in the red rich blood and in the dripping humidity and in salt-sticky sweat of its people—expels the Old South aristocratic myth in a move of its own regeneration: Blood on the leaves and blood at the root (Allen/Meeropol, 1937). Instead of Mencken's desert, or even Ashley Wilkes's classical idyll, Ayers (1992) offers a metaphor of the South as lush cultural jungle. He contends, "The South was not the Sahara, but the Congo. The South produced not symphony halls, but juke joints, holiness churches, and country dances. American culture proved richer for the imbalance" (p. 372). The South is richer, yet for all its lushness, "Southern trees grow strange fruit" (Allen/Meeropol) that begs for harvest. Black, the South is vibrant, fertile; white, it is sterile.

If the land is left to the harsh mercies of "poor white trash, now its masters," then we must tend the land, must "mind the South" (Reed, 2003, p. xi) by attending to the "strange and bitter crop" (Allen) it bears. Strange fruit—that powerful metaphor of lynched black male bodies that linger in Southern consciousness—might be elaborated to parallel—but not evaluate—other classed, gendered, sexualized fruits of the Southern spirit. This research confronts the ambivalences of Southern place by cutting through layers of romantic, nostalgic discourses that have come to shape the South, layers that befog how sense of place influences sense of self. Harsh mercies look not past but into the "pastoral scene of the gallant South" (Allen) so that by its strange fruit it may not only be known (Matthew 7:20) but come to know itself.

Aims of this Book

One place comprehended can make us understand other places better.
                    --Eudora Welty (1978) from "Place in Fiction," The Eye of the Story

This research seeks to encourage progressive conversation and social political movement in the South by attending to the anomalous forms of Southernness that emerge in the interrogation of feeling Southern. Toward that end, I explore and foreground a marginalized Southern curriculum of nostalgia, homeplace, grace, and queerness. I investigate aspects of Southern place, such as being and feeling Southern, that are submerged in conventional white patriarchal notions of Southern identity. My narrative—autobiographical, theoretical investigations—is an effort to allow some of these anomalous forms of Southernness to surface and, out of these forms, create a Southern curriculum of place. This work is necessary for displacing the dominant race-, class-, and gender-constricting conception of Southernness that perpetuates itself.

I identify as a Southerner; I feel Southern and feel a deep attachment to Southern place(s), but aspects of my experience, identity, desire, concern about the world are negated by constricting notions of Southernness. Southernness has been a form of identification that has protected racist, misogynistic, homophobic practices and mindsets by invoking small-town life, pastoral aesthetics, closeness to the earth, simplicity, and spirituality. It is against these Southern ways of being that I counterpose my concepts of Southern curriculum, concepts rooted in place yet disruptive of hardened conventions. Examining Southern place and conventional traits of Southern identity reveal a greater complexity to feeling Southern, which in turn further complicates the conversation of a curriculum of place.

The politics of place inform individual and collective Southern identities. As examining Southern place and conventional traits of Southern identity reveal a greater complexity to feeling Southern, attending to anomalous forms of Southernness creates a counternarrative of the progressive transformation of Southern place. The forms of

Southernness for which I have created curricular forum are as follows: 1) unsettling prohibitive nostalgia so as to disrupt rather than solidify identity/place norms; 2) homeplace as a site for the interrogation of the construction of identity rather than the consoling, pacifying mirror of identity; 3) queer Southernness, exemplified in the conjunction rather than the opposition of fundamentalism and queer desire; 4) grace that shatters rather than absolves traditional raced, classed, and gendered notions of Southern identity.

This study elaborates a curriculum of place set in the South, whose influence, according to a cross-section of scholars, spreads like kudzu throughout the rest of America. Second, the study is a journey of self—a self situated squarely in Southern place and the raced, classed, gendered, religious sensibilities of the place. Entwined yet discrete in relation to the first two, the third purpose of my research is to uncover sites of subjective and social transformation within the American South. Transformation is not a destination, but is itself a passage, forward motion that requires a continuing disruption of traditional Southern codes that leave the South with nostalgia, guilt, and pain. Applebome (1997) specifies some of the most prominent codes, to which I would add the code of white Southern womanhood:

> The tenets of the Lost Cause were familiar and inviolate: the nobility of the Southern planters and the romantic picture of the old plantation, the cult of the Confederacy—both the governmental entity and the men who died for it—and the evils of reconstruction. (p. 126)

Nostalgia is the legacy of the Lost Cause, the attempt to sustain a sense of being from restrictive traditions of race, class, and gender. It is the nature of white Southern nostalgia, then, rather than nostalgia itself, that holds white Southern desire captive and preempts love—loving the South and loving in the South, for instance. I attempt memory work that works the tensions between love and nostalgia and searches for causes by which we—self, self and South—are lost.

In the following chapter are themes I will revisit throughout the rest of the book: the feeling of Southernness, spirituality, nostalgia—

queered and entangled with desire, and grace. My fundamentalist
Protestant upbringing is never far from the surface, neither are my
working-class roots. Chapter 1, "The Measure of Days: Telling and
Feeling the South," also presents some significant literature that supports my claim that the past figures significantly into curricular studies of place. Southern aesthetics are to be found in the same spaces as
its privation: in Southern people. They inform each other, place and
people, through a past that needs re-claiming (Pinar, 1991, 2004); and
yet, I do not know exactly how to reclaim or even what needs reclaiming until I unpack the trunk. I carefully unwrap and unfold the
contents, look at them, and assess what they mean to me. Then I can
put the treasures on the shelf and sell the junk at a yard sale. My un-
claimed treasures are those artifacts of renewal and reconstruction
that, like my mother's Elvis wall clock with swinging hips, can be
counted on to start conversation among people.

Love and longing are disentangled in the interrogation of the
complexities of homeplace (Chapter 2), the complex, conflicting tension between the paradoxes of queer and fundamentalist Christian
discourses (Chapter 3), and the fundamental intransigence of a Southern Biblical vision (Chapter 4). Southern attachments to religiosity
and spirituality, sex and gender roles and homeplace have bearing on
how white Southerners feel Southern. Being and feeling Southern is
complex as it complicates, creating "affective structures that weld
emotional registers to a kind of regionalized epistemology, a southern
way of knowing and doing" (McPherson, 2003, p. 167). Feeling Southern is an indicator of being Southern; it shades our perception of self
and other, and forms the basis of what Gray (2002) calls, "a Southern
self-fashioning" (p. xxiii).

Each chapter allows some anomalous form of Southernness to
surface that troubles conventional notions of what it means to be a
Southerner, to feel Southern. Out of these nonconventional configurations—nostalgia, homeplace, grace, and queerness—I engage a Southern curriculum of place through which to elaborate contemporary
curriculum discourses. In each chapter I take up the often paradoxical
situatedness of my experiences and work through different tensions

rather than succumb to the temptation to disidentify with them completely or embrace and preserve them. My journeying of self-in-place-in-past displaces dominant race-, class-, and gender-constricting conceptions of Southernness that perpetuate themselves.

Chapter 2, "Season of Lilacs: Nostalgia and Homeplace(s) of Difference," interrogates the earliest, most intimate place where raced, classed, gendered, sexed, and religious conventions are maintained: home, or homeplace. I trouble the lingering presence of nostalgia in Southern homeplace ideology to situate homeplace as a site for the interrogation of identity construction rather than a soothing mirror of identity. Homeplace is the nest of Southern comfort, veiled in the promise of good old, better-than-now, less complicated days, when—and where—sameness and privilege are safely guarded. Homeplace nostalgia moored in white Southerners' deep desire for history steeped in Old South rhetoric and ideologies represses difference and the transformative opportunities it presents. Probyn (1996) notes, "The past is not there to explain the present; it is there to encourage forms of becoming" (p. 121). When white Southerners look to the past for explanations, or for points of origin that drive the present, we are discouraged from becoming—and from belonging; homeplace becomes a protective barrier, a sanctity of sameness. Through the reclaiming of memory and the confronting of nostalgia, home can be reconceptualized as a place where difference might be recognized and accepted.

Chapter 3, "Queerly Fundamental: Complexities of Christian Fundamentalism and Queer Desire," troubles the convergence of fundamentalist Christian sociopolitical thought with corporate models of curriculum and schooling. Talburt (2005) sites the "rise of fundamentalisms" as a phenomena whose relation to "class, race, national, ethnic, gender and sexual oppressions" have been dramatized (and theorized) in multiple spheres, including education" (p. 3). She emphasizes "...the need for researchers and educators to closely consider, among other concerns and issues in the twenty-first century, "the Christian-corporate nexus in schools..." (p. 4), an unholy alliance within the public school curriculum "that emphatically seeks to pro-

duce docile teachers, students, workers and citizens" (p. 5). It is my
contention that herein also lies the root of maintaining straightness in
schools and schooling. I take up the paradox of identity construction
and lived experiences as I reflect upon my upbringing as a member of
the Church of Christ from my peculiar, queer perspective. As the title
suggests, queer and fundamentalist Christianity converge in complexities and contradictions of identifications and desires. Further, the
title implies the play of language on the concept of "queerly fundamental" subjectivities. Queer and fundamental converge autobiographically as I consider myself as queer, fundamentalist, queerly
fundamental, and fundamentally queer. I consider not only the queerness of fundamentalism, but also its queer peculiarity. "Queerly Fundamental" is set in a small rural community where the two most
distinctive structures are the church and school, located side by side
with blurred boundaries of influence. A member of the church and an
English teacher at the school, I consider how the school, ensconced
within a staunchly fundamentalist community, cultivates a discourse
of straightness that reinforces and affirms straightness in its students
and faculty.

Chapter 4, "'The Price of Restoration': Flannery O'Connor and the
South's Biblical Vision," considers a social and cultural reconstruction
of Southern place and Southern identity and then names that price. If
white Southerners are to be liberated from constricting forms of
Southernness, we must become aware of our fundamental narrowness of vision and be accountable for the transgressions it affects. Discussing the South and white Southerners in terms of grace and any
sort of renewal requires a degree of the expression of sentiment, and,
as in preceding chapters on homeplace and religion, I am careful to
problematize the presence of sentiment in Southern nostalgia and my
own slippage into it. In fact, my referencing O'Connor functions as a
safeguard; as a literary critic, she voiced strong disapproval of the
writer's use of excessive sentimentality.

Do I privilege the South and Southernness in my work? Only, I
hope, inasmuch as the South represents the only regional perspective
I have. My goal has always been to confront the South in its complex-

ity, and it is this complexity that should call our lenticular outlooks of the South into question. On many levels, there simply is no uncomplicated standpoint to take. O'Connor facilitates an exploration of grace and the South, noting that the Southern writer must elaborate larger social contexts, even as the accent of the writing itself remains Southern. In O'Connor's work one finds explication of both grace and the South within the humor and grotesque—most particularly the Misfit—she uses to amplify her characters' intransigence.

Chapter 5, "Conclusion: Cosmopolitanism, Grace, and Communion," concludes by offering the idea of communion as a central metaphor for a Southern curriculum of place. I extend the notion of communion that emerges from my queered fundamentalist perspective to mean an intimate sharing—a common union—of feelings and ethical behavior toward each other. I propose communion as a responsible outcome of ethics in a world of strangers. Communion is a condition of thinking and feeling—of being—in which the participants are open to conversation and transformative motion. Anomalous forms of Southernness—disruptive nostalgia and homeplace, queer Southernness, and shattering grace—disorder traditional configurations of Southern identity buried beneath white patriarchal notions. Within the ruptures of unfitting Southernness lies the South's progressive social commitment.

Conclusion

My family and coworkers, as well as people I meet who want to chit-chat, all ask the same question: "What are you writing about?" For about a year, I could get by with, "Well, it's hard to say...." Later I changed to, "Well, it's about the South." My parents expected a more detailed answer when they discovered me taking notes just after Mother had called off the ingredients to the Elvis Presley cake that she set before me on one of my trips home. Sensing that she and the Elvis cake were becoming material, she asked again. "Well," I said, "It's about how some of the things that make us Southerners, like 'the old homeplace' and 'old time religion' and dwelling on 'the good old days' can influence how we look at things." Their looks became increasingly skeptical. Last Christmas my grandmother asked me, and I know that she needed a direct answer so she could call her sister in the nursing home who has a niece by marriage with a Ph.D. and a big-time job at the Centers for Disease Control. Geriatric sibling rivalry is serious stuff. It was time for me to give an account.

I look at the answer that I gave my mother as I was eating Elvis Presley cake, sitting at the table in the kitchen of my childhood home, and I noticed how old is in every phrase. And not just any ordinary old; this old does more than denote age (old dog), condemn as despicable (stupid old jalopy), or occupy space (silly old bear). This old is a term of endearment, giving place, religion, and time a whole different shade of meaning. It is what white Southerners cling to that clings to us right back. If old denotes nostalgia for white Southerners—a loving longing for things that make us feel Southern—then I write about different ways this is so, bearing witness to my singular Southernness. My grandmother just rolls her eyes and dials the phone.

Elvis Presley Cake

Ingredients:
1 box yellow cake mix
1 20-oz. can crushed pineapple
2 cups sugar
1 box confectioners' sugar
1 8-oz. package cream cheese
1/2 cup oleo
Chopped nuts

Mix cake according to directions. Bake in 13 X 9 pan.

Using juice and all, boil together pineapple and sugar for 3 minutes.

Punch holes in cake (Mother uses the handle of her wooden stirring spoon.)

Pour pineapple mix over warm cake.

Icing: Mix confectioners' sugar, cream cheese, and oleo. Spread over cooled cake. Sprinkle chopped nuts on top.

This recipe is passed along by my mother, Wonell Whitlock. According to her, wherever she takes an Elvis Presley cake, somebody always asks for the recipe, which delights her to no end.

Chapter 1
The Measure of Days:
Telling and Feeling the South

Lord, make me to know mine end, and the measure of my days, what it is;
That I may know how frail I am...

--Psalms 39:4

I love the South, and I feel Southern. I love it for those imbalances that Ayers (1992) credits for making it lush: the juke joint, country dance-, holy rolling-mindset. The South is eccentric, queer, proud of its food and its heat, its recreation and its sweat. I love the attachment I have to this place, layered in complexity, which is part of my identity. Still, I am asked, "Why do you love it?" meaning, How could you love the South, with its past—now its present—racial, heterosexist, misogynistic violences? The present South is not condemned to its past, yet might be reconstructed—through a disruption of constricting white patriarchal structures—to display a lush, black, queer South that might nurture the self and move self and other toward social change.[1]

Reconstruction is a volatile word in the context of Southern studies. Since I refer to reconstruction throughout the research, a brief clarification is in order. Historically, Reconstruction—with a capital R—refers to the period following the Civil War: the period of political reentry of formerly rebellious states, addressing the economic devastation of the South, inaugurating the education of freed persons. The period began before the war ended, with Lincoln's proclamation, on December 8, 1863, of amnesty and reconstruction for areas of the Confederacy occupied by Union armies. It offered pardon, with certain exceptions, to Confederates taking a loyalty oath and the re-establishment of statehood to conquered states wherein 10% of voters took the prescribed oath and organized a government that abolished slavery.

Republicans in Congress who opposed Lincoln's plan offered their own plan—the Wade-Davis Bill—that appointed military governors to rule Southern states and required a majority of citizens take the loyalty oath for the reestablishment of statehood. Following Lincoln's assassination, subsequent plans for Reconstruction that varied in severity—and degrees of implementation—toward the Southern states were proposed by President Johnson ("Presidential Reconstruction") and the Radical Republicans ("Congressional Reconstruction").

Reconstructed ended with the presidential election of 1876 and the Compromise of 1877, in which Southerners agreed to accept a Republican Hayes presidency in return for, among other concessions, the withdrawal of federal troops from the South. With the withdrawal of troops, Republican governments, that had included Black officeholders, were turned out of state offices. Democrats took back power in Southern states, and white Southerners called it "Redemption." Williamson (1986) observes the evangelical connotation of Redemption in white Southern minds. He writes,

> An identity that had been sorely burned in the Civil War and very nearly drowned in the swirling currents of Black Reconstruction was regained, and a positive image of Southern self took root and life again. As southerners looked back upon Reconstruction, they felt that they had been all but lost in a world that was all but lost, but then they were found…the term that they applied to regaining control of their states was as fully laden with meaning as the Christian view of the rebirth of the spirit. They called it "Redemption." (p. 39)

According to Williamson, Reconstruction was an "ordinance against nature and a denial of God" (p. 37) in its distortion of established Southern social order: "Bottom rail on top, Massah. Bottom rail's on top now" (Williamson, 1986, p. 37; Faust, 2004, transcript) was a boast of freed persons and Radical Republicans that iterated the degradation of white society. If Reconstruction was a fall from grace, then Redemption was, to white Southern minds, a rebirth, the reinstatement of a state of grace. He notes, "When they had caught their breath, they turned and moved on, "born-again" Southerners… [Restoration] proved to have lasting strength" (p. 37, 39). Thus, the secular, political era of Reconstruction and its ensuing demise took on theological proportions to Southern ways of thinking and being.

This research is an inquiry into contemporary Southern reconstruction—designated by lower case r—a curricular reconstruction of cultural renewal and social consciousness within Southern place(s). Curricular reconstruction is found, not in stringent forms of Southernness and binding structures of past-in-place, but in the particular, anomalous, queer ruptures of a people whose regional consciousness and identification with place is so strong, that we have forged intransigent attachments to it. Curricular reconstruction conjoins social psychoanalytically informed curricular processes to specific elements of Southern lived experiences that include narratives of place central to the renegotiation of past-in-place that might help provide the "psychology of social commitment" (Pinar, 1991, p. 180) lacking in the South.

As Cash (1941) sought to uncover the Mind of the South and Roberts (2002, p. 371) charts the "South of the mind," my autobiographical research considers the South of the subjective self, (my)self. I find that the mind of the South and the South of the mind are inextricable, converging within the spaces of subjectivity. As such, my research approaches South through self and vise versa. As the country music group Alabama so applicably sang, "I'm in the Heart of Dixie/Dixie's in the heart of me." I can isolate neither the mind of the South nor the South in the collective minds of its people; I do not presume to try.

This study does not demarcate all that it means to be "Southern." Regional sociologists such as Reed (1982, 1983, 2003), continue to speak to the issue. In addition to a sense of place embedded in regionalism, localism, and religion (1982, p. 136—137), Reed supports Phillips's (1928) earlier contention, although it seems to a somewhat less and less intense degree, that the "cardinal test of a Southerner" is "a common resolve indomitably maintained—that [the South] shall be and remain a white man's country" (Phillips in Reed, p. 83). Racial (or gendered, inferred from Phillips's inadvertent phrasing) segregation is not exclusive to the South, yet as resolute separatism is an indicator of regional identity consciousness, racism that underlies the resolve must be interrogated. Underlying issues of race inform anomalous forms of Southernness—homeplace, nostalgia, queer Southernness, grace—to which this study gives curriculum space.

My contribution is to offer my own perspectives on the problems of Southern culture toward the educational end of employing knowledges of place to articulate the "elusive conversation between place and curriculum theory" (Kincheloe & Pinar, 1991, p. 8). Bearing witness to these sometimes uncomfortable knowledges links the particularities of Southern ways of being to the social concerns of curriculum theory. And then these terms—being Southern, feeling Southern—fall short of the subjectivity I present, for even as I feel Southern, the South must surely feel my rootedness in it. Unraveling the tensions of self and South disrupts and illuminates both. Just as the politics of place figure into individual and collective Southern identities, Southern identities figure into a politics of place. McPherson (2003) suggests, "...a tendency prevails within the field [of Southern studies] to preserve the south, that is, to focus on those elements that unify the region rather than to pursue it in relation to national or global contexts" (p. 9). This study focuses on common elements that perhaps tend to unify white, very low middle- to low-class Southerners, but not with the goal of preserving the South in localized contexts that further isolate the South nationally and globally. Neither do I set out to analyze white Southern subjectivity; this project does not offer an explicit unpacking of race and racial issues. Rather, I use the particularities of white Southern subjectivities to subvert the preservation of unitary—and constructed—Southern ideals which themselves prescribe and preserve dysfunctional Southern identities, and, as such, race is intrinsic to if yet largely unarticulated in the conversation.

My research speaks to two autobiographical impulses: the need of many individuals to explain ourselves and the need of most Southerners—a rage, according to Hobson (1983)—to tell about the South. My questions about the telling echo Prufrock's: And how should I then presume? And how should I begin? I tell much of it through stories, vignettes, that, true to Southern style, often ramble, meander, and if they end at all, do so with questionable points. The story is the point. I tell most of it in my voice, the voice of a scholar, yes, but a storytelling scholar who is present in the text. I tell some of it in song, both in hymns and country music, itself a kind of spiritual. I tell a bit of it with Scripture and a bit with literature—some fiction, some not. Telling the South is more of a challenge than remaining true to my voice. My guiding principle throughout has been to confront the South without rejecting—or embracing—it, without excessive sentimentality or excessive rage. A detached confrontation would not be honest since my fondness for the region and its people is apparent, but then, so, I hope, is my distress toward historical raced, classed, gendered, sexual, religious cruelties. A reconstructed South must be framed by engaging both the attraction and the aversion.[2]

Wholly Spirit: Conceptualizing Spirituality

If spirituality is part of what it means to feel Southern, and spiritual renewal is key to new, more affirmative ways of feeling Southern that are not paralyzed by a Lost Cause, then a working definition of spirituality is in order. Definitions are as wide ranging as the disciplines from which they may be garnered. From Thich Nhat Hanh (1987, 1995), for example, one might interpret spirituality as mindfulness of the present moment. For fundamentalist Protestants looking for more "fundamental" descriptors, Unger's Bible Dictionary (1988) offers one theological definition:

> The quality of being spiritual as opposed to material. The spirituality of man refers to the immaterial part of his nature. The term is also used with reference to the disposition or internal condition of men when in such a state as prepares them to recognize and properly appreciate spiritual realities. True spirituality in the last sense is the result of the inworking of the Holy Spirit. (p. 1217)

Women's spirituality and medieval mystic scholar Carol Lee Flinders juxtaposes spiritual practice and politics, where spirituality is transformative selfhood imbued with elements of mysticism, "training the mind and redirecting desires, simplifying thought processes and life at the same time—the two efforts requiring one another" (Flinders, in Ruttenberg, 2004, p. 51). Spirituality is to be found in the transformative in-between spaces of balance, the inward striving for simplicity paired with the outward movement toward community, a sort of mystical interconnectedness.

Curriculum theorists acknowledge an element of the spirit in the search for understanding. Huebner (1999) looks for the language of spirituality within the idea of "moreness" (p. 403) He conceptualizes spirituality that transcends, goes beyond, "the known, the ego, the self" (p. 403). He continues,

> The "moreness" in the world, spirit, is a moreness that infuses each human being. Not only do we know more than we say, we "are" more than we "currently are." That is, the human being dwells in the transcendent, or more appropriately, the transcendent dwells in the human being. To use more direct religious imagery, the spirit dwells in us. (p. 404)

Huebner's is an abundant spirituality that occurs in the fullness of hope and love, faith and openness; it leaves the human vulnerable to the possibility that we may be overpowered by something that we do not cause or control, something greater than the sum of our parts.

Macdonald's (1995) "hermeneutic quest" (p. 173) is contemplative and transcendent of rationalistic methodologies; it offers "aesthetic, moral and metaphysical meaning through poetics" (p. 182). Situating curriculum theory within the meditative hermeneutic cycle, Macdonald continues, "The act of theorizing is an act of faith, a religious act…what defines [both theory and pedagogy] is the spirit and vision that shines through the surface manifestations" (p. 181). Theorizing is an act of faith, and faith is a fruit of the Spirit (Galatians 5:22). The spiritual is what shines through—not as unfounded hope or misguided naiveté, but as animating, vital dispositions through which we may enact change. Interestingly, Macdonald relates curriculum theory to mystery—"it is a mystery [to educators whose faith is in the scientific] because it deals with *the* mystery" (p. 182), but what is the italicized "the"? I suggest that the connection between curriculum and spirituality is found somewhere within Macdonald's *the* and Flannery O'Connor's *Mystery*.

O'Connor noted in her characters a distorted sense of spiritual purpose (HB, p. 32). Incidentally, O'Connor's notion of the spiritual aligns with elements of Unger's more legalistic definition above: 1) the a-material, 2) an internal disposition for recognition of grace, and 3) the indwelling of the Spirit. In O'Connor, it is from the distortions that the spiritual emerges.

For Christians, the idea of the spiritual begins—should begin—with what is at the core of the Christian's life: Christ. "The creative action of the Christian's life is to prepare his death in Christ" (1969, p. 223), O'Connor writes about her stories, "The meaning of life is centered in our Redemption by Christ and what I see in the world I see in its relation to that" (p. 32). Lives, then, are lived in preparation for redemption, which cannot occur except through grace. O'Connor explains the moment of grace in her stories:

> There is a moment...in which the presence of grace can be felt as it waits to be accepted or rejected, even though the reader may not recognize this moment....I have found, in short, from reading my own writing, that my subject in fiction is the action of grace in territory held largely by the devil. (p. 118)

Here O'Connor has situated grace within place; her focus is on the action of grace and the character's receptivity to it, conscious or not. Grace, as I use it in this research, has more to do with illumination and possibility than absolution. Rather than a bestowal of favor or forgiveness, grace is the overflow of the deep love of God. It is a glimpse at His heart.

Besides redemption and grace, O'Connor shapes the relationship between love and spiritual union, tempered by human distortions. She writes, "This action by which charity grows invisibly among us, entwining the living and the dead, is called by the Church the Communion of Saints. It is a communion created upon human imperfection, created from what we make of our grotesque state" (p. 228). The cultivation of charity through communion occurs as the Spirit works; the force of the Spirit is magnified, not diminished, by human grotesquerie. What shall we say then? Shall we continue in sin that grace may abound (Romans 6:1)? Paul, of course, says, "God forbid," but O'Connor shows abundant grace among and within transgressors. Redemption and grace, love and communion: these can be pondered to a point; the rest is the mystery that so intrigued O'Connor, the unnamable piece in the puzzle of the spiritual. She writes, "The fiction writer presents mystery through manners, grace through nature, but when he finishes there always has to be left over that sense of Mystery which cannot be accounted for by any human formula" (in Ellsberg, 2003, p. 139). That Mystery with a capital "M" is the spiritual.

"Paint Me a Birmingham": Embedded Nostalgia in Southern Studies

Paint me a Birmingham, make it look just the way I planned;
A little house on the edge of town, porch goin' all the way around;
Put her there in a frontyard swing, cotton dress make it, early spring
For a while she'll be mine again, if you can paint me a Birmingham...

(recorded by Tracy Lawrence, 2004)

Nostalgia sits on the South like fog on a spring morning, heavy yet elusive, so it is increasingly difficult to extract the one from the other. Scholars generally agree that Southerners feel a regional identity and consciousness, which suggests that there is indeed such an entity as Southernness, and it is based upon a condition that comes from being in and a part of the South. But much of this is predicated on a vaporous yearning that keeps seeping through the cracks of Southern past and place. What might white Southerners find out about ourselves and our histories once it burns off? McPherson (2003) writes,

> Nostalgia in and of itself is not a bad thing, for it can function as a wedge to introduce a critical distance into cultural practices and cultural theory. But the nostalgia that often tinges southern studies and southern culture is only rarely concerned with moving forward and with positively reconstructing

the past. Throughout [Reconstructing Dixie], I take the nostalgia that flavors many accounts of the South to task, asking in whose service such a sentiment finally plays. My aim is to discern when such a sentiment enables mobility or revisioning rather than (often mournful) reaction and stasis, underwriting a white racial melancholia. (p. 10)

In other words, what the world needs less than most anything right now is one more Southern study dripping with Lost Cause nostalgia, the kind that tries to justify and romanticize the past as it underwrites this "white racial melancholia" that breeds more nostalgia, and on and on. I have come to envision nostalgia, then, as process rather than product, one that can either feed melancholia or facilitate "critical distance" for revisioning past and place through its mobility of forward motion.

Boym (2001), who aptly names nostalgia "hypochondria of the heart" (p. 3), calls to mind McPherson's idea of lenticularity, a kind of cinematic double exposure, as she describes nostalgia as a "superimposition of two images—of home and abroad, past and present, dream and everyday life. The moment we try to force it into a single image, it breaks the frame or burns the surface" (p. xiv). What might happen to the South when Southern images are forced into single focus? Juxtapose rural and urban poverty to Old South money. New South enterprise and good ol' boy networks. Strip malls and flea markets. Rebel flags and black middle class. Redneck queers and Pentecostal preachers. By slothfully allowing exposures of false duality to coexist, blissful in the blurriness, the South maintains its somnolent existence of class, gender, race, laced together by desire.

Boym describes nostalgia as yearning for both place and time. She writes, "The danger of nostalgia is that it tends to confuse the actual home and the imaginary one. In extreme cases it can create a phantom homeland" (p. xvi). And as McPherson suggests a kind of dual function of nostalgia, Boym distinguishes between two types of nostalgia to illustrate its mechanisms of seduction and manipulation: restorative nostalgia and reflective nostalgia. Because the South shifts between the two yet is shaped primarily by the nostalgia in its restorative form, I cite her explanation below.

Restorative nostalgia stresses nostos (return home) and attempts a transhistorical reconstruction of the lost home. Reflective nostalgia thrives in algia (longing), the longing itself, and delays the homecoming—wistfully, ironically, desperately. Restorative nostalgia does not think of itself as nostalgia, but rather as truth and tradition. Reflective nostalgia dwells on the ambivalences of human longing and belonging and does not shy away from the contradictions of modernity. Restorative nostalgia protects the absolute truth, while reflective nostalgia calls it into doubt.

Nostalgia is seductive in Southern spaces; translating restorative Southern nostalgia into reflective social memory might make flesh the phantom homeland.

Queering Nostalgia

That was such a simple time and place. Bluebell tastes just like the good ol'days...
                                     –Bluebell Ice Cream Commercial, March 2005.

Nostalgia sells everything from ice cream to lemonade by tapping into the idea that not only time—the past as opposed to the present— was less complicated, but also that place was less complicated. Yet since place has nothing with which to place it in opposition, the implication is that place-in-past is simpler than place-in-present. What if there is a way of considering nostalgia, inasmuch as it is a yearning for home, or for a Lost Cause or Lost Horizon, and so on, that goes beyond acknowledging "good" and "bad" forms of it that either help or hinder awareness and interconnectedness with others? A way of forcing lenticularity into single focus? Is it possible to inspect self-social desire operating within nostalgia and extend nostalgia—and therefore a sense of self—beyond past and place into the present? There is, according to Probyn (1996), and it unsettles, or scrambles, the manners of order and origin that we work to maintain in the South. Probyn "inject(s) desire, and moreover lesbian or queer desire, into considerations of belonging" (p. 25), suggesting that the past might "quicken a lust for the present and for the possible" (p. 122). Perhaps a disrupting of nostalgia might also disrupt the dwelling of Southern codes in past and place, splitting hierarchies to allow a shifting of Southern desire, Probyn's lesbian lust. Perhaps we might consider this queering nostalgia.

This notion of queering nostalgia implies more than setting up a rainbow booth between the NASCAR and Confederate memorabilia booths at the flea markets that dot Southern landscapes like peach trees. It means engaging nostalgic thought within frameworks of desire, so that past and place might also be sites of present becoming—and belonging. Stubborn belonging contrives with stagnant nostalgia; both resist movement that "rearranges" and "disorients" (Probyn, 1996, p. 113—114). Perhaps what troubles the "mind of the South" is to be found within something buried deep in the heart of Dixie. We belong to the South and it belongs to us, and that is a way of thinking that accounts for a lot of trouble. It also keeps us from becoming much other than keepers of traditional culture; clinging to nostalgia makes us okay with that station in life, proud of it, even. There is safety and comfort in order and origins, of remaining "moored in time" (p. 103), and so we guard the South—Dixie—as a milieu of both. Approaching the South by considering it within contexts of nostalgia driven by movements of desire, as Probyn describes, presents the South as milieu of singularity, "the ground of desire, a ground that must be rendered in the very detail of its singular qualities" (p. 49—50).[3]

In an excessively sentimental yearning for an irrecoverable past place or condition—not an exclusive leaning of lower classes like mine, but discernable in country lyrics and bumper stickers across the South—the emphasis is on the going back. "Carry me back, Lord, while I've still got the time," sing the Statler Brothers, in one of several of their greatest hits with a nostalgia theme.[4]

Queered nostalgia, on the other hand, means that we "go back different" (Probyn, 1996, p. 112) to face an indifference of people, place, and past. It means that we go back expecting to be pained yet prepared for a disruption of perspective, for our desire to move distance of place and time "disconcertingly forward" (p. 114). And in this way we might revisit past and place queerly, with the "fervor of the possible" (p. 116). White Southerners seek to recapture a certain place-in-past that is replete with Old South tropes: gallant Lost Cause warriors beneath the Stars and Bars—which still flies freely in my community—white Southern ladies, land that is to be hallowed. Southern cultural relationship codes—those of race, class, and gender—perpetuate guilt by promoting memory loss. Pathologic nostalgia pathologizes memory, rendering the spaces of past, present, and future diseased in the claiming.

The reclamation of memory is different from, yet works within, nostalgia. Memory (home)work of identity-becoming is more than recollection; it is reclaiming. My own homecoming plays out differently from the nostalgic memories recounted by my mother and father about their own respective "old homeplace." Probyn writes, "...(queer) desire compels us to write fully of and within the milieux that give meaning to life, milieux that constitute the singularities of social life" (p. 62). In the queer rupturing of remembering my own childhood home, I see the embeddedness of the idea of home as an enveloping womb, a soft, safe place where it is better to remain. There is no room in this environment to forge homeplace into a present location of desires and mindfulness. Forging requires an almost assuredly painful grappling. Yearning anesthetizes, but it comes at a price: without the forging, home is more tomb than womb, and we are relics to be remembered perhaps fondly.

Two years ago, my father and I took a camera back to his "old homeplace." He wanted to get pictures before the old house completely fell in upon itself. At each photo site, he explained the special memory contained there. A tree, a field, a wellhouse—the yearning was palpable. The irony was not lost on me; I wondered what pictures I might take. I would depict a family who, without a doubt, feels and expresses love for one another, yet one in which the members guard our intimacies to protect soft spots of vulnerability. I would frame the gender role expectations that were strictly enforced, the religious dogma that remained unquestioned. My pictures would capture sites of missed opportunity and denial, of unexplored and unexpressed desires. But my coming out is incomplete; I remain in-between "in and out." Until I can "go back different," I can only become my past, what the repressed and denied desires wish me to be, the fruit of indifference. I am who my family needs me to be for the stasis of our/their homeplace; I might as well cap the lens.

There is no space for present be(ing) or future be(coming) when the present is past is present. As Boym differentiates between productive and prohibitive nostalgia, Probyn explains Deleuze (1989) explaining Bergson (1990/1959) explaining recollection-memory and contraction-memory:

> The present that endures divides at each instant into two directions, one oriented and dilated toward the past, the other contracted, contracting toward the future. Thus, of the two lines at work in memory, one veers toward the past (recollective-memory) and the other (contraction-memory)...is the tensing of things into a line of becoming. (p. 118)

I propose that the path of least resistance for white Southern minds is the bend of recollection—that like the old Jimmie Rodgers (1929) song, we keep "waitin' for a train" that is "goin' back to Dixieland." Queering nostalgia might be the cow on the track that will tense memory back upon itself and spring into lines of our own becoming.

Jerusalem, Jerusalem:
The Sounds of Unreconstructed Voices in the South

If this research is to suggest progressive conversation for reconstructing the South, then it must first present some idea of the constructions by which the South exists. In other words, what is the nature of the South, and what does it mean to feel Southern? McPherson's (2003) *Reconstructing Dixie: Race, Gender, and Nostalgia in the Imagined South* interrogates Southern whiteness as it is perpetuated through media portrayal, including the film, television, documentary, and tourism media. McPherson contends that Southerners have been complicit in the codification of traditionally Southern images that are derived from raced, classed, and gendered roles and stereotypes. We have a history of believing our own myths and publicity. The promotion of

Old South impressions shapes inhabitants' regional identity; it is one way to sell the South to ourselves and others—tourists and filmmakers, for example. McPherson explains how, through nostalgic yearning for an imagined South, the meanings of the South and home have entwined to shape Southern homeplace ideology. Her exegesis of Southern culture—a perpetual myth in the making—is invaluable, suggesting a curricular role for popular culture in reconstruction.

In *Dixie Rising: How the South is Shaping American Values, Politics, and Culture* (1997), Applebome argues that the South increasingly defines America with its distinctly Southern values, conservative politics, and culture. He frames a Southern sensibility akin to what Cash (1941) referred to as the temperament of the South, that which "lives on from generation to generation, while fashions, ideas, politicians, and movements come and go" (p. 160).

> Cash's South is one driven by a passionate identification of the average white Southerner with the region as a whole and its leaders…a sort of collective will to succeed as a region or a community particularly in distinction to the North. (p. 161)

To contextualize this Southern sensibility/aesthetic/temperament, Applebome, a non-Southerner and former *New York Times* Atlanta bureau chief, traces the roots of major national debates on conservative politics, race, and states' rights to the South. The South has shaped these central issues so that they may be embraced by mainstream, conservative electorate, thus recreating the "good-against-evil moral universe of Southern politics" (p. 109). For example, in "Montgomery, Alabama: Wallace's Revenge," Applebome traces the 1994 Republican takeover of Congress, an alarming change in America's political landscape, to George Wallace's 1968 and 1972 racially charged presidential campaigns, first as a Dixiecrat, then in a bid for the Democratic nomination.

According to Applebome, Wallace's politics of racism—in a famous quote after losing the 1958 gubernatorial race, Wallace vowed never to be "out-nigguhed again" (in Applebome, p. 99)—split the

Democratic bloc in the South along racial lines, destroying forever the Democratic Solid South. He describes Wallace's right-wing populism and suggests its legacy: "It was white. It was angry. It was Southern. Now the nation's political center of gravity looks exactly the same way" (p. 91). White, angry, Southern-style politics, appropriated now by the Republican conservatives, continue to prevail as voters select candidates on the basis of moral issues, strength, and safety—"fear factors"—as opposed to social and humanitarian values.

Although race is the central issue in Dixie Rising, the author offers a comprehensive view of a Southern culture that continues to influence non-Southern America, including country music, labor politics, and religion. Perhaps Applebome's journalistic training or his coming of age outside of the South allows him to imagine a Southern culture that complements Caldwell's earthy trash and Grizzard's tailgating male utopia—two seemingly incongruous interpretations of the same region. He writes,

> [Caldwell's characters] had an almost mystical attachment to the land and to the past...[his books] defined the Depression-era Savage South.... In the end, [Caldwell and Grizzard] were like mirror images, looking at the same text and coming up with entirely different readings. Caldwell seeing the Savage South, Grizzard seeing the sunny one....Grizzard, with much of the insight but little of the venom of George Wallace, turned his mythic South into the quintessence of the good old days. (p. 325—330)

Applebome makes an observation in Dixie Rising similar to Pinar's (1991, 2004), that a reconstruction of America begins with reconstructing the American South, that to understand America one must first understand the South. Applebome looks at how the South's music, conservative right-wing politics, and "New South" brand of commerce and industrialization have contributed to the Dixification of America, a proposition similar to that of John Edgerton (2004) in "The Southernization of American Politics."

From the local histories through which he chooses to portray the South and Southern culture, Applebome emphasizes what Pinar (2001) and Kincheloe, Pinar, and Slattery (1994) declare: that the

South is an African American place. Applebome writes, "James
Baldwin was right…when he said…'we always on each other's minds
down here, because we live so close together, so if there's ever going
to be a resolution of the race problem in this country it's going to be
in the South because everything is so intertwined'" (quoted in Applebome, 1997, p. 170). He quotes Ralph Ellison, who was even more direct: "You can't be Southern without being black, and you can't be a
black Southerner without being white" (p. 330). How deeply is this
regional identity forged in a Southern will to survive? Applebome
draws his inference from Richard Wright's Black Boy:

> …he knows he can never get rid of the South. The best he could hope for
> was to take some aspect of Southern culture and make it bloom; make some-
> thing good come out of it. That same intensity is common to blacks and
> whites. They never lose that sense of identity, no matter where they go. (p.
> 292)

Perhaps the intense need for grace among whites is racial guilt at
trying, not to be rid of the South, but to suppress and control the
blackness intertwined in its regional identity. A Southern reconstruction means finding common curricular ground for this common sense
of identity by recognizing not only the impossibility of unraveling
black-white identity, but also the undesirability of doing so.

Applebome's interviews with anti racist activists strengthen his
point that Northern schools were not integrated (p. 170, 352)—that
the battleground for desegregation was Southern schools. He argues
that current moves toward resegregation mean that the South "was
really backing away from segregation. In the 'liberal' North, segre-
gated by class and housing patterns, had never really integrated at
all" (p. 352). In his discussion of O'Connor's treatment of racial
themes both in her fiction and personal correspondence, Wood (2004)
notes, "Many people, black and white alike, believe that the project of
integration has been a massive failure. It has produced an official
equality but a practical inequality, and thus a de facto resegregation"
(p. 131). Like Pinar (1991), Applebome acknowledges both the South's

lack of social commitment and its complexity (p. 257), arguing that if racial issues that continue to plague American schools are to be resolved, the resolution will probably occur in the South (p. 170).

The South of Dixie Rising retains the grotesquerie that O'Connor portrayed a half century ago, one that grapples with its demons when it is not dancing with them. Applebome lays bare the New South—grotesque in its recalcitrance, if not its immorality—how it continues to subvert and deny the intertwined races that define its culture. However, the notion of a "New South" is oxymoronic; the interplay of nostalgia with Southern culture is a critical element of the South that shapes the larger culture.   Concerning culture, the white South abhors newness, and white Southern nostalgia allows for the conflation of past and place, religion and politics that drives the Southern—and as Applebome suggests, the American—political agenda of conservatism.

Nostalgia and the Tangles of Desire

One of the most frightening recurring images and themes in Dixie Rising is that of the nostalgia of contemporary neo-Confederate white male culture. Applebome links together Old South history with white supremacism—the neo-Cons—and what he calls Confederate nostalgia. Confederate nostalgia produces Confederate iconography, the ubiquitous Confederate battle flag, for example; being so conceived precludes the iconography from existing in neutrality. Thus, the white feigned bewilderment at the controversy over battle flags waving from capital buildings throughout the South. "Pride, not prejudice," reads one bumper sticker on one pickup, reinforcing what Applebome believes makes Confederate nostalgia suspect at its root—the white Southern assumption that "their South is the South" (p. 136) and that of "The South" as a political imagery at all. He portrays a "war of images" in which symbols of Confederate nostalgia are viewed with "suspicion or contempt" (p. 132). He surmises,

> The bottom line is that other than the occasional tributes to blacks who
> fought for the Confederacy—invariably trotted out as transcendent proof of

> the racial sensitivity of the Lost Cause world—the neo-Cons view history
> and the past through a totally white prism, as if the view of what constituted
> Southern culture in 1861 holds true [today] as well. (p. 136)

A sunny South where the flag waves freely is the image held in common by Grizzard and the neo-Cons; Applebome describes this place as one of "feel-good nostalgia, easy answers, and painless solutions, forever looking backward through a pale mist and seeing only the soft-focus outlines of what it wants to see" (1997, p. 344). The nostalgic white South is Blanche Dubois, always in the soft lighting of the paper lantern, avoiding the stark lightness of the naked bulb that might reveal her for what she fears herself to be: a pallid relic subject to her own fiction.

Nostalgia is the underlying motif within the vignettes exemplifying the wave of conservative Republicanism that has made "traditional Southern positions on crime, welfare, states' rights, and conservative values mainstream ones" (1997, p. 348). Applebome's language suggests that nostalgia shapes the same themes that surface in O'Connor's fiction; it is the white Southerner's faith in the yearning rather than his faith in redemption that allows him to deny his moral culpability, and thus his social and political responsibility. Political solidarity is required to maintain the collective hallucination that we are "saved" from "sin"; that is, the past and its embeddedness in the present. Applebome explains the precursor to Southern politics:

> It's a very Southern story, one of redemption through faith, in a region
> where there was a solid religious South before there was a solid political
> one...[quoting a Presbyterian minister], 'The new South does not exist. As
> long as the religion of the Southern Protestant Church remains what it is,
> nothing new will be conceived in, or issue from, the Southern womb.' (p.
> 28ff)

Southern fundamentalism is the vanguard of Southern past by its nostalgic appeal to nineteenth century ideologies of race and gender. The minister's sentiment disrupts gendered images of a feminized church as the bride of Christ, invoking instead a masculinized, patriarchical church that penetrates Southern culture. Nothing new will be conceived as the South is already inseminated by its past, now its present.

Amazing Grace

God, whose law it is that he who learns must suffer. And even in our sleep pain that cannot forget, falls drop by drop upon the heart, and in our own despite, against our will, comes wisdom to us by the awful grace of God.

--Aeschylus, in Hamilton (1930), *The Greek Way*

Grace is an anomalous form of Southernness that surfaces when conventional forms are disturbed. The South is no stranger to grace, believing that God's grace will come to a suffering and deserving South, that whom the Lord loveth he chasteneth (Hebrews 12:6). Flannery O'Connor's depiction of a sudden, violent onslaught of grace, for example, unrests notions of a passive, impotent grace white Southerners await in part for atonement for sins—slavery, segregation, social hatred. The shattering grace visited upon the South disrupts unfounded hope of redemption without the seeking of forgiveness; the myth of Southern redemption is that it will occur apart from the asking for forgiveness and the making of restitution for past sins, that it will occur without memory. "What has given the South her identity," O'Connor (1969) writes,

> ...are those beliefs and qualities which she has absorbed from the Scriptures and from her own history of defeat and violation: a distrust of the abstract, a sense of human dependence on the grace of God, and a knowledge that evil is not simply a problem to be solved, but a mystery to be endured. (p. 209)

Desire is suppressed in the Southern identity struggle of "manners under stress" (1969, p. 208), and it is through the violent act of grace that the Southerner might become aware of its very existence.

Just as the expectation of grace contributes to a Southern collective identity, so also does restoration. I fear that the South believes in a restoration of a Southern culture that it has imagined and cultivated into being. White Southern nostalgia has helped fashion myths of restoration. Yet, in the end, the nostalgia is for the restoration. The desire of the South is greater than merely for an antebellum way of life; the mind of the South, or the "South of the mind" (Roberts, 2002), desires more than nineteenth century ideals. I suspect the South desires nothing less than restoration to what it believes is its rightful place as God's chosen people, His chosen place. An anomalous, shattering grace dispels myths of restoration with the promise of becoming; from the rift of grace comes the possibility of reconstruction.

Place Markers:
Race, Class, and Fundamentalist Protestantism

In light of Cash's (1941) well-worn yet accurate proposition that there are at the same time one and many Souths, Southern perspectives and sensibilities are multiple and diverse. In her discussion of post—Civil War race (re)construction, *The Making of Whiteness: The Culture of Segregation in the South*, 1890-1940, Hale (1998) declares, "the central moment in the making of a white southerner, the primal scene of the culture of segregation, then, was one of learning the meaning of race" (p. 96). The central moment in the (re)making of a white Southerner and the primal scene of a culture of common unity and diversity will occur in that same learning. Constricting conventions of Southern identity construction obstruct racial understanding from which progressive individual and social change might emerge.

Because whiteness was for so long invisible and therefore normative to me, the acquisition of racial awareness and meanings occurred through other identity constructs, such as class. I continue to grapple with what class might teach me about race, for I have always known that I came from the cotton-pickin', factory-working class. While I cannot recollect the moment when I realized that I was white, I remember precisely the day I was grouped in with the collective "lower class" in a conversation. The remark was not a slur, just a fact. I remember thinking, "I am not low class. I may not read *Southern Living*, but surely I fall somewhere in the middle." After all, although my parents did not belong to the Twin Pines County Club in Littleville,

Alabama, they knew someone who did, and I went swimming on their guest pass. My instruction in class had begun; it continues today. "But I'm educated...."

Class and race are deeply embedded ways that I feel my Southernness, and it is through their complicated interplay that other anomalous ways of feeling Southern emerge. For, as Pinar (1991, 2004) concludes, race, class, gender, and I would add sexuality and religion, "converge and conflate in southern culture and history" (p. 106). Concerning class and race, he writes,

> In the South, there is a persisting issue of class, intertwined as it is with race...Poor whites have allowed their racial prejudice to keep them politically complacent. No matter how poor whites are, their view is that there remains a class underneath them.... (p. 106)

Sometimes, the convergence was in living color, right in our living room.

For example, my family watched *The Dukes of Hazzard*—"At last, something worth watching on television!" My brother and I identified with the rugged, cavalier, yet kind and sensitive Duke Boys, Just two good ol' boys...fightin' the system like two modern-day Robin Hoods. He got a model of the General Lee, their orange Dodge Charger with a Confederate flag on the roof and a horn that played Dixie. Daisy Duke was the sensible sex object, whose only apparent role was to tend to Uncle Jesse and inspire a name for very, very short, tight cut-off denim shorts. Race, class, gender, and a great theme song—"Just the good ol' boys/Never meanin' no harm" (Jennings, 1979). I do not have to look far for the convergence and conflation: white Southerners are just good ol' boys, even if we are good ol' girls, meaning no harm, not responsible for history (proudly displayed on our vehicles) nor accountable to the socio-cultural-political "system" for social commitment. In fact, fighting that system is allowable because we are loyal to peers and family.

Acknowledging and exploring the complex relation between race and class and gender, I locate myself in complex relation (Gilmore,

1994b, p. 5) to the South and examine unfitting forms of Southernness that emerge. Growing up a white Southern fundamentalist Christian woman in a blue collar home prescribes for me certain roles, identities, attitudes, and behaviors that I trouble by infusing queerness, a profession in the academy, and social activism into the mix (I stop short of moving "Up North"). The ruptures feel suspiciously to me like betrayal: to my class roots, to my family, to my femininity, to Christ. Being queer puts me at odds with conventional Southern being; being a scholar creates a rift with family and homeplace mindsets; being anti racist sets me in opposition to place-in-past.

Gilmore (1994b) speaks to such ruptures of relocation in which the subjects—women writers—negotiate boundaries of belonging and becoming. She writes,

> ...the community into which one is born is not, ultimately, the community to which one belongs. Women who join convents, who cross classes and regions, who politicize female identity, and who are lesbians locate themselves in complex relation to their communities or homes of origin and to the communities they join. (p. 4—5)

With whom, where, are my comm(on)unities? I occupy in-between spaces of class and gender and race, still struggling with the polarities on either side. If I locate myself in one, am I cut off from others that have shaped my identity? Crossing borders, transversing and transgressing race and gender, home and community, I navigate toward "self-invention, self-discovery, self-representation" (Gilmore, p. 42). I connect my was and is, searching for coalitions of affirmation—through place—of Southernness, as well as Southern spaces of convergence of race, class, gender, and so on. So this glimpse at the South as place and as site of curriculum is complicated by the harsh mercies (Mencken) of a working-class academic, my best negotiation of the world of my birth and the world of my making.

Southern fundamentalist Protestantism, too, converges and conflates with class, and race and gender and sexuality. Historically it has been raced and classed and gendered and heterosexual. Religion is one way of being and living in the world; likewise, Southern religion is a way of being and living in the South. Hill (1999) notes the cooperative relation that exists between Southern religion and its surrounding culture. He explains, "The southern church is comfortable in its homeland, and the culture sits comfortably in its church" (p. 30). Richardson (2003) adds, "...the lingering Calvinistic allegiance to a sovereign God with the Baptist election as God's people prepared the psychic groundwork for the emergence of a regional consciousness, which became the South" (p. 78).

Although there are hundreds of fundamentalist sects and denominations of Christianity, when we fellow queer fundamentalists meet one another in the line at Wal-Mart or at the beauty shop, or even at curriculum conferences, we can nod knowingly at experiences we share in common. I suppose it is somewhat the same sensation Graceland pilgrims feel during Anniversary Week. When queer fundamentalists meet, we each know of the other's stations of ambivalences—the light darkness, the dark lightness that is the love and hate entwined together in our desires. We commune. I explore the paradox of my experience and try to work through the tension between queerness and fundamentalism rather than deny the complexity and contradictions between my identifications and desires, thereby exploring the promise of a different, unfettered communion.

Literature on Southern Place and Curriculum

If place is crucial to understanding the self and society, then it is central to curriculum studies that relate the individual and the social. A concept of place brings the particularistic into focus by linking the understanding of the individual to the social forces that flow through him or her. Place embodies the social and the particular. Employing the South as illustration, Kincheloe and Pinar (1991) introduce the notion of place as one organizing idea for political, autobiographical, racial, and gender issues in curriculum, and they propose a progressive political Southern curriculum theory that is grounded in the particularity of place. Their collection of essays illustrates these themes by focusing on the place called the South and the unique distortions remaining from its history. From a synthesis (Pinar, 1996, p. 291) of self and situation, the individual and the social, which they characterize as social psychoanalysis, Kincheloe and Pinar (1991) explore the possibility of cultural and educational renewal through social psychoanalytic Southern studies.

In addition to voice, community, and gender, the concept of place has emerged as a means to understanding curriculum autobiographically and biographically. In *Curriculum as Social Psychoanalysis: The Significance of Place* (1991), Kincheloe and Pinar consider the question of place by examining its autobiographical aspects. In the collection, seven writers examine issues of curriculum as related to place, and in particular, the place that is the American South. Quoting Eudora Welty, Kincheloe and Pinar note that place and human feeling are intertwined. When events take place, they achieve particularity and concreteness; they become infused with feeling. Fiction expresses daily human experience, situated in concrete places with specific characters. Kincheloe and Pinar (1991) write: "place is the life-force of fiction, serving as the crossroads of circumstance, the playing field on which drama evolves" (p. 4). Place and time are intertwined: "Place is place only if accompanied by a history" (p. 8).

Edgerton (1991)[8] writes autobiographically of her childhood in northern Louisiana, attempting to situate her understanding of the South as place in her life history and in her reading of the autobiography of Maya Angelou. Edgerton shares a fundamental experience of displacement and "otherness" with Angelou, despite their racial difference. She appreciates certain positive elements of the Southern experiences: "nature, smells, risk taking, and music" (p. 96). In the distinction between alienation and angst, Edgerton distinguishes her experiences from Angelou's and establishes the centrality of her own embedded Southern experiences to her autobiographical research. She concludes,

> While some of my negative experience of the South is tied to alienation—
> discomfort with Southern sexism, racism, and fundamentalism—my most

embedded experiences...are closer to angst....Our difference functions as a foil, forcing me back onto myself. (pp. 96—97)

In "Willie Morris and the Southern Curriculum: Emancipating the Southern Ghosts," Kincheloe (1991b) draws upon the autobiography of Willie Morris, as he responds poetically to the Southern ghosts that "haunted his mind and body" (p. 123). Kincheloe characterizes Morris as a student of Southern traditions, constantly linking his life history to a history of place. He concludes that without autobiographical self-remembrance, Morris might not have understood how Mississippi remained in his soul. Kincheloe writes, "Without self-understanding, however, he could not see the connections between himself and Mississippi; he had to transcend it to find it. He had to transcend it to find himself" (p. 145). Kincheloe suggests that the social psychoanalytical element of Southern curriculum might allow us, as it did Morris, to come to the source of "modern alienation" (p. 145).

Pinar's (1991) essay in that volume depicts interdisciplinary Southern studies programs at the universities of Mississippi and South Carolina which express in curricular form repressed historical and cultural elements of the South. According to Pinar, when such elements surface and are reintegrated culturally and politically, impediments to psychosocial development will be removed. Via this process of cultural renewal, the general educational level of the South might be raised. Pinar argues that what the Southern literary renaissance achieved in the early decades of the twentieth century must now be achieved in Southern mass culture; namely a restoration of memory and history of the Southern place so that it can be understood as distinctive historically and culturally. He suggests a program of interdisciplinary Southern Studies—organized thematically around race, class, and gender, employing autobiography—that might eventually engender "a psychology of social commitment" (p. 180).[9]

Situating life history in the cultural context of the South, Slattery and Daigle (1994) explore "Curriculum as a Place of Turmoil" in twentieth-century Louisiana fiction. The apparently divergent life histories of Jane Pittman in Ernest Gaines's (1972) *The Autobiography of*

Miss Jane Pittman and Walker Percy's Tom More in *The Thanatos Syndrome* (1987) are juxtaposed in their struggle to break free from the bondage of Southern social boundaries. Slattery and Daigle proposed that the barrier of the Mississippi River that separates Jane's world of slavery in Pointe Coupee Parish from Tom's world of melancholy in the aristocracy of Feliciana Parish is actually the force that unites them. Slattery and Daigle write, "As we deconstruct the anguish in Pointe Coupee and Feliciana, we will also explore the response to the turmoil that allows Tom and Jane to meander across boundaries in order to transform the anguish of their societies" (p. 443). Slattery and Daigle link the meanderings of the river and the two literary characters and suggest that from this example of border and boundary transgression, educators and curriculum specialists might move toward a deconstruction of institutional borders.

In "A Last Dying Chord? Toward Cultural and Educational Renewal in the South," Kincheloe, Pinar, and Slattery (1994) link contemporary curriculum discourses in a curriculum theory of place; as meaning cannot be separated from context and the knower cannot be separated from the known, so, too, does the process of understanding curriculum occur within the context of place. Following a brief sketch of the problematic of the South as place, they elaborate on a curriculum of Southern studies that centers around the concept of identity. They suggest that a social psychoanalytic curriculum of Southern studies would not sentimentalize Southern history or culture by isolating them historically, abstracting their particularity and specificity, or denying their distortions. The authors write, "Southern studies would work, as does psychoanalysis, to enlarge the social ego of southerners so that distortions can be acknowledged, psychologically accepted, but socially and politically suspended" (p. 434). The suspension of Southernness as a form of identification that has safeguard and preserved racism, misogyny, and homophobia by invoking place-in-past not only reveals a greater complexity to feeling Southern, but also opens a space for reconstructive social and political movement in the South.

Camping Toward Canaan:
On the Significance of the Study of the South

At a time when race, not just black and white, but the whole emerging, multicultural stew of twenty-first century America is the underlying social issue in America, no place has been so defined by race, alternately enobled and debased by it, as the South. The South's past may offer up more wrong turns than right ones, but its experience…is as good a distillation of the nation's search for its soul as we are likely to find.

—Applebome, (1997, p. 344)

February 14, 2004, was the Valentine's Day of an election year, which would be, ordinarily, an unremarkable pairing. This year, though, love and politics proved a volatile mix. In the middle of primary season, the Supreme Judicial Court in Massachusetts declared that recognizing unions between couples who are gay/lesbian as anything less than "marriage" is unconstitutional. State legislatures began scrambling to define marriage by law.[5] Throughout the long Valentine's weekend, hundreds of same-sex couples gathered at City Hall in San Francisco, where Mayor Gavin Newsom ordered that licenses be granted to gay couples. James Parker and Eric Oliver, a couple from Mobile, Alabama, my home state, had traveled across the country to legalize their two-year union. Says Parker, "If it doesn't stick this time, it will—eventually. Either way, it was the best feeling you could ever have" ("More Gays, Lesbians Marry on Eve of Court Hearing," 2004). As one state after another, fourteen in all, passed same-sex marriage amendments and proceeded to re-elect the President, it became apparent that it would not stick this time, either.

We live in the reign of W, with radical, rather than compassionate, conservatism validating the power bloc of the Religious Right.[6] President Bush kicked off his campaign with an appearance at the Daytona 500; pundits observed that he wanted to shore up the NASCAR dad votes. "Gentlemen, start your engines," he decreed. And the race is on. As if on cue, spokespersons for the Right appeared on network news programs with engines, and mouths, running full throttle. They represent groups with words like "family," "American," "citizens," and "values" in their names. The argument against gay marriage seems to me primarily a religious one, cloaked in civic and cultural politics so that it will not appear to be about religion to the media and "mainstream America." The underlying objectives and motives for making the gay marriage argument in the first place are political, cloaked in religion and morality so as to appeal to a strong conservative religious voting bloc. To nudge the electorate along in making the appropriate connection, one campaign sign, hand painted and nailed to a telephone pole in my parish, read, "Bush, Christ, Hope."

During Valentine's weekend, one man speaking about the San Francisco weddings declared that the disturbing issue was a renegade mayor's disregard for the law, that only secondary was the concern that marriage was to be between a man and a woman. On another network, a spokeswoman was interviewed. She seemed primarily bothered by the chaos in San Francisco, a kind of vigilante matrimony running rampant in the streets. Oh, and by the way, marriage should be between a man and a woman. Neither fooled me. The Right Republicans were hoping that people would vote their hearts in November, not about anything so base as war, or gas prices, or employment, or health care for the elderly, but about whether or not they could stomach the idea of men having sex with men and women having sex with women. Patriotism, it seems, is straight.

And that is exactly what happened on November 2, 2004. The whole nation was poised for a close election that hinged on a handful of swing states. The Republican strategy had been brilliant; President Bush had come out early with his stance on marriage and then said little more publicly about it. He did not have to; conservatives had not only placed marriage amendments on state ballots, thus drawing the public's attention to the issue in the voting machines, they had also promoted conservative ideology so that moral issues had moved to the forefront of voter concerns. And they had made the people's moral champion George W. Bush. *Choose you this day whom ye will serve* (Joshua 24:15).

Except for the interview of two grooms from Alabama, there is nothing overtly Southern about the San Francisco story, or about gay marriages, or about homosexuality for that matter. But then, some of the most delicious insights may be found within the indirect observations. I am a Southern woman, even when watching the news. To complicate things, I am a Southern fundamentalist Christian lesbian woman, blue collar past, white collar here and now. To be truthful, sometimes I hardly know what to think about anything anymore. I have a secret hope that gay rights initiatives fail, so deep does the conservative fundamentalist indoctrination run. A part of me still thinks like "they" do, and it terrifies me. A queer fundamentalist, my concern is that my repressive thinking comes from my Southernness; my consolation is that my free thinking is Southern too, but from anomalies of Southern identity that work against white, patriarchal, misogynistic, heteronormative frames. Positioned subjectively and socially within the fissures of fundamentalism, I am not completely disidentified with it totally, but reveal internal contradictions of fundamentalist discourse, determined to emerge with faith and desire through queer Southernness—a location for transformation self- and social change.

Britzman (1998) poses this question concerning curriculum, "What would curriculum be like if the curriculum began with the problem of living a life?" (p. 49). I suggest that it might begin to resemble more life itself: it would be curriculum that takes into account the bodies, voices, interactions, spirits, and desires of people. It would be a curriculum in which those people—their behaviors and feelings—are contextualized by time and place. Curriculum continues to be "complicated conversation" that, when seized as an opportunity of reflection and engagement, becomes, according to Pinar, an action of "private meaning and public hope" (2004, p. 188). Part of the reason that curriculum is "complicated" is that place is significant to it. My research into a curriculum of place begins with the problem of living a life—my life, as a white, lower-class, Southern woman—within the context of past and place. Unlayering dysfunctional nostalgia for place that sentimentalizes the past and thereby keeps us living it, contributes to shaping what Pinar (2004) calls a "curriculum of southern studies whose educational point is...a psychoanalytically-informed interdisciplinary study and re-experience of the past" (p. 241). An understanding of the South is a necessary requisite for educational reconstruction in the United States; without the reclaiming of history and memory, the South might maintain—in denial—its history of defeat and defeatism.

Curriculum and schooling—like living a life—do not take place in isolation, but in the every day. Students and teachers are who we are in large part because of where we are; we are shaped by place; we believe, behave, speak and desire in place; we interact with each other in place. Schubert (1986) states, "The curriculum is the interpretation of lived experiences" (p. 33); as such, the concept of place continues to emerge as a means to understanding curriculum autobiographically and biographically. Our lived experiences take place somewhere. And this somewhere is significant to interpreting lived experiences. Adams, Hoelscher, and Till (2001) refer to this sociospatial context within which communication takes place as "textures of place" (p. xiv). That is, place transcends its literal and visceral attributes; woven into its texture are social and cultural communicative and interactive processes that continue to define and create place, even as they contextualize those very actions. Because place and human feeling are intertwined, a political curriculum of place must negotiate the politics of place, which are to be found in the day-to-day lives and voices of its people.

The autobiographical study of a Southern curriculum of place has practical significance as it disturbs monolithic notions of the South. When Southerners re-member, re-collect, and re-claim the stories of our lived experiences, we disrupt identity politics that creates a "consciousness of commonality" (Hackney, 2004, p. 189) by prioritizing difference (p. 181). Southerners and non-Southerners may come to see through the impermeable veil of mythology and manners that surround the South. Williamson (1986) names place as a key element in the organic society of the Old South and central to maintaining postwar Conservatism. In a "rage" (p. 34) for white identity, place figured then, as it figures now, in maintaining conservativism toward race, class, gender, and sexuality as white Southerners seek not to reconstruct but to restore a "placeness in time" (p. 22). Examining lived experiences as they are contextualized in place might help us understand the people of this region, a place that continues to live out its tumultuous history of raced, classed, and gendered strife.

By posing the question, "What and when is 'there'?" St. Pierre (2000, p. 263) further strengthens the idea of interconnectedness between past-in-place and the white Southerner's attachment to both that is central to a study of the South. She writes, "The point here about attachment to places, and our histories in them, is that home is not a haven; identity can never be a refuge" (p. 260). St. Pierre considers the *where* of *when* and the *when* of *where* by calling on Deleuze and Guattari's (1987/1980) "nomad deterritorialization of striated spaces" (in St. Pierre, p. 263). As a location where past and place are coded and performed in identity construction, the South may be confronted as such a striated space. Within the smooth spaces of South, without coded interiority and with only a "milieu of exteriority" (p. 264), are found anomalous forms of Southernness that offer new ways of feeling Southern.

Perhaps by "confronting the constraining framework" (St. Pierre, 2000, p. 260) of our geographically situated past with the objective of deterritorializing the bounded striated codes of the South, we might move toward smooth spaces of consciousness that are uninscribed, affirmative, and joyous (p. 266). I use "move toward" rather than reach because smooth spaces are spaces of means, not spaces of ends. They are spaces of questioning and uncertainty, spaces of disruption and discomfort. Working toward smooth is risky; we embark expecting to employ a generative "practice of failure" (Lather, 1996, p. 3). Of this identity-based memory work, St. Pierre writes,

> (It is a voyage that) always seems to involve painful desubjectification, joyful disarticulation...It is an affirmative, joyous space, perhaps the most thrilling of all the fields in which we work. (p. 260, 266)

Troubling Southern codes and boundaries might allow us to make meaning about how those codes have functioned as identity constructs that code and bound us as well.

Entwined with a regional history of "The South" are the histories of countless individuals lived out daily in schools, factories, banks, churches, law offices, bedrooms, malls, and so on. The juxtaposition of the two histories might lead to awareness and understanding—of self, self and other, and self and society—by Southerners and non-Southerners alike. Kincheloe, Pinar, and Slattery (1994) argue that the major contemporary curriculum discourses—the political, the racial, the autobiographical, the theological, the aesthetic, the poststructural, the phenomenological, and the gender-focused—can all be linked in a curriculum theory of place. As meaning cannot be separated from context and the knower cannot be separated from the known, so does the process of understanding curriculum occur within the context of place, or within its textures, if you will.

Slattery (1995) writes, "[These] curriculum landscapes and experiences of transformative pedagogy challenge the educational community to reevaluate the traditional understanding of the learning environment" (p. 215). Place is a curriculum landscape that brings the particularistic into focus by allowing us to examine ourselves much like the hypnosis patient: we can see ourselves as subjects within a particular setting. On the count of three, we may also begin to fuse and/or defuse events to emotions and make meaning. This is curriculum that begins with the problem of living a life by taking into consideration where the life is lived, a landscape ready for the groundbreaking for educational and social reconstruction.

The South is one and many, and from the voices of its one and many people a multidimensional reconstruction of Southern structures might emerge to inform curriculum. Reed (1982) examines the social-psychological nature of Southern identity and regional consciousness. According to Reed, Southern affection for religion and localism, for example, contribute to a group identification that exceeds that of American Roman Catholics and trade union members and approaches that of Blacks and Jews. He writes,

When survey researchers find in a region a variable that makes more difference in responses, on the average, than occupation does, more than religion does, more than urban-rural residence does, as much as race and probably as much as education does (all these are Norval Glenn's findings), when they find a variable like that, how much longer can they treat it as a nuisance and pass it off with ad hoc explanations? (p. 41)

Reed positions the South as a distinct sociological region with a regional identification and consciousness; certain of us identify as Southerners, and we answer research surveys with responses distinct to the region.

Reed's sociological studies of the South over the past three decades show the designation Southerner to be not only a regional, cultural, and political category, but also an ethnic one. He suggests that Southern regional studies be contextualized within "the conceptual and methodological apparatus of ethnic group research" (p. 4).[7] People who are Southern for the most part consider themselves to be—or perhaps it is just the other way: perhaps those of us who consider ourselves to be, are. Considering my perspective as a researcher of things Southern as well as things curricular, my quest is increasingly to delve into what it means to feel Southern. I consider myself to be many "things," but I am each of these things, I am finding, as a Southerner.

Notes

1   Sociologist John Shelton Reed (1982, 1983, 2003) supports the idea of sense of place in his regional studies of Southern regional consciousness and identity. He considers religion and localism ("the tendency to see communities as different from each other and to prefer one's own) to be "enduring aspects of Southern culture" (1982, p. 133).

I also want to add a note on capitalizing South and Southern. I agree with Reed, as he explains, "The work I have been doing since the publication in 1971 of a book called *The Enduring South* is based on the conviction that the South remains as much a sociological phenomenon as a geographical one. Despite the determination of most publishers to spell Southern with a lowercase s, I believe that the

South is still a cultural and cognitive reality of considerable, and in some ways increasing, importance" (p. 3). I use capital S based on these same principles.

2   Williamson (1986) examines a "rage for order" in black-white relations in the South by tracing the primary roots of race relations in modern America to Southern past. He describes a "crucible of race" (p. viii), a Southern story of race relations featuring a combination of race, sex, and class.

3   We might also begin to see the South as sites of queer, desire, belonging, and becoming. From a Deleuzian conception of desire and movement, Probyn looks at the singularity of queer desire that is to be found in how it uses the body to "connect and reconnect relations" (p. 53). I am very interested in her notion of how desire as movement might be used and in the connection she makes between desire, milieux, and the self. She writes,

> Beyond a taxonomy of good or bad manifestations of desire, what interests me are questions about how to use queer desire in such a way that it is not condensed in an individualizing logic and measure. Put another way, the question is how to use desire so as to put it to work as a singular and queer form of movement....As a theoretical strategy, and as a mode of cultural criticism, desire compels us to write fully of and within the milieux that give meaning to life, milieux that constitute the singularities of social life. The challenge of writing is to become what one is describing becoming. (p. 61—62)

4   Besides "Carry Me Back," the Statler Brothers greatest hits album from 1975, *The Best of the Statler Brothers*, featured songs that plucked the heartstrings of those who yearned for the good old days, such as "Whatever Happened to Randolph Scott." "Do You Remember These," "The Class of '57," and "Pictures." The album cover itself is a study in nostalgia: an oval portrait in sepia tones of four very staid-looking ladies. Their hair and clothing are circa 1890; each looks at the camera as if holding a pose for a daguerreotype. Catching the appeal to backwards-looking generation is not much of a stretch.

5   The Louisiana state senate passed a measure by a vote of 31—6 that would allow a vote on a constitutional amendment to ban same-sex marriages and forbid the recognition of civil unions. Despite the ruling by a district judge in New Orleans that the proposed amendment could not be placed on the ballot, on September 18, 2004, by a large margin, voters approved the state constitutional amendment. Although Louisiana already has a law recognizing marriage only between a man

and a woman, this amendment gives constitutional protection to that law. It also prohibits state officials and courts from recognizing any out-of-state same-sex marriages or civil unions.

6   What is the compassionate conservatism that President George W. Bush espoused during the 2000 election? According to Stephen Goldsmith, former Governor of Indiana and domestic policy advisor to Bush's 2000 campaign,

> Fundamentally, compassionate conservatism is a form of political conservatism. In other words, compassionate conservatives believe that government should have a limited role in people's lives and that competition in the marketplace is the most effective means of producing social and economic progress. Consequently, compassionate conservatives believe in low taxes, limited government regulation and the vast power of the free enterprise system. (Goldsmith, 2000, http://www.hoover.stanford.edu/publications/digest/004/goldsmith.html)

Conservative writer and former Bush speechwriter David Frum puts it another way: "The phrase itself is wonderful. [It has broad appeal because] it combines the left's favorite adjective with the right's favorite noun, creating an almost irresistible popular appeal" (quoted in Kuypers, et al, 2003, http://www.acjournal.org/holdings/vol6/iss4/articles/kuypers.htm).

7   *In Southerners: The Social Psychology of Sectionalism* (1983), Reed advocates Southern regional studies that fit Southerners into ethnic social science models analogous to those used to study American immigrant cultures. He suggests that scholars study not The South, but Southerners within the contexts of "ordinary concerns of ethnic group research—questions of identity, stereotyping, prejudice, social distance, and the like—and to see how well the analogy fit" (p. 4). He writes,

> These inquiries generally supported the basic assumption that it was indeed worthwhile to apply the conceptual and methodological apparatus of ethnic group research to the study of Southerners. Although some of the differences between Southerners and groups more commonly thought of as 'ethnic' are obvious (and others, less obvious, need to be emphasized), there are enough similarities to suggest that searching for others might be a productive line of work. (p. 4)

8   See also Edgerton (1996) *Translating the Curriculum* for Edgerton's demonstration of the significance of place within autobiographical theory.

9   Pinar may or may not have had in mind events such as the annual Elvis Conference held at the University of Mississippi. Applebome (1997) describes the event as

> ...wholly in keeping with the liberal takeover of Southern studies on college campuses that had taken them from the misty-eyed Old South hagiography the neo-Cons were belatedly trying to revive to a celebration of the pop culture of the South, with the clear subtext that the pop culture of the South had largely become the mainstream culture of America. (p. 290)

Chapter 2
Season of Lilacs: Nostalgia and Homeplace(s) of Difference

Down home, where they know you by name and treat you like family,
Down home, where a man's good word and a handshake are all you need.
Folks know when you're fallin' on hard times you can fall back on
Those of us raised up—down home.

--Alabama (1985)

Prologue

When my grandmother died, it was April, and the lilacs were in full bloom. I think back on those lilacs now, realizing that they, like the women in whose lives they played such a part, define homeplace for me. I realize that I cling to them, the flowering, decadently scented lilac that stands at the doorway like the angel at the Garden of Eden, and the women of Big Mama's. But the angel armed with flaming sword was placed at the Garden's entrance by God to keep people *out*, so homeplace, even as it beckons, has its own fiery barriers. I can no more cross the threshold of home guarded by the lilac than Adam and Eve could get past God's messenger. And yet, just as the searchers have sought the now mythic Eden, Southerners like me spend an endless quest yearning for homeplace, trying to go home.

It was around my grandmother's table that I first learned about homeplace, as she and her 5 remaining daughters, the sisters, recollected the old hard days and made plans to go back. In the same way that bell hooks (1990) contends, "houses belonged to women" (p. 41), for me, home is made by them. On Sundays, over coffee and caramel cake, they lovingly described the house and place where six babies were born. I learned that the old homeplace was a location of enshrined desire. And it is within nostalgia, a yearning for home, that desire and homeplace ideology intersect.

Daddy's people did not like Mother's people. My father's father had finally left the farm, got factory work, and moved inside the town limits. When his son, my father, fell in love with a girl from "the mountain," it appeared to them like a step backward. My mother's home was a place of noise and music and laughter and hard liquor—everything that Daddy's fundamentalist Christian mores denounced as sinful. The pact was made: when they married, she would disavow that lifestyle, stay away from home. I knew very little of my maternal family until I was 12 years old and my mother could not stay away any longer. She took me with her to Sunday coffee at Big Mama's.

By the time I met them, Big Mama had left her job at the local truck stop, and the sisters had divorced the wild young men who drank and played music on Saturday nights. I returned to a Sunday afternoon matriarchy that had resigned itself to calm. Now the sisters and their daughters returned to sit around the same table, now cluttered with chipped coffee cups rather than bottles of Jack Daniels. Big Mama's house was not quiet or orderly. The old house creaked and heaved with determination as it enveloped the lives it cradled, including, again, Mother's, and now, mine.

I write "Big Mama" when I refer to my grandmother, but it is a habit that I had to work to acquire. Because I met her when I was 12, she and I lacked a certain familiarity: I had to learn to call her a name. Daddy smirked when Mother approached him about how I would know my grandmother. I remember his remark that 20 years ago the local bootlegger was known as "Big Mama." I was my father's daughter even then and ignored the pain on Mother's face when I referred to "my mother's mother." Since I was not encouraged to call my grandmother what all the other grandchildren called her, I felt set apart and distanced, displaced. I went for coffee anyway and forged my own relationships.

Some images never leave us. When Big Mama got sick in 1983, the sisters rallied. Nobody was taking care of their mother except them, and they stayed with her around the clock for a year. On a Sunday very different from those spent around the table, I saw death still in the claiming. Big Mama had no appetite and was drinking only a little milk. Mother was at her bedside trying to get her to eat yogurt. I could not bear to go into the dark bedroom, witnessing the scene instead from the next room, as close as I could get but not nearly as far away as I longed to be. My mother coaxed her mother to eat, tiny spoonful by tiny spoonful, cooing to her as she had to my own baby, to me as an infant. She tenderly spoke words of love to her mother, words devoid of joy, words sickeningly rich with heartache. I had never felt so low and empty and sick, and I never have since.

After she died, I was wracked with remorse because I missed so many years. I loved her, and I treasure the time I spent with her. But regret and guilt are old friends who call often; there would be no moving forward. Then I dreamt my dream. She and I were alone in the darkness, and I, grown and helpless, was sitting in her lap. She enveloped me in an old string quilt, soft and comfortable with age. Her words and her body soothed me; I knew that I had known her. And my heart and mind rested easy.

When the sisters finally made the pilgrimage back home, some 50 years after leaving it, they carried with them buckets and tools. They came for artifacts, tangible memories. Each collected cuttings from foliage that remained, now overgrown with scrub bushes and weeds. My mother and her four sisters cut through the wild vines and tall weeds to reclaim their mama's garden and take it home with them — old plants: mock orange, iris, forsythia (yellow bells), and lilac. Since then, wherever Mother has lived, wherever I have lived, we have dug up a piece of those plants, with good roots so they will live. "They won't ever even know they've been moved," she tells me. I do this because wherever I live, it comforts me to know there is a lilac by my door.

"Something About the Southland…"

What is the lure of home? I allude to the seduction above, by evoking powerful, lasting images of home and place in a narrative that effectuates what Gilmore (2001) calls "the power of narrative to heal" (p. 7). Homeplace is an aspect of Southern place and feeling Southern

inundated with conventional notions of Southern identity; a curriculum of place should consider the socially constructed sense of place
that arises from homeplace experiences. This chapter situates homeplace as a site for the interrogation of identity construction rather than
the consoling, pacifying mirror of identity. When the idea of home is
sacred to those who long to return there for sanctuary, it paralyzes us
to growth, to our own becoming; we might, however, reclaim home
by re(memory)ing it. I suggest that the white Southerner's sense of
place, of *home*place, might begin with an interrogation of self, place,
difference, and (dis)locatedness.

My analysis of homeplace narrative weaves autobiographical narrative—in this case a reading of the lived experiences of one rural,
working-class, queer-lesbian-feminist fundamentalist Christian—with
literary texts and curriculum theories. Southern place is the context by
which these hyphens of identity construction may be worked; home
informs place as place informs home. Both inform the self by contributing to the sense of place within white Southerners. Homeplace
identity has particular embedded meanings for white Southerners,
and there are diverse and varied Southern homeplace identities to
account for. As research on Southern place insists on maintaining
connections among race, class, and gender, this study of homeplace
within place maintains those same connections by engaging memory
to encounter nostalgia, desire—not just for home, but for the *idea* of
home—for, as Probyn notes, desire remembered is "deeply imbri-
cated in the structuring principles of race, class, gender, and place"
(p. 110).

From what do we seek to be healed by a transformative journeying home? Perhaps from what we imagine—or have made—
homeplace to be: the journey's end, the place that was over the rainbow all along, complete with our own Uncle Henry and Auntie Em.
Memory (home)work demands a negotiation of past and place, a
grappling with nostalgic episodes of downhome, so that we might
make meanings and cultivate awareness within locations of home and
place. We might, as Asher (2003) terms it, "engage the possibility of
transformation" (p. 242) by "developing self-reflexive awareness, and

working through the splits of self and other" (p. 237) regarding homeplace. The healing, then, is of the illusion of comfortable sameness, of a unitary belonging that thwarts the potential of transformation and integrity of the self—of becoming.

Home culture is an identity construct to be approached and mined for the singularities of homeplace experience rather than as the source of metanarratives of identity and ultimate origin, Probyn's "founding status" (1996, p. 116). Rather than go home to "create order from the point of beginning" (p. 113), to sit under the shade and sip my cool glass of sweet tea, I disrupt past and place with memory, reclaiming them, past and place, "with the fervor of the possible" (p. 116). In other words, I try not to succumb to the temptation to look back and explain the present or assign causality. *Ah, so because this happened, I am this way or that; I did this thing or that...*Home(be)coming is a recursive journey which looks at the past-in-place with an eye toward the future. It is a journey of deliberate displacement, in which the sojourner becomes, to coin Flannery O'Connor's term, "the displaced person" (1971).

Throughout this chapter, I purposely link displacement to dislocatedness in relation to a curriculum of place-through-self. Dictionary meanings of displace and dislocate are similar: both mean to remove or expel from the usual or proper place. *Displace* has the added dimension of the physical forcing of one to flee one's home or homeland; while *dislocate* means more particularly a forced change in normal/usual connections, status, relationships, or order (Merriam-Webster, 2003). I use them interchangeably to draw the focus to the notion of *place* within each. The displaced person in O'Connor's story is displaced due to war—he is a foreigner. This displacement, and that of genocide, flood, and so on, is different from the displacement from home that I describe in this chapter. Rather than suggest, for example, that the displacements of immigrants and war refugees are similar to or at least parallel to that of white Southerners, or to the displacement of blacks and queers, I point to a displacement of the self-within-place, perpetrated and perpetuated by the over identification and attachment to past-in-place. The displacement of white

Southerners, for example, may be characterized by the devotion to the Southern Lost Cause.

The Lost Cause is a romanticized idea of the South, the persisting legend of a lost civilization, one that never was and is always in the future. It is a celebration of what white Southerners see as the pinnacle of the Confederacy: "its nobility, its Christian virtues, its leadership, the loyalty of its men" (Ayers, 2004, transcript). According to Blight, white Southerners forged the Lost Cause, "not as a story about loss, but a story about victory. They might have lost the way, but they were now winning the ultimate victory, over control of their own society and against Reconstruction" (2004, transcript). White Southerners, in the attempt to continually maintain separations and expel the abject other (Sibley, 1995, p. 8) are ourselves abject, other, separate— displaced.

Another sense in which I employ *displaced* and *dislocated* is as displacement within displacement, that of one who by her acknowledged difference—and the rejection of that difference by home—is removed emotionally, physically, relationally, and so on, from the place. This is the context of my discussion of Minnie Bruce Pratt's and Dorothy Allison's respective returns home later in this chapter, and of my recognition of myself as Misfit that marks this research. As Edgerton (1991) describes what she experienced during her childhood: "The displacement becomes significant in that one cannot simply choose another place that is truly home. The place called 'home' is in many ways closer to being a part of the anatomy than mere geographic location" (p. 92). The homecoming of the displaced to the displaced home disrupt rigid boundaries of exclusion and separation.

Indigo Girls (Saliers, 1990) sing, "There's something about the Southland in the springtime...where the waters flow with confidence and reason," but *what* is there? The lure of the South is conflated with that of home, giving particular meaning to *homeland* for white Southerners. McPherson (2003) notes, "...the meaning of South often slides into the meaning of home [through the] tight interweaving of tropes of home, femininity, and region" (p. 216). And both South and home slide into the homeplace feminine ideal of Mother: *How's ye mama nem?* [1]

This shifting by which it becomes no longer possible to differentiate between South and home—and Mother, fuels the dynamic tensions that designate *homeplace,* or *downhome.* As I make my own home-journey, I confront and disrupt "dominant constructions" (Gilmore, 2001, p. 13) of home and conceptualize new meanings by loosening the interwoven tropes. It is difficult, for example, to explore the home-trope of femininity without confronting the pervasive forces of masculinity that are also present in the person of the father. If emancipatory meaning may then be made of homeplace, then so may it also be of the South, with which it is indistinguishable to white Southerners. Homeplace—the journey toward reclaiming home—is a metaphor for the South. Parallels between South and self are uncovered by disrupting the comforts of home, by tossing a rock into the waters flowing with confidence and reason. Home is in the ripples, not the flow.

Telling: Homeplace as Narrative Text

The interplay of nostalgia, homeplace, and sense of place perpetuates a Southern sensibility cultivated through a pervading sense of other. In *Reconstructing Dixie: Race, Gender and Nostalgia in the Imagined South,* McPherson (2003) interrogates Southern whiteness as it is reified through media portrayal, including the film, television, documentary, and tourism media. She uncovers the recursive connections between race and Southern femininity and offers her own interpretation of how each informs and is informed of the other within Southern historical and cultural structures. In much the same way that race and Southern womanhood are enmeshed, McPherson explains, the meanings of the South and home have entwined to shape homeplace ideology. Within a spiral discourse of place, home is one construct of feeling, and therefore of being, Southern.

Home becomes a conversion narrative in the working through of tensions. Born of guilt and seeking forgiveness, home as conversion narrative manifests the Southern compulsion, not only to "tell about the South" (p. 217), but to also tell the South. In order to tell the South, we go home to find voice that we might speak ourselves as well, and in familiar language that soothes and comforts. McPherson cites Hobson's (1999) contention that the racial conversion narrative borrows, "from earlier, often Puritan conversion tales in their appropriation of religious tropes, in their confessional tone, and in their pursuit of redemption, though here the salvation is secular" (in McPherson, 2003, p. 217). But is it secular?

McPherson's positioning of the Southern conversion narrative in terms of Colonial Puritan conversion narratives opens up the dialogue of race, class, and gender to the implicatedness of religion in Southern identities, including homeplace identities. From out of Southern narrative appropriations of religious tropes, homeplace has itself become a trope and a significant anchor in the storying of Southern redemption. A homeplace narrative that unrests and unsettles, one that evolves out of multiple meanings and discomfort, might be a transformative conversion narrative. A homeplace narrative of a reconstructed South might employ a discourse of convergent spaces, of transcending a downhome that mires the South in past and place. When memory work is a self-reflective interrogation that facilitates, as Asher suggests, "understanding [one's self and one's narrative] in relation to different others instead of apart from them (2003, p. 245), familiar Southern sensibilities may themselves be unsettled by a rupturing of the comforts of home.

The Discomforts of Home: Minnie Bruce Pratt and Dorothy Allison

Reclaiming home as a network of difference from which the (dis)placed self emerges—of-the-place, but not *unto*-the-place—suggests the interrogation of self, place, and homeplace-yearning in terms of larger contexts. For this study the socio-cultural-political contexts that underlie homeplace narratives are race, class, gender, sexuality, and religion.[2] Edgerton (1996) credits Toni Morrison with naming the working through of place, people, and past *re-memory* (p.

141) and describes this work as an "intellectual and intersubjective" uncovering of place—with issues of "desire, guilt, privilege, and domination" (p. 152—153). Pratt (1991) calls this "practicing memory" (p. 22). The South, site of desire, guilt, privilege, domination, and defeat, is fertile ground for cultivating an aesthetic of memory; and, thereby, through intersubjective recursivity, it uncovers *itself*. I interrogate homeplace-yearning by engaging the self-transformative narratives of poet/activist/essayist Minnie Bruce Pratt and self-proclaimed white trash feminist Dorothy Allison on their personal and intellectual journeys home. Both are of-the-place—selves shaped by place, time, and other, yet (re)turning to (re)member homeplace with discomfort, agitation, displacement. Home is no safe harbor; it is the storm into which they sail.

Pratt's intellectually and emotionally powerful collection of essays, *Rebellion: Essays 1980-1991* (1991), which includes the 1984 "Identity: Skin, Blood, Heart," disrupts homeplace nostalgia by critiquing Southern white women's identity constructions entangled in racism, classism, and heterosexism. I chose the *Rebellion* collection, rather than access "Identity" from the often-cited *Yours in Struggle: Three Feminist Perspectives on Anti-Semitism and Racism* (1984), co-authored with Bulkin and Smith, for reasons regarding scope. As a later edition spanning over a decade of work, *Rebellion* presents a broader scope of Pratt's writings. It includes essays in which she elaborates on themes touched upon in "Identity," her mother, for instance, and her lesbianism.

Pratt's personal and political, transformative memory work, in which she recounts and reclaims past and place, illustrates the *place* of place narratives in a curriculum of place. In *Rebellion* she attends to place-in-time, illustrating ways in which the past is present in the South and exerts its influence over the reproduction of white Southern homeplace. In the title essay, Pratt juxtaposes excerpts from the diary of Mary Boykin Chesnut and poetry in praise of Confederate heroes with episodes of her girlhood in Alabama and her antiracist activism in North Carolina. While the themes of unsettling traditional white Western feminist thought regarding anti-Semitism and racism are as timely and thought-provoking now as 20 years ago, Pratt's narratives may be read for the significance of place, within which home is situated, in elaborating larger socio-cultural-political contexts and identity construction. Pratt's themes are enhanced rather than diminished by their contextualization in a curriculum of place.

In configurations of homeplace where home, region, and femininity are interwoven, Mother is central to the telling of homeplace, and thus to the uncovering of homeplace identity constructions. While Pratt confronts her own dislocatedness primarily by re-memory(ing) home-as-father, Dorothy Allison's displacement is borne of mother-yearning: a daughter's love for a mother who cannot save her. Allison's transgressive trauma narratives are important to this study, as I employ her work to suggest home as a metaphor for, as Gilmore (2001) phrases it, "the persistence of love" (p. 47, 66), as exemplified in the complicated bond between mother and daughter. Allison's complicated bond with her mother is further complicated and underscored by poverty, illegitimacy, and incest. Her mother-yearning is representative of nostalgia, a mournful, persistent yearning for home.

Allison's queer and classed subjectivity unsettles traditional narratives of home and in so doing points to anomalous forms of Southernness that might further a marginalized Southern curriculum. Set against violent conventions of Southern identity—white, masculinist, patriarchal, heteronormative, Allison's stories converge at the site of mother-yearning, where she hopes to make meaning of the complexity of her own identity. The memoir-performance piece *Two or Three Things I Know for Sure* (1995) and the essay "Skin, Where She Touches Me," from the collection *Skin: Talking About Sex, Class, and Literature* (1994) particularly illustrate the centrality of mother to home. Both pieces depict Allison's persistent love and admiration for her mother and the unspoken tensions among their relationship, her longing, and a past-in-place of poverty and violence. Allison works the tensions with the telling; if there is meaning to be made, it will be made in the telling. She can reclaim past and place by mourning her own and her mother's loss. Vulnerability is risky, but it is the price, Allison seems to say, of understanding and love, both of/for self and other.

I wear my skin only as thin as I have to, armor myself only as much as seems absolutely necessary. I try to live naked in the world, unashamed even under attack, unafraid even though I know how much there is to fear....I tell myself that life is the long struggle to understand and love fully....I have to try constantly to understand more, love more fully, go more naked in order to make others as safe as I myself want to be. (*Skin*, p. 250)

Allison does not go home to find a comforting mirror of identity; in fact, this prospect terrifies her. She disrupts this notion and embraces difference by reclaiming her mother.

The obvious point in common, besides home themes, between Pratt's and Allison's texts is skin. Skin is the outer covering of identity; for Pratt, it is an outer layer of "false identity" (p. 61), indicator and protector of privilege. For Allison, skin is "the boundary between the world and the soul" (p. 225), protective barrier of the vulnerable interior self and as far as the world can penetrate. Conventional aspects of white patriarchal identity construction go no further than the skin; the survival lie is that of course they do—these traditional constrictors cut to the core of identity. Yet beneath the skin are the constructs of mother-home in which Allison hopes to find affirmation. "Skin, Where She Touches Me" is an account of how her mother's death pierced the skin they had in common, penetrating the surface and laying bare secret intimacies of home. Pratt's and Allison's narratives embody Britzman's (1998, p. 19) "difficult knowledges" of self and South that must be disclosed in the foregrounding of a marginalized curriculum of Southern place.

Getting Home

The journeying home to the past is often not merely to the place of childhood—of our immediate nostalgia—but to fictional cultural, social, and value structures of a century ago. Getting back home means recapturing fictional truths, fed by the simplicity of sameness, that predate critical concerns and uncomfortable knowledges. Kincheloe, Pinar, and Slattery (1994) probe "the complexity of the contemporary

South—a place at once a first and third world, a place at once pre-modern and postmodern with a flickering modernity almost skipped" (p. 420). It may be these things at once, yet the friction that results from the three trying to occupy the same place and time is as hot as a Louisiana August sidewalk. The South—sometimes proclaiming itself The New South—casts a technological and economic eye to the future as it tentatively edges into the present, all the while anchored culturally to the nineteenth century.

The complexity of the contemporary South lies within the raced, classed, gendered, sexual, and religious tensions of place-in-time. The underlying complexities sometimes manifest openly and publicly, at the voting booth, for example. When the "solid South" went solidly and not surprisingly Republican in the 2004 election, voters cited "moral issues" as their deciding factor. Morality represents the codification for maintaining nineteenth century ideals toward sexuality, gender, and religion. With the casting of a vote, we are told by conservative politicians—and preachers—that we can reclaim old-fashioned values by reclaiming a *time*, a time, for example, when gay people would not dare peep out of the closet, much less propose marrying one another.

What the conservatives advocate is a reclaiming of the male-dominant home, the comfortable, safe, protective home. When patriarchal structures of gender within the home are affirmed, homeplace as sanctuary of sameness is also affirmed. Sometimes this sentiment is stated outright. For example, the Promise Keepers' Tony Evans, African American Pastor of the Oak Cliff Baptist Fellowship in Dallas and friend of President Bush, leaves little doubt as to the place of gender-dominance in the home or the violence permitted to reestablish it as he scripts a husband's statement of reclamation to his wife. Evans suggests,

> Over the last thirty years, [this] role reversal has given rise to a feminist movement specifically designed to assert the role of women. Now a lot of women don't like to hear me say this, but I believe that feminists of the more aggressive persuasion are frustrated women unable to find the proper male

leadership...sit down with your wife and say something like this, 'Honey, I've made a terrible mistake...I gave up leading this family, and I forced you to take my place. Now I must reclaim that role.'...I'm not suggesting you ask for your role back, I'm urging you to take it back...there can be no compromise here. If you're going to lead, you must lead...Treat the lady gently and lovingly. But lead! (www.webpan.com/dsinclair/promisekeep-ers.html, http://www.now.org/issues/right/promise/quotes.html)

A home of security and protection, one of sameness, is a place where proper male leadership may flourish and perpetuate itself. The lady, after all, is treated gently and lovingly, soothed into gracious submission. A home that affirms itself as a network of difference and dislocatedness might *in itself* be a location of affirmation and emancipation, a place where its people might "veer into the past and organize a present becoming" (Probyn, 1996, p. 118). Even frustrated feminist women, *lesbian* feminist women, like me.

Pastor Evans' remarks bring to mind a conversation I had recently with a taxi driver in San Antonio. In the space of 12 minutes he told me that he was a confederate reenactor who had been reported to the NAACP for putting a small confederate flag on the bumper of his cab. He said, "Now, I ain't ashamed of my past. If they can fly African flags here, and Mexican flags, why can't I fly mine?" I told him that, well, many people look at that flag and what they see is slavery. He fell back on the centuries-old, Evans-esque argument: "Listen," he said, "they was treated better than most whites. They was treated like family." "Happy darkies" on the farm and "Southern Ladies" in the home are myths in common of Southern place. My cab driver had claimed for himself a Confederate past; he not only clings to it as a source of pride, he performs the crowning point of its Lost Cause existence: the Civil War battlefield. He is home on that battlefield, and he and his band of brothers share a sameness much deeper than their period piece gray uniforms. They are still fighting for a way of life centered on time-in-place, the source of their pride, power, and privilege. Ironic that Pastor Evans would appeal to the same line of thinking as my Confederate cabbie.

Homeplace may be reclaimed as a site for questioning narrow identity constructions through the disrupting of nostalgia. While embracing nostalgia solidifies identity and place norms, disrupting nostalgia allows anomalous, fluid forms of Southernness to surface that might corrode hardened, intransigent Southernness. As Doll (2000) notes, "No one ideal is grasped—not love, not home, certainly not purity—because to grasp is to begin a hardening process" (p. xix). Going home, going to homeplace restores the spirit with the richness of love, family, community—of *not* grasping. Yet the common unity must be borne out of a harmony of difference; the place is dynamic in its displacement. Home can be the restorative fulfillment of yearning (hooks, 1990), the site of agency, consciousness, and intimacy, yet the constricting threshold of the white Southern homeplace ideology of sameness as a site dictates what the dweller can do, think, be, feel—and, as important, what she cannot. Uncovering the self's dislocatedness within (home)place might reveal the lure of home and the source of yearning: the homeplace quest is a way to get to love.

Reconciling the conflicting cultures of Southern homeplaces is reconciling the perception of love. And love is the greatest fruit of the Spirit (Galatians 5:22), the impetus of spirituality. According to Thich Nhat Hanh (1995), "A life that is too comfortable makes spiritual growth difficult" (p. 171). Love and comfort are not to be conflated. When I retreat to locations of downhome because it is numbingly comforting, nostalgia makes what I *feel* feel suspiciously like *love*. I look back fondly on the old homeplace and feel love for it, yet it is nostalgia that prompts the fondness. In the comfort, for love, I am moribund. Love is at the same time a condition of being and a condition of purpose; when love is distorted by nostalgia, purpose and being are similarly malformed. Unsettling nostalgia might reveal Southern (dis)comfort, as Minnie Bruce Pratt illustrates, but it might also reveal love unencumbered by conditions.

Minnie Bruce Pratt: Honorable Rebellion

Pratt discloses the "underside of the rhetoric of home" (Martin and Mohanty, 1986, p. 204) as she negotiates her own Southernness, recounting the complexities of being a white Southern woman who struggles with place and the experience of homeplace. By exposing the underside—the side of fallen tree trunks where the maggots crawl and feed—the raced, classed, and gendered foundations that bolster Old South ways of "being at home," she refuses nostalgia and challenges white Southern "desire for the kind of home where the suppression of positive differences underwrites familial identity" (p. 205). There is little differentiation between kinds of differences, positive or otherwise; it upsets the structure. Gilmore (1994b) observes, "Pratt constructs the home as a duplicitous site of acculturation which violently binds differences together under the sign of the same" (p. 238). A gay child, "crazy" aunt, alcoholic brother, a convert to a different religion, an educated sister, a liberal—differences are diverse, yet the familial identity of sameness lures us home. Violent blood ties of belonging color the truths we tell.

Difference-in-place emerges from a decentered perspective that has shifted from lived experiences, and the telling of difference dispels illusions of homeplace refuge. Pratt revisits the privileges and apparent security of the white, middle class, male-dominant home, and "repositions" (Gilmore, 1994b, p. 239) herself to tell her own truths. But these truths are as fluid and recursive as the self-in-place in which they are contextualized; truths told by the displaced self are borne of the same difference that they promulgate. It is Pratt's struggle to tell rather than absorb the discourse told to her by the traditional homeplace text that signifies a curriculum of difference.

As home is central to Pratt's politics, a theme of sameness-difference-dislocatedness within the context of home is central to her work. Fear of displacement contributes to the reluctance to confront difference and change. She writes,

> This is a fear that can cause us to be hesitant in making fundamental changes or taking drastic actions that differ from how we were raised. We

> don't want to lose the love of the first people who knew us; we don't want to be standing outside the circle of home, with nowhere to go. (p. 65–66)

Going home queer, for instance, as she did, as I do, is one of those drastic actions. When the first people who knew us know us only within the confines of sameness, they become unsettled by the difference. This, in turn, unsettles the homeplace. Ironically, if we go back closeted, in whatever capacity one closets oneself, then how well is he or she really known. *I want them to know who I am* remains a leading motivator to come out to parents, siblings, friends, and so on. Still, it is a powerful attraction—to embrace the sameness of the circle of home, and the greater irony is that we can sometimes be standing *inside* the circle and *still* have nowhere to go. Containment within a circle of sameness hampers our becoming.

Going home to difference and asynchrony displaces the self by destabilizing the contexts of (home)identity construction. De Lauretis (1990) notes that in Pratt's repositioning herself within various "historical situations and discursive positions" (p. 135), she decenters her identity as she knows it and undergoes a "dislocation of consciousness" (p. 135). As she disrupts the idea of personal and historical unitary identity, she negotiates the space between home/not at home, which in turn refutes Southern ideals of homeplace as unitary community. Therefore, identity of self within home and regional geographies is discursive, can be negotiable and fluid. Further complications arise when the *thought* of homeplace is elevated, suggesting not only a colonized ideal of autonomous, patriarchal home, but also a stance of Enlightenment transcendence so that it exists as an ideal that is out of reach and beyond honest memory. Like the South with which it is conflated, home becomes yet another Lost Cause.

Pratt's *Rebellion* (1991) is a transformative conversion narrative that not only works for change, but also "finds new ways of being Southern" (p. 240). McPherson cites Pratt in a call for a "radical conversion" (p. 224) that is based, not on impotent, guilt-laden nostalgia, but a conversion of action in which the meanings of homeplace are "reworked" and "rerouted" (p. 219) so that the "emotional tugs of homeplace" (p. 227) are used to enact change. McPherson writes, "*Rebellion* names guilt in order to move through it, acknowledging the lures of ambivalence or nostalgia, but also expressing their limits" (p. 228). Pratt interrogates ways of feeling Southern by disrupting memories of home as a haven of sameness and stability that reinforces the self-evidence of white identity. She concludes the title essay, "Rebellion," with her reconstructed truths:

> I begin to understand that a white woman of the South can live and write, but not of the dead heroes. She can live and write a new kind of honor, the daily, conscious actions of women in true rebellion. (p. 135)

Home (Dis)place(ment)

A homeplace narrative that unrests and unsettles might be a transformative conversion narrative if it evolves out of multiple meanings of difference and displacement. Probyn (1996) notes, "The past is not there to explain the present; it is there to encourage forms of becoming" (p. 121). Pratt confronts and then refuses the identity effected by her home experiences, and in the process uncovers the underlying violence and pull of nostalgia that are incongruous with her becoming. Gilmore (1994b) notes, "The stability of home is rendered through this violence and so wields its power through its continuous reproduction and the suppression of its reality" (p. 238). The violence of homeplace is essentially represented by the racist and anti-Semitic behavior of her father. Her growing-up experiences with her father are those against which she measures her adult interactions with self and other. The troubling incongruity between Pratt's home culture—the comfortable site of her raising—and her increasing involvement in social justice activism draw out her awareness of her difference in perspective from that of her father.

As the stability of home is rendered through violence, so also does violence execute the rift between father and daughter. In a scene from "Identity" reminiscent of the account of Christ's temptation on the mountaintop (Matthew 4), Pratt's father takes her to the top of the county courthouse to look out over the town below. She was supposed to see the place, her heritage, all that had been laid before her, secure in an established raced and classed hierarchy. She contrasts what she, as a child with a lineage of privilege, would and could not have seen from the pinnacle of the established seat of civic justice, where her grandfather had presided as judge for 40 years.

Pratt's narrative takes a violent shift as the rite of passage of privilege recognition is interrupted, for she is afraid to ascend to the top. That moment marks a significant moment of recognition for father and daughter, when both distinguish and must attend to the gendered component of privilege within the social matrices of race-class-gender.

> This is what I would and would not have seen, or so I think: for I never got to the top. When he told me to go up the steps in front of him, I tried to, crawling on hands and knees, but I was terribly afraid. I couldn't, or wouldn't, do it. He let me crawl down; he was disgusted with me, I thought. I think now that he wanted to show me a place he had climbed to as a boy, a view that had been his father's and his, and would be mine. But I was not him: I had not learned to take that height, that being set apart as my own, a white girl, not a boy. (p. 33)

As the incident shatters the facade of sameness and accentuates the gendered differences of expectations and privileges, it threatens to expose fissures of race and class as well. What she would not have seen is *difference*, obscured by the trappings of privilege. Father and, eventually, daughter recognize this imminent danger to a homeplace culture of protection.

Pratt reconsiders the moment with what Probyn (1996) calls a "necessary distancing" (p. 113) that counteracts the pull of nostalgia when she exercises honest memory. She becomes aware of the constricted view and domain offered to her by her father, and her greater worldview shifts to one "more accurate, complex, multilayered, multidimensioned, more truthful" (Pratt, "Identity," p. 33). She concludes, "To see the world of overlapping circles, like movement on the mill pond after a fish has jumped, instead of the courthouse square with me at the middle, even if I am on the ground" (p. 33). Yet, memory is complicated; Pratt possesses also the memory of her father's sorrow and pain—also her heritage—"disclosing to me his heart that still felt wrongs" (p. 62).

> I honor the grief of his life by striving to change much of what he believed in; and my own grief by acknowledging that I saw him caught in the grip of racial, sexual, cultural fears that I am still trying to understand in myself. (p. 71)

Place, nostalgia and going home are instrumental to displacement; Pratt grieves her father's despair as, we will see later, Allison mourns her mother's loss. Their anguish is inextricable from place.

The self who confronts difference from home culture, the (dis)placed person within a home of origin, knows either the dread or terror of being outside sameness, when homeplace is exclusive of positive difference. When Pratt writes, "We don't want to lose the love of the first people who knew us; we don't want to be standing outside the circle of home, with nowhere to go" (1984, p. 65), she invokes an image of Christian disfellowship, or excommunication—as powerful a tool in families and communities as it is in congregations. The threat of being cut off, cast out from the fold is a strong motivator, and the apostle Paul encourages the early Church to use it when transgressors refuse to repent for their sins (I Corinthians 5:2). Martin and Mohanty (1986) speak to the desire for sameness strengthened by the impending fear of rejection by "one's own kind, by one's family, when one exceeds the limits laid out or the self-definition of the group" (p. 208). They continue,

> The tension between the desire for home, for synchrony, for sameness, and the realization of the repressions of violence that make home, harmony, sameness imaginable, and that enforce it, is made clear in the movement of the narrative by very careful and effective reversals which do not erase the positive desire for unity, for Oneness, but destabilize and undercut it. (p. 208)

It is common unity that we seek from the downhomeness of feeling Southern. Thus, the desire for home is displacement, even as the craving to belong keeps us in bounds. The same traditional homeplace discourses of sanctuary and sameness that define the boundaries of Southern belonging often "cage us and keep us from shouting for changes" (1991, p. 24), according to Pratt, when we go back with difference.

But what of the home(comings) of the dispossessed? In "Death of a Hired Man," Robert Frost declares, "Home is the place where, when you have to go there, they have to take you in." But what if they do not? What if they will not? What are we willing to do or feel or ignore or accept so that home will take us in, or that we might enter it anew, queer? The degree of compromise is one measure of Southern homeplace. Probyn (1996) writes, "Going back different, going back to people indifferent to your difference, the past indifferent to your present, your presence superfluous to the past, being haunted by places past...there is much pain here" (p. 112).

A homeplace that reproduces itself through the perpetuation of sameness discourages and castigates difference within and without, whether that difference is detected in the individual or in social, cultural, ethnic, religious, or political groups that threaten what it perceives as its sanctity. When we "go back different," we are going to more than place; we go to place-in-time, where the past is present. The displaced person, subject of difference and subject to indifference, unfits time-in-place by (dis)claiming a past to which his or her presence is "superfluous" and (re)claiming a past requisite for a necessary self.

High Cotton: Homeplace in Dixie

We were walkin' in high cotton. Old times there are not forgotton.
Those fertile fields are never far away.
We were walkin' in high cotton. Old times there are not forgotton.
Leavin' home was the hardest thing we ever faced.

–Alabama, 1985

Pratt's personal and intellectual journey home demonstrates that home is a filter not only for what we may or may not think, feel, do— but for what comes in and what goes out; in the filtering, home does the work for us. It is also a filter of memory. When memory is Dix-iefied, grounded in Old South "lies of normalcy" (Segrest, 1985, p. 57), we become complacent—and complicit—in the lies, protective of the veil that makes home and Dixie the Most Holy Place (Exodus 26:33) in homeplace ideology. Reclaiming home as a generative place requires a tricky recursive dance of returning and stepping back, of delving and surveying. For the white Southerner, memory (home)work means uncovering indicators of conflation of home land and home place with the Dixie ideal. hooks (1990) writes, "I had to leave that space I called home to move beyond boundaries, yet I needed also to return there" (p. 148). In other words, how much of our nostalgia, our yearning for home, is a yearning for Lost Cause ideals of race, class, and gender structures? Moving beyond the boundaries that contain the illusion of the privilege of sameness suggests a distancing by which home may be observed in the larger context of Southern place.

Home is for me as much a Southern place as it is a place where my family interacts. I had forgotten, for example, that when I was a child I longed for a Confederate flag to display in my room. One of my family's earliest pilgrimages was to Shiloh battlefield.[4] I remem-ber being awed by the stories: the bloody pond, the hornet's nest, the old Shiloh Church. After our tour, Mother and Daddy let my brother and me choose one souvenir apiece from the gift shop, and we each chose a Confederate infantry cap, gray, with a black bill and Confed-erate flag on the front. I wore mine for the rest of the day and then retired it to a place of honor in my room, which was fast becoming a shrine to the Lost Cause in my love affair with the Civil War.

But I had not really forgotten; I had just filtered it to poignant an-tiquity. I had done what all great Lost Cause romantics had: treasure Civil War artifacts as triggers of melancholia by splitting them from the embedded historical structures of race and gender, yearning for what the Old South must have been: beautiful, uncomplicated, gen-teel. Without the filter, I have little doubt that had I lived in North

Alabama in *1863* instead of 1963, I would have had nine kids and a truck patch. I would have also picked cotton in a landowner's field. And so I bought into Dixie, romanticizing an essential Southern way-of-being, dismissing racial, gendered, and sexual implications that were wrapped up in the Stars and Bars. I hung my flag.

White Southerners' collective sense of self-in-place is constructed both from the history of our homeplace experiences and from a romanticized, regional history of defeat and yearning. Kincheloe, Pinar, and Slattery (1994) describe a curriculum of place that rejects the mythologized history of past and place in favor of one based on Southern "particularity of place" (p. 410). Opportunity for renewal arises with the confronting of Southern myths that anesthetize us to painful cultural and historical conditions and to the "complexity of human acts" (p. 411). Southern myths embedded in homeplace experiences translate into a homeplace myth of a unitary way of feeling Southern, which, in turn, diminishes the complexity of human acts as it anesthetizes them. The complexity of homeplace, for instance, arises from both sameness and difference, from being-in-place and being-displaced. The perpetuation of Old South identity lore privileges the general over the particular, the same over the different, the collective home over the complex networking of its individual members. The South, and a Southern curriculum of place, might enliven social consciousness as it "recovers, affirms, and celebrates" the land's best "living symbol" (p. 410), the harmonious diversity of its people within Southern homeplace.[5]

Southern myths and confederate iconography, shrouded in nostalgia, had the anesthetizing effect of giving me space—within a South, within a home—in which to fit. My parents bought me that Confederate flag—a full-size battle flag, the Stars and Bars, which I promptly hung in my room for decoration. I thought it was lovely; I was filled with pride. It was a colorful addition to my life-size poster of Vegas Elvis in a black jumpsuit that glowed when I flipped on the black light. My flag and my poster were both icons in my shrine to the South, not to mention tasteful decorations in a teenager's room. They attested to my acculturation and complicity with raced, classed, and gendered structures in the striated locations of downhome. I took them to heart more than I knew. Gilmore (2001) writes, "Difference does not establish itself all at once, but by degrees" (p. 46). I go back queer and feel the difference, which leads me to ever-so-tentatively delve into other conventions of traditional homeplace, like desire and emotion, that intensify the degrees of difference. To that end, I turn to Dorothy Allison's intense trauma tales of home desire, centered around her persistent love and yearning for her mother, by which she negotiates sites of difference where she as queer-feminist-intellectual-activist can make meaning from the discomfort.

Two or Three Things: Dorothy Allison

Although homeplace is a form of Southernness submerged in conventional, white patriarchal impressions of Southern identity, it is, as hooks (1990) and McPherson (2003) suggest respectively, woman's space, belonging to women and inextricably Southern. Maintaining paradoxical gender dynamics of power and influence requires a constant repositioning of the homeplace feminine through regressive and progressive acts. As any Southern girl learns from a young age, a woman can have her way regarding almost any decision—as long as she ensures that her husband thinks the idea is his. Negotiating her agency involves compromise, trade-offs that favor and promote the masculine patriarchal status.

The disruption of the gendered dispositions of home—which Pratt undertakes by distinguishing her father's grief and privilege from her own—discloses spaces of feminine subjective agency as it uncovers deviative forms of Southern homeplace. Dorothy Allison interrogates agency within the feminine home and unrests homeplace nostalgia through her mother narrative. She writes, "I have written stories about people like [her mother and first lover] out of my need to understand them and re-imagine their lives. Better to mythologize them, I have told myself, than to leave them with their fractured lives cut off too soon" (1994, p. 225). A similar sentiment may be held regarding the South and Southern homeplace. Left alone, the women's lives were already mythologized, regardless of social, cultural, and material deprivation. Their living selves are located within the fractures; telling and understanding and reimagining demythologizes the cut-off lives of Allison's women. Likewise, silence—not-telling—upholds mythologies of a cut-off, Lost Cause, South. Hope for a progressive South lies within the stories from the fractures.

In her recursive proclamation, "Two or three things I know for sure," Allison unsettles the known; there are no truths to be known for sure, only telling. Allison seems to ask, "What can be known from accounting lived experiences?" She writes, "The story becomes the thing needed" (p. 3), and yet, "Behind the story I tell is the one I don't" (p. 39). Both the told and untold stories are narratives of homeplace, and transformative homeplace lies in the community of women who are there. Love and admiration for her mother, apparent from the recounting of her mother's tenacious struggle to subsist within social structures of class and gender, endure despite the encumbrances of those structures that prevent her mother from saving her. "Women run away because they must," she writes, but, "My mama did not run away" (p. 5). Instead of relocating, she and the women of homeplace remained to pay the cost of "hard compromises": loss and entrapment of being-of-the-place. Home, place of subversive feminine strength, is a site of disruption of sameness rather than site of hardening of identity/place norms.

Examining homeplace as a *form* of Southernness that *perpetuates* Southernness requires not only interrogating the homeplace for which one yearns, but also interrogating the love through which the yearning occurs. Sometimes that love is seemingly inexplicable, yet its persistence lures us to place. For example, when I was called to question on what felt like an innocuous remark, "I love the South," I clung to those Southern entities that seemed given to love—people, home—wrongly severing them from place-in-past. Allison reconciles this unfitting love by moving toward love for self and other as subjects. In *Skin* she writes,

> The first rule I learned in writing was to love the people I wrote about—and loving my mama, loving myself, was not simple in any sense. We had not been raised to love ourselves, only to refuse to admit how much we might hate ourselves…it was my mama's life, the madness that love had thrown at her, the violence, the grief, and the shame. (p. 237, 240)

Loving the South is no simple matter for much the same reasons as Allison's; we are often raised with the abnegation of self-loathing, passing for a love that in its madness throws white Southerners violence, grief, and shame. To tell the mother, Allison tells the pain. To tell homeplace, I tell the mother, to tell the South. "Two or three things I know for sure," writes Allison, "and one of them is that telling the story all the way through is an act of love" (1995, p. 90).

When I read Allison, I picture my mother's family. In fact, the photographs Allison includes in *Two or Three Things I Know for Sure* could have come from Mother's picture box. My favorite photograph of Mother was taken around 1960; in it, she is lined up with four of her five sisters, shoulder-to-shoulder, slightly facing right. They were getting ready to go to town when going to town meant fixing up, and the array for each is the same: form-fitting sweater and skirt, black pumps, rings, watches, bracelets, painted fingernails. Incidentally, whenever the baby sister, now 59, looks at the scene, she remembers distinctly that they would not let her tag along, a kid at age 13. The most striking feature of the tableau is the line of dark lipstick that runs from sister to sister. And although the photo is in black-and-white, I can picture its deep red shade. These are women, like Allison's, who would not run away.

Other photos in common are of the tragic young men—the uncles in Allison's family, pained, restless, and angry—who "gave themselves up to fate" (1995, p. 28). These were the men who came into my grandmother's home to claim her girls. I have seen them in photographs, too. Angular, sitting with legs apart and arms relaxed and draped over a chair back or a sister's shoulder. The men have the same expressions on their faces: raw, wild glints in their eyes, cocky grins that masked disappointment and fear. They came at night to the house with whiskey and guitars and played music. Sometimes they put on records and danced with the sisters. They were dangerous boys who would become "hard-faced men" (p. 28).

My mother was not a willing dance partner. My daddy was not a dangerous boy. They worked together at a local café, and against his parents' wishes, they began to date. In 1961, she told him if he would marry her and take her away, she would not go back, promised that she would not go back; this is my daddy's version of the story, for my mother has never spoken of the promise. For a time she kept it; there are pictures of them as a young couple. He is grooming a horse as she, pregnant with me, lingers in a housedress and flip-flops. But I was witness to her yearning for home. When I was six years old, my grandmother and oldest aunt came to our house, but not to visit. They came to collect a sewing machine that Mother had taken with her when she married. It sat on a black base with a white cover that latched on. I remember what it sounded like when my mother used it, and I remember her sobbing as they left with it. Then Daddy, protector of the promise, took us to Sears to buy a new one, the same one she sews on today. That was my first awareness of Mother's longing, of her displacement, and it is the strongest yearning that I have ever known her to have.

The years passed, and as I tell in my opening narrative, Mother's homeplace changed. The sisters exchanged their hard-faced men for tired, earnest men who worked hard for a living and who had outgrown dancing on Saturday night. Every Sunday they gathered, until eventually, my mother went home—with me in tow. My brother went with us rarely; this was women's space, where mother love and sister love fortified them/us as subjects. Mother had taken me into her homeplace narrative, a child both parentally and self-identified with the father. For years, whenever Mother was aggravated or flustered with me, even in amusement, her retort was the same, "You're just like your daddy!" And for years, it made me chuckle, until I realized it was at those times that my mother expressed her contained resentful anger at Daddy in acceptable code—language that reinforced his gendered, patriarchal stature, assuring him that there was none of her in me. My daddy might never understand her yearning, might never have access to the part of her that held her deepest desire, but I would be invited in to make meaning of it for both of us. I am my father's daughter, yet it is my mother's pulse I feel through my skin. "Put your hand here," writes Allison. "Hear the echo of my mama's pulse, her laugh, her songs. While I live and sing she does not die..." (1995, p. 243).

For a time, five of the six sisters worked at the VF Plant, where they sewed Lee jeans. It was work that made backs and legs ache, wrists and fingers deformed, and soon Sunday conversation became about their lives as working women. Because she was strong, deter-mined, and level-headed—nothing much outwardly fazes my mother, but she holds a great deal *in*—she was elected president of the local garment workers' union. She was proudest of two things: 1) the re-spect afforded her, and thereby the workers, by management and 2) her participation in contract negotiations that resulted in agreements and benefits more favorable to local workers than contracts in other states had been. In fact, the VF plant in Russellville, Alabama, was one of the last in the United States to be outsourced to Central Amer-ica. I like to think Mother's skills as a leader and negotiator helped keep it here for as long as it was.

The sisters "talked Lee" at Big Mama's because of its largeness in their lives; my mother had no other place to tell it. Daddy's resent-ment was visible whenever she got a union call or when she had a union meeting that kept her an extra hour after work. He aimed his comments toward home, asserting that he was not weak and control-lable like the sisters' husbands. After my grandmother died and the sisters continued their Sunday afternoons, he began to say that he wished that the old house would just burn down—that everybody would be better off if it did. He did not understand what they all con-tinued to cling to or why they did not devote themselves to their "own" families. Mother graciously submitted by saving her agency— and her life—for Sundays. After church, she and I went to Big Mama's, the homeplace where women negotiated their subjectivity and their subjection, ways they could lead in public and submit at home. It was then I realized the homeplace of the child's yearning is not the same one yearned for by her parents.

In the classed, gendered, fundamentalist narrative of my mother, I find the hope of a homeplace of affirmation and solidarity wrought from different life narratives, a place for telling. It is not a perfect place, nor a place of perfection. The lives there are often fractured; the place ruptures at the seams. It thrives because of—not in spite of—the schism. Allison writes,

> What I am here for is to claim my life, my mama's death, our losses and our triumphs, to name them for myself. I am here to claim everything I know, and there are only two or three things I know for sure. (1995, p. 52)

Within a homeplace of difference and positive disruption, we might, as Allison, suggests, "honor the truth of each other's stories (1994, p. 251). Life stories, narratives, cannot be told if they are not honored, nor honored if not told. The self-in-place who names and claims lived experiences of difference and displacement (pro)claims her own truth as a subject. While a homeplace of sameness projects its own truths, a homeplace of difference is a homeplace of the different truths of its subjects.

Home (Be)Coming

Allison and Pratt turn to home, rather than from it, to find ways that honest self-respect, the "positive self" (Pratt, 1991, p. 59), may be formed within Southern geographies, including places of home. A new honor of rebellion lies in our acknowledgment that home has been, for some of us as white Southerners, the space where we "sit in the darkness of White privilege" (Doll, 2000, p. 16); it lies in our willingness to open the windows and air out the permeating mustiness of nostalgia. Lorde (1984) reminds us that racism and homophobia are inextricably linked and present in place and time, urging women to "reach down into that deep place of knowledge inside herself and touch that terror and loathing of any difference that lives there. See whose face it wears" (p. 113). Nostalgia, which speaks the desire of time-in-place, conducts the deep-seated fears and hatred of difference from within the self into the collective illusion of unitary homeplace. As nostalgia bears out the desire for reconciliation of past and present—a centering on the past to reinforce present truths—the sanctity of sameness, at the expense of identity—individual, social, cultural, political—is preserved.

Homeplace may be celebrated—honored/recognized/acknowledged—as a site for restoration and resistance, as hooks (1990) proposes, but to do so requires a rethinking of the ideal of the Southern homeplace. As Pinar (2004) notes the convergence and conflation of raced, classed, and gendered domains within Southern culture and history, we might uncover these sites of convergence within the home. Home is a most immediate and intimate Southern place; home(as)place is a category of social and individual experiences situated within larger Southern place. A home-based curriculum of place becomes "a curricular embodiment and contradiction of peculiarly southern experience...demystifying southern history and culture" (Pinar, 2004, p. 94). It employs confrontation and interrogation of lived experiences—through the recovery and grounding of memory—to enhance self-understanding and social reconstruction. Home-based curriculum of place, underscored by difference and (dis)place(ment), might facilitate home-based social justice.

We may consider home as a place for rootedness without falsely idealizing home with sentimentalized, nostalgic yearning in which it is severed from larger social contexts (McPherson, 2003), with racism and heterosexism left outside on the porch with the dog and wet boots. Thich Nhat Hanh (1995) suggests that "Learning to touch deeply the jewels of our own tradition will allow us to understand and appreciate the values of other traditions" (p. 90). There are jewels in Southern culture, including, of course, the Southern homeplace, that we might excavate and touch deeply. Separating them from the debris of "other" is the dirty work. Honest memory work yields both.

The spiritual, and in turn desire, is to be found within the libidinous geographies of place and identity. The common unity of displacement strengthens bonds that lure us home. Home offers community, not with the seduction of the security of sameness, but with the promise to celebrate diversity within. Might not the (dis)comforts of home "veer into the past and organize a present becoming" (Probyn, 1996, p. 118)? Going home, going to homeplace can restore the spirit, quicken the seeker with the richness of love, family, community, yet going home can also mean confronting pain, guilt, loss, melancholia. As home is a location of displacement, it can satisfy yearning as a site of agency, consciousness, and intimacy. When the lure of homeplace rests in the common unity of difference, home will be not only a place we love to go, but a place we go to love.

Home-yearning, according to Honig (1994), "never goes away" (p. 595), and, given the traditional, conventional images of homeplace, the past-in-place offers a comfort and security of privilege elusive to the present self. Home welcomes us in with the alluring promise of sameness—*Come, we are of like mind here*—yet the price is the same promise—*Be of like mind here*. When the sojourner crosses the threshold from the spaces of her own life experiences and subjectivity—as subject of difference, as propagator of difference—the journey home becomes tentative. That same threshold becomes a border to be breached, where knowledges and silences are unsettled in the transgression. Without recovery of homeplace, there remains little hope of a transformative homeplace narrative in which self-in-place and the place itself might move toward progressive change.

Home-yearning is powerful, appealing to the heart as well as the senses. As strong as the food and flowering images remain to me—coffee, cake, the smell of the old house, the shade and scent of the lilacs, day lilies that sway beneath the kitchen window—the emotional yearning for something greater than the images is stronger still. Revisiting a glimpse of my own homeplace narrative, I see the yearning for a community for sameness that exists among the sisters and, then, by me. And yet, within the woman's space that they cultivated—literally—for themselves, there is room for new growth, for the recovery of the generative components of home. These women were not unitary subjects; they had different life narratives, experiences so varied they sometimes had to find ways to negotiate in order to find their common ground.

Pratt and Allison challenge us to confront the yearning and interrogate it without rejecting it. We have no need to turn from home; neither author suggests such rejection. Rather, each illustrates the disruption of (home)place on her queer journey home. We might disrupt conventions of sameness, much as Big Mama would stand on the front porch and shake out the old throw rug, and see what dust drifts into the sunlight. Home, then, is a place of difference rather than the submergence or erasure of differences. When I, academic, gender-, class-, race-, and sexuality-traitor, rememory home in discomfort and displacement, the yearning shifts toward a desire for dialogue and coalition building, for communion. I go back now different, as Misfit, and I seek something more than being embraced if only I do not speak my difference. My desire is for communion of love *because of* my difference; until that is so, my homeplace narrative is incomplete, home is not yet.

Epilogue

It is April, and once again the lilacs are in full bloom. My daughter asks me about my work these days. Until now she has shown only a distracted interest, so I am delighted and excited when she questions me. "Do you ever write about me, Mom?" she asked; I was too quickly dismissive. "No, baby, right now I have so much upbringing baggage I have to work through that I write mostly about growing up." At 2 in the morning a week after her last visit, I realize that was not exactly right; I realize the interconnectedness of it all, past and present, being-child and being-parent. Being home and being away from home.

I am suddenly aware of the other woman who inspirits me with a fiery breath to write: my daughter. I have created with greatest passion during her, not my, crises, realizing now that our connections *makes* them mine. And it is then that I know why I return home: it is to draw from it, draw from it, draw from it—and in so doing, rework it. I talk to my daughter and write for her, and for me, exhorting her to return, not so much to Jesus—as my mother and father would—but to home. I am reproachful toward her for turning her back on home, family, upbringing, culture; home is the spiritual, religious, sacred sanctuary that I accuse my daughter of rejecting, that I live in terror of rejecting myself. It is home where I am sure that everything will be better, where Mother will put on a pot of coffee and a skillet of corn bread and just let me *tell*. Then maybe later we will go again to Big Mama's house, where three aging sisters will talk hometalk—of people past and present, of food and quilting, of Walmarts and shopping trips—until I am strengthened by the community and can pass it forward, to my daughter who is caught in the torrents.

I write to shape homeplace into an idea that I can embrace, one that will embrace me right back. It is as if by clinging to home as a sacred space—holy ground—we might manage to hold onto the love and desire that eludes us; likewise, a rejection of one means loss of the other. Perhaps the intimacies that we humans seek from and for each other—intimacies to feel, speak, receive love—may be found down home. Intimacy is *what* we first desire; memory work that accounts for intimacy illuminates *how* and *why* we desire. Homeplace, a location *where* we first desire, may also be a site of convergence for desire and intimacy, for love and loving. My daughter, distant from me as I may feel, is not altogether lost from me if she and I share a homeplace.

And so the homeplace connection between past and present, between places then and places now becomes apparent. Home is not a sanctuary; it is not a place of safety and comfort. It is a place of reconstruction, of the working through. I see it as plain as the mud-dirty Mississippi River that drives itself past my office window on its way to salty water. Heraclitus would say that I can never step in that same old river twice; likewise, the ebb and flow of homeplace renews its inhabitants if we but reclaim it with open spirits. I have stepped in the new river, no longer writing *about* my mother but writing *as* mother, past and present linked as the waters of confidence and reason wash over me, bearing me home, far away from home.

Notes

1   Translated, "How are your mother and relatives?"

2   The common definition of unto is to, yet I purposely use unto here in its anti-quated, formal, Biblical forms: 1) extent, limit, degree of comprehension, inclusion as far as, and 2) effect, end, consequence. These suggest the finality of destination of being unto-the-place.

3   For a juxtaposition of South American Catholic pilgrimages with pilgrimages of the American South, see Richardson (2003). He offers treks to Graceland and historical Natchez, Mississippi, as examples of the Southern metaphor of pilgrimage in which historical representations of the Lost Cause South replace the sacred in the white Southerner's journey.

4   Southerners must forge an accurate sense of history and historical consciousness coupled with an authentic sense of self within Southern culture. Authenticity is far too complicated for me to tackle here, but I am immediately mindful of a prime example of an unauthentic emotional Dixieland trigger. In Ken Burns's epic prototype for all documentaries that were to follow, The Civil War, there is the now-famous letter from Major Sullivan Ballou, "My Very Dear Sarah." Burns said in an interview that he kept a copy of that letter in his pocket while making the documentary as inspiration—a reminder of the scope of the project.

5   In the episode, "Honorable Manhood," Paul Roebling reads a voiceover of the final letter that Major Ballou wrote to his wife before he was killed at the first Battle of Bull Run as a melancholic violin plays strains of the haunting "Ashokan Farewell." Makes me cry every time. And incredibly, with one swift, sure tug at the heartstrings, the narratives of lives who peopled roughly one third of the South in 1860 (1860 U.S. Census Data, http://fisher.lib.virginia.edu, 2003) are erased through showmanship and cinematography.

Chapter 3
Queerly Fundamental:
Complexities of Christian
Fundamentalism and Queer Desire

I am almost sure I was the favorite topic of conversation that summer. After all, it is not every day that one of the school's teachers "turns into a lesbian." That's the way some of the parents in the community put it; folks from my church were much more direct and matter-of-fact with their revelation: "Well, you *know* she's *gay*," a double emphasis for a double life. Well-meaning colleagues approached me and offered to tell me the latest gossip; a former student even e-mailed me about "this rumor that's going around." Some people embark upon their journeys of self-discovery in private; mine was more of a public matter. I was a teacher. More specifically, for 9 years I was a Grade 11 English teacher in a conservative Southern rural community. In fact, the high school was located next door to the church where I worshiped with my children. School functions began with prayer, and the Fellowship of Christian Students (FCS) was one of the largest organizations on campus. In more ways than one it was often difficult to distinguish where the churchyard stopped and the schoolyard began. No wonder my story was breaking news.

Queer Southernness

Queer Southernness is one aspect of being and feeling Southern engulfed in conventional heteronormative notions of Southern identity. Compounding fundamentalist Christianity with an already anomalous, queer Southernness reveals a complexity of being-in-place from which to question dominant, constricting conventions. This chapter examines the normalization of straightness, through doctrine and practice, within fundamentalist Protestantism. Straightness in this case is contextualized by exploring the meanings and practices of straightness as it is enacted in one secondary school setting. I employ a recursive, spiral—a queer—approach to straightness as normalized identity: queer me looks back at straight me in a queerly straight world or a straightly queer world as I myself become increasingly queered and the recipient of my own straight gaze. Sumara and Davis (1999) argue, "Curriculum has an obligation to interrupt heteronormative thinking—not only to promote social justice, but to broaden possibilities for perceiving, interpreting, and representing experience" (p. 191). In this instance, much of the heteronormative thinking to be interrupted was my own, as I began to autobiographically explore the notion of queer Southernness that is to be found in the tension from the interplay—rather than the opposition—of fundamentalism and queer desire.

If, as Luhman contends, "Normalized identities such as straight and stable gender identities work through, invoke, produce, constitute, as well as refuse its other" (1998, p. 151), what is the impact when the field upon which such epic warring takes place is within one little Southern gal? What overt and covert discourses from conservative ideology and political activism by the Religious Right are the vanguards of straightness in teachers and within curriculum? How might we designate such ideologically based activism *oppressive* without succumbing to the delicious bitterness of vengeful confrontation? What possible range of discourses can be produced to construct a transformative straight teacher? While I interrogate intolerance and condemnation as they may be employed for control—a kind of *piety for power* strategy—for me to make any meaning, any meaningful application, from my Protestant upbringing, I evoke the very best it has to offer, that which is at its heart: the fruits of the spirit. Love, joy, peace, patience, kindness, goodness, faithfulness, gentleness, self-control—against such there is no law (Galatians 5:22—23). It is with a spirit of love and hope that I negotiate the brick wall of dogma because love is, as Edgerton contends, "a very real and necessary condition" (1996, p. 67).

I interrogate a paradox of my experience and grapple with the complications rather than deny the complexity and contradictions between my identifications and desires. I was raised in and found a means for spiritual growth through my identification with a fundamentalist religious discourse. My sexual identity, the very foundation of my desire, collides with this fundamentalist discourse. I have claimed and continue the project of claiming my queerness. And I continue the spiritual journey I started within a fundamentalist religious framework, though that spiritual journey now embodies a very explicit critique of fundamentalism. While I want to name and challenge the violence embedded in fundamentalist thinking, I do not want to hold myself in antagonistic opposition to those who claim it or to the religious discourse itself. I have emerged from it and it remains a force in my life. I therefore want to reveal the complexities, paradoxes, anomalies of spirit and desire that I bear witness to as a queer fundamentalist—not a fundamentalist, not a lesbian woman void of other identity experiences, not a critic with an overdetermined attachment to one theoretical discourse, perspective, or ground for thinking—but as a person with truly problematic and contradictory identifications and desires.

I am writing ethically from within the tension of these contradictions, trying to speak the disturbance of my own subjectivity that might reveal the real danger of fundamentalist thinking, a danger that binds the lives, not only of religious fundamentalists, but also of those "progressives" who use a "hermeneutic of transparency" (Moss, 2001, p. 1315) to position those who practice social discourses of hatred as objects rather than subjects. I do not take the position that these forms of hatred should not be critiqued and undermined; instead, I argue that we need to acknowledge and understand their subjective complexity in order to work toward their disruption. I am positioned subjectively and socially within one of the fissures of fundamentalism. Rather than disidentify with fundamentalism entirely, reducing those who practice fundamentalist religions as beyond transformation, I am revealing the internal contradiction of fundamentalist discourse, its fragmentation, fear, and possibility for change by bearing an often

pronounced discomfort from my continued identification with fundamentalism.

A Peculiar People:
Fundamental Fundamentalism

On September 12, 2004, televangelist Jimmy Swaggart delivered a
sermon in a Toronto worship service that was televised throughout
Canada. In the broadcast, Swaggart was discussing his opposition to
gay marriage when he said, "I've never seen a man in my life I
wanted to marry. And I'm going to be blunt and plain: If one ever
looks at me like that, I'm going to kill him and tell God he died" (Associated Press, September 23, 2004). Footage of the sermon was
replayed on American television, and audio recordings began circu-
lating on gay-themed web sites. Complaints were filed with the Ca-
nadian Broadcast Standards Council—and with Swaggart Ministries
in Baton Rouge.

On Wednesday, September 22, Swaggart apologized for his remarks; he said he has jokingly used the expression "killing someone
and telling God he died" thousands of times, about all sorts of people.
He said the expression is figurative and not meant to harm. "It's a
humorous statement that doesn't mean anything. You can't lie to
God—it's ridiculous. If it's an insult, I certainly didn't think it was,
but if they are offended, then I certainly offer an apology," he told
reporters (Associated Press, September 23, 2004).

A few things in particular—besides the obvious—are troubling
about Swaggart's remarks. First is the violent nature of the words
themselves and the spirit in which they are spoken, and although he
dismisses them as humorous, as jokes, the message was duly con-
veyed. Even if that were the case, humor is a most effective way to
impart meaning and intent. Sentiment lies beneath the quaintest "old
saying." *She cut off her nose to spite her face* has nothing to do with
noses or faces, but it denotes a weighty idea. There are many kinds of
violences, murder being only one. *Kill him and tell God he died*, similar
to Cain's strategy in the ancient story, justifies not only that violent

act, but a violence of spirit—all in defiance of God's nature and will. Sad that Swaggart would use his phrase about all sorts of people. One cannot help but wonder what sort.

Also troubling is Swaggart's use of *they* in the last sentence. Could he, would he have spoken the statement had a queer been seated in the front row? If his child were queer? Perhaps. While humanizing *they* will not end violences—Matthew Shepherd's murderers knew his face as they tortured him—a face might return to the transgressor. I am offended, and I understand figurative language, and I have a sense of humor, and I have a face and a name. Swaggart's statements are devoid of love and humanity, and for that, I am offended.

Finally, the most disturbing aspect of the worship service lies not with Swaggart at all. If one listens carefully to the recording, one can hear the reaction of the congregation. As he says "If one ever looks at me like that, I'm going to kill him and tell God he died," there is a perceptible ripple of laughter in the background. Its minister has just jokingly implied that he would do violence to repay a look, and the congregation giggled when it might have roared him down. History makes clear the devastating consequences that result when collective populations entertain the violent agendas of radical public figures. What is most troubling, then, is the laughter behind.

Not all fundamentalist Christians hold such extreme feelings as Swaggart expresses. *They* are individuals, no more unitary than Swaggart's *they*, and uncovering the humanity within the group is as momentous as individualizing queer. As there are varying kinds of fundamentalist Protestants, there are varying degrees of conservatism to which they ascribe gender roles and sexuality. According to Reed, approximately one-half of Southern Protestants are Baptists (1982, p. 236). Of these, most are affiliated with the Southern Baptist Convention, which originated in 1845 when it split off from the Northern Baptists over the issue of slavery. If asked to visualize what Southern Fundamentalism looks like, the general reader would likely imagine the Southern Baptists, Word of God in one hand and political agenda in the other, or perhaps the charismatic Pentecostal Holiness groups that Reed denotes as having experienced phenomenal growth in the

South (p. 241). Jimmy Swaggart is affiliated with denominations of the Pentecostal Holiness Assemblies of God and has certainly helped generate public awareness—for good or ill—of this denomination.

Growing up fundamentalist means different things to different fundamentalists. I was raised in the Church of Christ, a denomination with roots firmly in the Age of Reason (Hughes, 1996, p. 341). *Raised* is appropriate as my family unfailingly attended worship services twice on Sunday, Bible study on Wednesday evening, two Gospel Meetings, and one Vacation Bible School during the year. *Train up a child in the way he should go: and when he is old, he will not depart from it* (Proverbs 22:6). I cannot depart from it; moreover, it is difficult to look back upon it free of the veil of nostalgia. Often, the scenes of my remembering are like Rockwell tableaus: brightly lit Sunday School rooms, descending creaky stairs that led to the dank basement, a baptism. To this day, I can remember the smell of the "dinner on the ground," held each year before the a cappella singing that lasted all day on Sunday. I trace my life through Church—earliest friends, family, elderly folks. Flannery O'Connor once wrote about the Catholic Church, "You have to suffer as much from the Church as for it" (1979, p. 90). The same holds true for growing up a Protestant fundamentalist, for it has shaped my self and life in pernicious ways. Still, it was a source of joy, and something there nurtured my spirit, including, I am finding, my queer spirit.

I grew up going to Church three times a week, and the gender lessons began at the threshold. "Let your women keep silent in the churches" (I Corinthians 14:34) prohibited women from having authority over men, religious or otherwise. I learned my lessons well, embracing the literal language of fundamentalist teachings on divorce so well that I remained in an impossible marriage for 16 years. In fact, I had a "shotgun engagement" because my mom and dad held an emergency conference and decided that it would be better for me to "marry than to burn" (I Corinthians 7:9) in sinful lust, and from that point on, the wedding was a work in progress. I was 17. I had internalized an association between sexual activity—not just intercourse, but desire, experimentation, awareness/curiosity—and shame, believing that guilt accompanies sex for a good healthy dose of conscience that would deter illicit behavior. So, just being disappointed in marriage was not an option; I was expected to stay. To get to my queer life I had, as they say in the country, "a long row to hoe."

So how *does* a fundamentalist Protestant counter deeply engrained gender and sexual expectations? I can negotiate the tensions apparent in, for example, my Southernness or my white-working-class-woman status and make some meaning of self, self and other. But in matters of sexuality, I find myself grappling with fundamentalism much as Jacob wrestled with the angel. It has shaped my identity and informed my pedagogy, so my examination of straightness, in this case within the educational setting, of necessity includes forays into fundamentalism. Admittedly, I have done my share of ranting against the patriarchal structures within organized religion, sometimes wallowing in self-pity as a victim of doctrine.

I share Minnie Bruce Pratt's sentiments about the totality of indoctrination, the images so deeply imprinted on us as children that they shape our spiritual beings as adults. She writes, "I fear those images, embedded in me with the words of hymns, the scriptures, the images of sacrifice and purification, of power and dominion. I am skeptical of attempts to redeem the images, the system of belief contaminated by centuries of misuse" (1991, p. 212). Indeed, fundamentalist Christianity cultivates the propensity toward skepticism that sharpens my gaze, even as the faith to which I cling is as much a part of my identity as my queer-ness. They are both my ways of being in the world. I love the simple elegance of the Church of Christ's worship and fundamental doctrine. I am comfortable with this no-frills religion that has as its heart "walking in the light" (I John 1:7). Hawley (1994) muses, "Many important questions remain to be asked...most obviously, one ought to ask what differences are apt to ensue when women, not men, speak the language of fundamentalism" (p. 34). Fundamentalism is my native tongue, and I speak it now, but queerly.

Fundamentalists generally hold conservative, traditional views toward gender roles and sexual behavior. I know this because I grew up hearing quite a bit about sin and, of course, hell. For me, it has always been perfectly normal to believe, for example, that women are forbidden to hold positions of authority over men in the Church, that the only grounds for divorce is adultery, and that homosexuality is a sin. I was taught to be in gracious submission to my husband long before the Southern Baptist Convention exhorted Baptist women to do so; after all, man is the head of woman as Christ is the head of the Church (Ephesians 5:23—24). Hawley (1994) and Balmer (2000) consider the nature of American fundamentalism and the "ideology of gender that reconstructs an idealized past and attempts to reshape the present along the same lines" (Hawley, p. 30). According to Balmer,

> American fundamentalists remain on the defensive, trying to shore up what the broader culture now considers a quaint, anachronistic view of women. Whatever the merits of their arguments, the fundamentalist political agenda...may represent, at some (albeit subconscious) level, a battle for their own survival, as well as a struggle for the preservation of a 19th Century ideal. (p. 59)

Women had to find more creative ways to exercise their agency— often as we denied that we were doing any such thing—within structures that were defined, in part, by the suppression of that agency.

While Hill (1998) observes, "interpretation is no issue" for fundamentalists, fundamentalists' literal interpretation of the Bible is itself an interpretation. The Church of Christ, for example, claims to "speak where the Bible speaks, remain silent where it is silent." Pratt, raised Presbyterian in a small Alabama town, terms it this way: "But I was taught something...insidious: that unlike Catholics who lived by myth and legend, we Protestants lived our faith rationally, grounded by grace in the inerrant Bible, to be taken as the literal and infallible word of God" (p. 195). Historically, the Church, as the Church of Christ is simply referred to by its members, believes that the New Testament makes its requirements clear by, what Hughes terms, a "threefold hermeneutic" (1996, p. 62): through direct command, through example, or through necessary inference—in that order. Without openness to broader, contextualized interpretation, there is no avenue for dialogue, whether it pertains to the spiritual or the secular. Dialogue, intertwined with desire and questioning and the space of possibilities (Martusewicz, 1997), is itself interpreted by the fundamentalist as betrayal to the literal, divinely inspired Word. If pushed on matters of, say, Sears' "isms": evolutionism, ecumenicalism, secular humanism, and multiculturalism (1998, p. 41), conservative Christians will side with whoever has the Bible open to an applicable verse, and this will usually be the "high profile," (Sewall, 1998, p. 78) "secondary-level male elites" (Lawrence in Hawley, 1994, p. 38). Since the 1980's Regan era, high-profile leaders have shaped their flock into a political bloc, particularly in Southern states—all "red" Republican states in the most recent election.

Fundamental Perspectives

My journey into queer Southernness began when my queer and straight worlds converged during my last two years teaching at a rural Southern high school, to which I have lovingly assigned the fictional name Lick Skillet High School (LSHS). (There is actually a Lick Skillet community in Alabama, and the name was too good not to use.) Although compulsory heterosexuality was the understood state of affairs at LSHS, a queer reading of place as text discloses cracks in the wall of straight pedagogy. I propose that the non-queer stakeholders were blind to the queer fissures, as I myself had been for most of my tenure there. I return for a reflective visit to Lick Skillet's hallowed halls, but this time with a "queered gaze" (Doll, 1998, p. 287) of memory.

Lick Skillet is a rural and growing community on the expanding border of a technologically significant city in the Deep South. It is a community that very much enjoys reaping the benefits of its proximity to technology, yet its members wish for the conservatively close-knit cultural makeup to remain intact. There is no greater representation of this than the two buildings, the largest in greater Lick Skillet, that stand side by side in the middle of a flat expanse of what was until recently farmland. The first, LSHS, is a state-of-the-art education complex and the prototypical flagship high school of the

county. The other is the Clearview Church of Christ, also an architec-
turally elegant compound made up of several buildings, including the
Bible education building, the fellowship hall, daycare center, benevo-
lence thrift shop, and, of course, the auditorium that seats up to 2,000.
A queer duality in its own way for sure, considering the penetration
by church into state, yet a good vantage point for looking at the same
duality that is found inside those very same buildings. I know about
what is contained inside because for several years, much of my week
was spent in one or the other; I taught at LSHS and worshipped at
Clearview.

I kept one shirt. Hanging in the back of my closet with the outgrown or out-of-style clothes that I cannot bear to part with is a red
button-down cotton shirt with *Lick Skillet High School Spartans* em-
broidered on the left pocket. This was the teachers' Friday uniform,
my teacher costume, suitable for casual day and pep rallies. I put it on
again in order to take myself back, way back, to a time when I was
Ms. Whitlock, when I was other things to myself and others *before* I
was a lesbian. Putting it on, I can almost feel the crisp fall night air
and hear the drum cadence as the band takes the field for halftime. I
also feel emptiness of loss and denial, and the determination to find
some space from which to reconcile my queerly fundamental self. In
my 14 years of teaching, I never once considered myself as a straight
teacher, much the same way as I never considered myself as a white
teacher. Part of the privilege of being a member of the dominant culture is a blind presumption that yours is the natural, preferred enti-
tlement. Moreover, I taught in a rural community socially and
culturally dominated by a triumvirate of conservative churches:
Southern Baptist, Methodist, and Church of Christ. As I "queer the
gaze" (Doll, 1998, p. 287) through which I examine Lick Skillet
straightness, religion is a weighty presence. I hang the shirt back in
the closet, this time toward the front, for remembering.

So I return, mostly in memory, to a place where I never thought I
would. My teaching home shifted for me from being a place that felt
like family and home folks—a place of belonging—to a place the
gaze, including my own, was so intense I could feel it. I feel it now as

I think back. And yet in that shifting, school and curriculum transformed into a site of becoming. Sumara and Davis (1999), who propose a move toward a queer curriculum theory by interrupting heteronormativity, make this point about queer theory as it relates to pedagogy,

> "Queer" functions as a marker representing interpretive work that refuses...the cultural rewards afforded those whose public performances of self are contained within that narrow band of behaviors considered proper to a heterosexual identity....Queer theory does not ask that pedagogy become sexualized, but that it excavate and interpret the way it already is sexualized—and, furthermore, that it begin to interpret the way that it is explicitly heterosexualized. (p. 192)

Teachers are public performers, some of whom exhibit not only a narrow band of behaviors but a narrowness of behaviors and mindset characteristic of hetero(sexual)normative identities. Queer awareness of the public performance of heterosexualized pedagogy suggests that my colleagues, students, their parents, and community members did not change. Institutional life is notorious for *not* changing. Rather, my evolution into queerness was like putting on those 3-D glasses as a kid that let you see secret messages on an encrypted page. In my rural Southern fundamentalist Christian world, the straight message had been written within the school culture clearly and plainly all along; but I could not see it until my gaze was as queer as those old 3-D glasses with one blue and one red lens.

A Queer Obsession

According to Hawley, fundamentalists "see themselves as a holy remnant of an idealized past and as the vanguard of a future yet to be revealed" (1994, p. 21). Restoring this idealized, mythical, straight way of life is what allowed Robertson and Falwell, for example, to speak for God after September 11, 2001, when they declared that America "got what it deserved." The terrorist attacks, according to them, were natural consequences—the wages of sin (in Harris, 2001).

Conservative Christian organizations such as the Christian Coalition, Focus on the Family, and Concerned Women of America often seek to advance a political agenda by professing great love for the sinner, positioning their family organizations as the "good cop" to Falwell's bad. As Mel White and Soulforce prepared to enter the America's Center in St. Louis at the 2002 Southern Baptist Convention (SBC), SBC President James Merrit admonished delegates to respond with grace and love. "We love homosexuals. God loves homosexuals. But he loves them too much to leave them homosexuals" (Miller, 2002).

In 1998 the Southern Baptists declared that a wife should "submit herself graciously to the servant leadership of her husband" (CNN, 1998). Later that year, the SBC in its official statement of *Faith and Message* prohibited women from becoming pastors. The same statement urged Christians to oppose racism and homosexuality (CNN, 1998). (What a difference the official policy might have made if it had denounced *sexism* instead of *homosexuality*.) The president of the convention, Dr. Paige Patterson, offered a bold justification: "Somebody said the other day that we were trying to set things back 200 years and we felt like that was a big mistake. We're trying to set them back 2,000 years. We want to go all the way back to Jesus and the Bible" (1998). However, as Hawley observes, although fundamentalist ideals are rooted in nostalgia, it is not a nostalgia for that of Jesus' time, "but of home and community life in the small towns of rural, nineteenth-century America" (1994, p. 16). The intent is clear: the yearning is for a simpler, socially defined time; without twentieth century complications leading us into temptation, we might have remained pure children of God—all of us: individuals, families, communities, America. Yet the idea of a premodern, moral utopian American society is the fundamental myth.

But why are gay people the principle targets of these campaigns? Of all kinds of evils in the world—war, poverty, racism, violence—why malign people solely based on sexuality and gender issues? I borrow a connection Arthur Miller (1953) notes in Act I of *The Crucible*, as he seeks explanations to why the Puritans of Salem could persecute (mostly) women of the community for being witches.

...the necessity of the Devil may become evident as a weapon, a weapon designed and used time and time again in every age to whip men into a surrender to a particular church of church-state....Our difficulty in believing the—for want of a better word—political inspiration of the Devil is due in great part to the fact that he is called up and damned not only by our social antagonists but by our own side, whatever it may be....A political policy is equated with moral right, and opposition to it with diabolical malevolence. Once such an equation is effectively made, society becomes a congerie of plots and counterplots and the main role of government changes from that of the arbiter to that of the scourge of God...Sex, sin, and the Devil were early linked, and so they continued to be in Salem, and are today. (p. 33—35)

Of course, *The Crucible* draws its parallels between Puritan theocratic structures and the radical conservatism of the McCarthy era, yet the *Devil* remains a potent weapon, one still linked in fundamentalist ideology, the scriptural standard for morality, with sex and sin. But why the gendered embodiment of evil? Consider again Miller's observation: "Sex, sin, and the Devil were...linked" (1953, p. 35). The Devil as weapon becomes gendered because sex and sin for fundamentalist Protestants are so deliberately conflated and thus, gendered.

Pinar (2001) observes that gender as a social construct completes a "triumvirate" (p. 1157) with racism and misogyny. He further argues that antiqueer prejudice is, in fact, mutated racism and sexism. Fundamentalists play the "queer card" because, unlike outright racial or sexist sentiments, they *can* do so without penalty of public outcry. He writes,

Do they (the Religious Right) feel cornered, desperate for an issue which they fantasize will bring down God's wrath and make America the heavenly state they imagine it was always meant to be? Homosexuality appears to be that issue. Does this issue come to the surface now in these reactionary groups because the other two elements of the 'triumvirate,' 'race' and 'women's bodies,' are beyond their grasp?... the right wing clings to what's left of their hatred, that is, what's left that they can express publicly: that which is the 'queer.' (p. 1157)

While Miller rightly links the sexual, religious, and political, Pinar *queers* the configuration, suggesting that power and passion are therein intertwined. Sex sells. It sells shoes, clothes, and soft drinks—and it sells a message to disenfranchised evangelicals that sexually liberated (and therefore male-threatening) feminists and sexually perverted queers have infiltrated the schools and are influencing—even recruiting!—their children. Christians react to the taboo—the titillating—the thing that good girls and boys do not do or even talk about or even "lust in their hearts" over. The trigger here is the deliciously forbidden universal obsession: sex.

Through a Glass, Queerly

LSHS is an interesting place to deconstruct straightness. Of the approximately 50 teachers and administrators, at least 4 of us were queer. I am designating queer here myself; none of the people referenced, unless otherwise noted, has publicly stated that he or she is gay. I use queer in a broad sense, based in part on Morris's (1998) idea of the queer aesthetic, or queer sensibility: "Queer suggests a self-naming that stands outside the dominant cultural codes; queer opposes sex-policing, gender-policing, heteronormativity, and assimilationist politics." Queerness, as I examine it, subverts the heteronormative codes pervasive in the everyday business of schooling. Lick Skillet pedagogues who exemplify queerness are those who do not overtly perform straightness. It is not my intention to solidify a queer/straight identity binary; rather, establishing queer is the proactive act by which to examine straightness within the school culture. This time, queerly off center is where I am aiming. Of course, when we completely extract sexuality from queer and broaden it to encompass those who do not practice patriarchical conformity, then our little school, as do many others, becomes a much queerer place.

Miss Knight was the first woman inducted into the state Sports Hall of Fame for her 32 years of success as a girls' high school volleyball coach. In addition to the esteem in which she was held professionally, Coach Knight was beloved of her girls, the Lady Spartans.

She is a spinster who, despite a very public and celebrated professional life, keeps her private life closely guarded. In a world where heterosexuality is worn like a badge, the absence of het proclamation may distinguish one as queer. Although Pollak (1994) suggests that a role model who is in the closet is not a role model at all" (p. 132), when the role model is not merely a part of the institution but an institution herself, something much more important than a message of sexual identity is modeled. Talburt (2000) explains that, "to codify queer…is to doom ourselves to repeating the terms of our identities, to keeping the 'space of the possible' small and contained" (p. 10). There was nothing small or contained about Coach Knight. Thirty-two years and a case full of state championship trophies was how she navigated her own possible spaces.

Miss Knight is a peculiar presence—distinct from the faculty pack—who artfully coaches her team until it performs with a ruthless, graceful precision. She is one of Doll's "crones" (Doll, Wear, & Whitaker, 2006), yet within the school culture she is a kind of "grand dame," an icon, a fitting presence in a search for straightness. Her longevity has put her in the position of having taught many of the members of the community, those same members who attend the fundamentalist churches on Sunday. Icons may not be ridden out of town on a rail. Doll writes, "The two characteristics of separation and art endow the crone with a potency different from but equal to that of the phallus; therefore, she is suspect in the eyes of the patriarchy, seen as demented, if not demonic" (Doll, Wear, & Whitaker, forthcoming). On the other hand, winning icons are local treasures. Coach Knight, like Miss Dove, is formidable; when they are in her presence, school board members, central office administrators, and church deacons are once again 14 years old and have that tardy-to-class feeling. I only remember having 2 conversations with her that could remotely be considered queer. It was the same conversation, twice. Late in my year of queer transition, she asked me twice if I had made any men friends online whom I planned to meet. Looking back through my handy-dandy decoder glasses, I can feel the stress on the word *men*, see the slight nod of her head and raised eyebrow. A stretch, I know, but a queer one.

Lick Skillet's queer quotient was significantly raised because its principal was himself queer, also by default. Mr. James, LSHS principal for 12 years, never married, although he frequently tells the story of the painful breakup with the beautiful woman that ended with his flinging the engagement ring from the car window, off the bridge and into the river below. Mr. James shares his palatial home with his elderly mother and his roommate of 8 years, whom he refers to as "Coach." Coach accompanied the boss to athletic events, his well-worn lawn chair occupying the same spot during state baseball play-off games. The only time that I ever saw the normally calm and clever principal unnerved to tears was when Coach was charged with lewd behavior after being picked up at a state rest stop. Coach was employed by a neighboring school district; his arrest was news, complete with mug shot at 10 o'clock. This and one other publicly queer incident marks the year before my own full transition into lesbian life.

Again, Mr. James was at its center. Every year when scholarship recipients are announced at Senior Awards Day, it seems there is always a golden child who receives multiple scholarships that total in the thousands. A few years ago, that young man was Randy Starr. Randy was, of course, bright, but he was also an active Christian youth. Friendly and quiet, Randy's Bible was at the top of his stack of books; I never recall seeing him when he was not wearing a small cross around his neck. Randy's scholarships totaled approximately $80,000 his senior year. He had his pick of major universities. Fast forward one year. This time, the assembly was a motivational, academic pep rally to pump up the student body for the upcoming standardized tests. Mr. James asked Randy, who had since become active in campus politics and social activism, to return from college and speak at the assembly. I had been to that same assembly a thousand times. And then the big finish. I listened in amazement at our speaker's skill in whipping the crowd into a frenzy. Randy's speech went something like this: "Don't you let anybody tell you that you can't reach your dream. Don't let anybody hold you back from being everything that you can be. I'm here today to tell you that you can. I'm here to tell you not to listen to those people who will tell you that you can't succeed because of who you are. Don't let anybody tell you that you can't because you are from the country. (Cheers.) Don't let anybody tell you that you can't because you are black. (Very loud cheers.) Don't let anybody tell you that you can't because you are a girl. (Crescendo of cheers. And finally...) Don't let anybody tell you that you can't because you are gay. (Climactic roar.) Because I'm here today to tell you that you can. Thank you."

While the student body continued to be carried away in the excitement of the moment and crowd dynamics, the words had actually registered with us teachers. I was sitting in a row of about 6 colleagues; I remember that our first reaction was of the dropped jaw variety. We were stunned at what we had just heard, both that the word (gay) itself had been uttered in a school assembly right smack in the middle of Lick Skillet, and because the returning conquering hero was apparently a queer activist. Assembly dismissed, the teachers had an emergency regrouping in the lounge just to see if we had heard what we thought we had heard. We had. And just like letting students gather at the window to look at snow that begins to fall on a Southern winter school day, we teachers did not even bother fighting the inevitable class discussion about the gay (their assumption) speaker at the assembly.

By the end of the school day an electric current was running through the community. This was the opportunity that the conservatives had been looking for to reclaim their school. The story began to circulate that the principal had knowingly exposed a captive audience to a gay speaker. Since this was considered a breach of the "don't ask; don't tell" understanding that existed between Mr. James and the good people of Lick Skillet, his sexuality was now the topic for open conversation. The incident culminated in the basement of the local Baptist church, where deacon and board member Tommy Alverson vowed to his adult Bible students that he would not rest until he got rid of Mr. James. Khayatt (1992) maintains that schools function as one of society's "established tramsmitter[s] of dominant ideology" and as such they not only embrace patriarchal values overtly through curriculum requirements but also implement male privilege and compel [heteronormativity] covertly by offering the behavior of those allowed to teach and administer as examples of what is acceptable (p. 69).

By allowing Randy to offer a message that included queer students, Mr. James, however unknowingly, had broken the transmitter code with which students, parents, and faculty (including me) felt comfortable. I learned a lot that day about ruptures along the surface of normalized straightness in school and curriculum by listening to students in my class and colleagues in the hall. We teachers are always delighted when serendipitous teachable moments arise, but I let several slip away in the aftermath of that assembly. Not only did I not come out, neither did I teach tolerance or engage my students in conversations about social justice—equally radical moves. I stood mute and felt homophobia—theirs and mine—wash over me. And I made the decision not to return.

The last conversation I had with Mr. James was when I told him I was leaving LSHS, and Alabama, the following fall. My sexual odyssey being no great secret because of a highly efficient grapevine, he knew my reasons. Not ordinarily given to serious personal conversations with faculty—he much preferred light banter—his concern was touching. He suggested that my friends would remain loyal and supportive; he assured me that I would never have to worry about my job. But protection was not what I sought. I was ready to run. I did not realize that by running I had solidified, rather than queered, the moment: the transition that might have led to growth for all of us, the faculty community and me, was prevented. No natural course of things, whether afterglow or aftershock.

The Right and Prejudice

In light of Britzman's (1998) question, "What would a curriculum be like if the curriculum began with the problem of living a life?" (p. 49), my life-curriculum began during my last year at Lick Skillet. That marked the first time I recall feeling the weight of prejudice upon me, and it felt mighty queer. It happened so suddenly; one day, I was part of the fold—by gosh, people liked me. Next day, I was still me, but I felt something that I came to recognize as distance. "But it's me," I wanted to cry, "me!" I realize that internal and external homophobia were working together to amplify my emotions, but I was incredulous about two things: that the turnaround was such a marked about-face by some of my closest colleagues and that they would abandon *me*. The question arises: How can people, who as New Testament Christians believe in a "law of liberty" (James 1:25) and a loving God, buy into rhetoric that targets somebody like me as a threat to the moral fabric of America? The Religious Right is able to capture the public's attention and play upon its collective emotions because queers (and feminists, and others) are tangible representations of the forces of darkness, again, Miller's *Devil* (1953, p. 35). The problem of living a life for me, then, was that not only was I no longer walking in the light, but I was part of the darkness.

Fundamentalist Christians who ascribe to antiqueer rhetoric do so because queer sex is sin, but what of the "sinner"? How are we so easily vilified? One answer lies in the relationship between religion and prejudice. Hunsberger (1995) speculates that the extent to which fundamentalist people are authoritarian generally determines the extent to which they are also prejudiced, primarily because both "religious fundamentalism and authoritarianism encourage obedience to authority, conventionalism, self-righteousness, and feelings of superiority" (p. 121). People who demonstrate the characteristics of right-wing authoritarianism are often likely to become fundamentalists; at the same time, religious fundamentalism tends to foster the right-wing authoritarian personality (p. 121).

Hunsberger is careful to leave open the possibility of free agency for the individual Christian; he appears to realize the sensitive nature of the empirical research and its margin of error before he would use it to generalize that all fundamentalists are doomed to lives of prejudice. Rather, he holds that prejudice is most likely to occur when the two factors, fundamentalism and authoritarianism, are entwined. He

explains, "Religious people who hold that their religious beliefs represent the absolute truth, that they must constantly be alert to Satanic
influence in the world around them, that the world can be divided
into 'Good' and 'Evil'...and who also tend to be high right-wing au-
thoritarians, tend to hold prejudiced attitudes" (p. 124). Although all
fundamentalist Christians are not prejudiced—the radicals do not
represent all practitioners—Hunsberger clearly shows that they/we
have the *propensity* to be. With the soil so very fertile, all that remains
is the mobilization under authoritarian leadership of today's political
Religious Right.

Straighten Up and Gaze Right

I somehow did not win an Academy Award for "Best Female Queer
in the Role of a Heterosexual" during the 6 months following my divorce and six months *before* the queer assembly, despite the "cast of
thousands" in the production. The whole school community was
supportive, offering encouragement, as well as dating hints and "fix-
ups." One important tenet of compulsory heterosexuality is the assumed participation in the gendered mating rituals, including the expressed and implied gender expectations. Brownmiller (1984) writes,

> ...in this patriarchal culture, women socially have to validate their female-
> ness in addition to their gender. In other words, to emphasize gender iden-
> tity, you have to dress, to behave, to think, to react, to emote, to fear, to love,
> to nurture, and to look 'like a woman' in order to be a woman. (p. 212)

After a respectable time had passed, I began to date again; the
women faculty made ready the offering. I remember well the day of
the makeover consultation. It happened, of all places, in the principal's office. I have reproduced their tips on "How to Attract a Man"
here so that others may benefit from them:

"Let your hair grow; get a softer cut."

"Walk (stand, etc.) more like this." (Demonstration following.)

"Get him to talk about himself."

"If you have to wear slacks, then get some nice outfits with really feminine pants."

And this one from Principal James himself:

"Wear sandals and paint your toenails. There is nothing sexier than a woman with painted toenails."

The piece de resistance:

"Be yourself."

I bought those sexy sandals; I spent a hundred dollars on Merle Norman makeup ("It's thick so it covers difficult blemishes."). I bought a little black dress for the faculty Christmas party because the band director was single, but I consider my lowest point dying my hair in the sink in the faculty bathroom before the Homecoming game. Performing het can be hell. Very near this time I had a queer epiphany: if I completely remake every fiber of myself, voice, hair, clothes, gait and mannerisms, attitude and personality, then I just *might* be presentable enough for a man to find me attractive. I change; he chooses.

While I have made every effort to prevent this from being a coming-out story, two telling indicators of straightness discourse occurred to me as straight teacher transitioning to queer. It is the way in which two different colleagues responded to my taking them into my confidence. The first is a happy surprise; the second is a sore disappointment. The very first friend and coworker to whom I sounded out the idea of maybe being not so very heterosexual was Joy. She appeared to be an open-minded person, and she was. Although married to a traditional head-of-the-household man 20 years her senior, Joy fought hard to carve for herself a niche as a slightly bohemian teacher. Perhaps because she practices pedagogy with a queer aesthetic (Morris, 1998, p. 276) or because of her fascination and belief in people, I felt safe in declaring to my friend that I was not entirely revolted by the thought of loving a woman. She responded with all of the warmth and support that every het-on-the-brink could hope for in her time of emotional flux. It is important to note here that my queerly eccentric and accepting friend is not a fundamentalist Christian, no Sister in Christ.

My first queer conversation with a Clearview Christian came a few weeks later, after a failed fix-up date with a fellow who had found me to be, in his words, "peaches," while I considered him more of the pits. At the time, my work had been suffering because my personal life was severely testing my professional one. Sensing this, Dora, who had arranged the date, gained my confidence by relating her own divorce and aftermath stories, including confronting the expectations and demands of parents, church, and community. I ventured softly into the same territory as I had with Joy: that my intrigue and titillation had led me to approach women online to talk to. As I write it today, I feel foolish. Dora's expression never changed from one of sweet concern as I naively sought some sort of validation for my actions. I remember thinking what a swell person she was—*and how easy this was going to be after all.*

One of the recurring themes in fundamentalist Christian doctrine is that God "hates the sin but loves the sinner." That principle is the guiding force behind the Christian Right-supported ex-gay movement, in which gay people are welcomed into the flock where they undergo an onslaught of reparative, or conversion, therapy. Straightness is the state of loving the sinner and hating the sin, whether the sin is being queer, poor, non-white, different, and having below average intelligence or ability. So out of concern and for my own good, Dora went to her old friend, our assistant principal of curriculum and instruction, and informed her of my confusion about my sexual orientation. Now, I am sure that the reader saw that coming, as well as the spreading of the glad queer tidings like seed thrown into the wind, but I did not.

So Shall Ye Also Reap

The Christian Right molds straightness in curriculum and stakeholders through educational policy that is decidedly anti-queer, further solidifying conventional notions of straight notions of Southernness. Witness the Texas textbook adoptions in which publishers Holt, Rinehart and Winston and Glencoe/McGraw-Hill changed wording in its textbooks at the behest of the Texas Board of Education. Phrases such as "married partners" and "when two people marry" ran counter to Texas law prohibiting civil unions and were replaced by the phrases "husband and wife" and "when a man and a woman marry." Publishers stopped short of adding all the changes for which Republican board members pushed. One proposed passage for a teacher's edition read: "Opinions vary on why homosexuals, lesbians and bisexuals as a group are more prone to self-destructive behaviors like depression, illegal drug use, and suicide" (ABC News, November 5, 2004).

Conservative Christians would openly hearken back to a nostalgic ideal with traditional back-to-basics, family values-laden public school curriculum—nothing hidden there. I contend that it is much more effective for the Right to infuse, rather than impose, straightness into education structures. The curriculum is not so much hidden as it is subdued. Rodriguez writes, "Indeed, combining heterosexism with schooling is an insidious way of educating youth to promote 'sexual facism'; no doubt it is part of the moral right's 'hidden curriculum'" (1998, p. 177). Straightness, compulsory heterosexuality, and by extension heterosexism, are quietly nurtured in the school culture in much the same way that team pride is built by the football players wearing suits and ties on game day.

The Right finally recognizes what Freire knew: education is political (1970, p. 127), and it is the medium through which capitalism, and thus patriarchal democracy, will be perpetuated. Or perhaps we/they have always known and have, over the last three decades, mobilized to "clutter" curriculum and pedagogy with non-issues to more easily make and hold it transparent. And so we see more overt measures, apparent in the quantification of school accountability and in the zealous fixation on standardized test scores. Publish district test scores and promise merit raises or school choice based on performance; pedagogy, and curriculum become centered around content standards, leaving the children on the margins in their own classroom. Where is the participatory and transcendent education (Darder, 2002) of fellowship and dialogue? Conservatism and corporatism, the "power of commodified identities within capitalism" (McLaren, 2000, p. 187), have bound the wonder and inquiry of teachers and students in the classroom, holding them hostage to the "bankrupt logic of standardization" (Darder, 2002, p. 58). The suppression of zest keeps things straight.

When overt measures are undertaken, according to Lugg (2000b), they may take the form of re-Christianizing the schools. Re-Christianizing public schools would replace the secular with the Judeo-Christian version of the spiritual by promoting religious activities and curricula—a "redemptive mission" (p. 622)—within the schools. Textbook censorship that lobbys for creationism and an abstinence-only sex education curriculum falls into this category. Multiculturalism would be eliminated, yet religious-sponsored school activities would be endorsed. The school prayer movement and the 1999 Hang Ten promotion, sponsored by the Family Research Council (Dr. James Dobson's Washington lobbying group), that set out to post a copy of the Ten Commandments in every public school in America are attempts at re-Christianization (FRC quoted in Lugg, 2000b). The introduction of Bible electives, particularly those developed and marketed by the National Council on Bible Curriculum in Public Schools (NCBCPS), into public school curriculum is a current example.

To achieve its education policy goals, the ultra-Right finds ways to induce the public out of its voting apathy so that conservative elected officials can then advance this far-reaching philosophical and curricular/pedagogical agenda. The formula that seems to yield the greatest results contains 1) variables to which the public will react passionately: children, sex, and queers, and 2) the threat of disenfranchisement of the fundamentalist population by school policymakers.

Such polarization pushes Christian voters to an ultimatum, and they answer by turning to the safe, known entity: the fellow holding the Bible. We make a choice because we perceive no other choice, when, in fact, issues such as those above do not represent the "normative desires of traditional Christians in school reform" (Sewall, 1998, p. 78). The alternative is risky: Christians must resist the militant, reactionary, exclusive course, acknowledge that there are issues in question that conflict with a literalist interpretation of the Bible, and turn to dialogue.

What may on the surface appear to be a return to old-fashioned Christian values—a focus on the family, rededication of husbands and fathers, the promotion of abstinence—is actually a very modern political strategy. A closer examination of what these value-laced ideals stand for will uncover what they stand against. Fundamentalist activism goes beyond a nostalgic back-to-basics, back-to-God campaign, for in order to entice the people to embrace this agenda, the movement must vilify those responsible for the falling away. People like me. Such an ascribing of blame and shame has made me—female, white, queer—suspicious, as Pratt (1991) terms it, "of the images of power, domination, submission given to me by Christianity" (p. 212). Queers are easy targets because gender-related issues make up what Bowman (2000) calls "the last acceptable prejudice" (p. 1). The conflict is gendered, with implications that cross the threshold of the classroom. And for the sake of advancing a conservative political agenda, the last acceptable prejudice has led to the last acceptable form of oppression.

The Pedagogy That Dares Not Speak Its Name

How is straightness infused into the school culture? The key, I think, lies within the curriculum. "When values become institutions," writes Doll, "they become dangerous. Whoever controls the accepted notion of God, presides over what is socially acceptable" (2000, p. 43). When that notion is of a heterosexual God with nineteenth century ideals and when the institution is the school culture, then it is straightness that is socially acceptable. What actual curriculum undercurrents propel accountability, "scientifically" based research, standards-based curriculum, and Highly Qualified Teachers (*No Child Left Behind*, 2001)? How is it that we can expect to close the achievement gap between white, middle class children and minority sub-groups (*NCLB*, 2001) with Norm- and Criterion-Referenced Test mandates? Education in this country is rooted in patriarchal structures; pedagogy, curriculum, and epistemology must not be. *NCLB* is the culmination of 20 years of conservative Right political activism that began during the Reagan administration. *NCLB* is legislated straightness. The queerly fundamental course of action that I propose for education is based on love, and love seems like a deceptively uncomplicated creature.

An educator for 16 years, I see a decided absence of love in pedagogy and curriculum at all levels. A conservative wave of corporatism and performance propels education; we are in the *business* of educating youngsters—we always have been preparing workers, but the jobs have become more sophisticated. Now, three- and four-year-old prekindergarten students have mandated performance standards, and reading is taught from scripted, directed "curricula" (Open Court, Language, Voyager), endorsed by federal "experts," such as President George W. Bush's "reading czar" Reid Lyon. There is no room for the dialogue-sparking spiritual element just beneath the surface of human nature, no room for what Noddings calls "moral education as a form of life" (in Sears & Carper, 1998, p. 124). Dialogue might lead to critical consciousness, which might in turn engender unity in diversity in our students, which might finally result in our acceptance and appreciation of each other. Freire maintained that if we would live free—whatever our oppression, whether pedagogical, societal, political—we must "risk an act of love" (1970, p. 35). Love is not to be found in a quest for higher scores; it is present when teaching becomes a "personal calling to actualize the transformation of identity" (Wexler, 1996, p. 149).

Love-in-action, revolutionary love, inspires conversation, dialogue that effects understanding. Love without dialogue is a theoretical ideal, fruitless, and dialogue without love is talk, analogous to the

Biblical syllogism in James: faith without works is dead; works with-out faith are barren (2:14—18). Strike (1998) suggests, "The key to dialogue is the virtue of reasonableness" (p. 68), the belief that both parties approach the dialogue with openness that is based on faith and trust. Dialogue grounded in reason is supported by precepts that are undeniably embraced by Christians: faith, hope, love; and the greatest of these is love (I Corinthians 13:13). Along with openness, reason, and love that we bring to the dialogue table, we must also, however, come with the expectation that we might leave the table in (dis)comfort.

The concept of conversation in which I am investing such hope is based upon that of "analytic dialogue" (1997, p. 115), which Ellsworth (1989/1994, 1997) incorporates into her discussion of the "repressive myths of critical pedagogy" (1989/1994) and pedagogical "modes of address" (1997). She positions dialogue as a form of pedagogy that is a practice "historically and culturally embedded" (1997, p. 48) in raced, classed, and gendered "networks of power, desire, and knowl-edge" (p. 49). She dismisses simplistic, unquestioned tenets of dia-logue, as well as the neutral understanding that is assumed as its logical outcome, as not only ineffective, but repressive, doing more harm than good to efforts at critical pedagogy. Neither phlegmatic nor unitary, Ellsworth's analytic dialogue embraces ruptures and un-settles its participants as it moves participants toward the *play* of un-derstanding. The task may be, she suggests, "building a coalition among the multiple, shifting, intersecting, and sometimes contradic-tory groups carrying unequal weights of legitimacy within the cul-ture" (1989/1994, p. 317). It is from *processes* of analytic dialogue that we grapple toward the self-understanding from which "self-mobilization in the service of social reconstruction" (Pinar, 2004, p. 201) might spring. It is a queered dialogue for social justice.

I call on fundamentalists to dedicate ourselves to the principles as teachers and citizens, as selves and others, to which we have dedi-cated ourselves as Christians: "As I have loved you, so you must love one another. By this all men will know that you are my disciples, if you love one another" (John 13:34—35). I propose the following roadwork: fundamentalist Christians must acknowledge that homophobia and the other "isms"—racism, sexism, classism, ageism, etc.—impede spirituality, and recognize that celebrating the agency of all people strengthens the spirit—both our individual and collective spirits. When the discourses that construct straight teachers become instilled with openness, trust, and propensity for dialogue, then unity in diversity might also emerge. Perhaps then the sacred might permeate pedagogy then culture then society, which might then lead to Wexler's (1996) exploration of the "implications of religious theory and practice for creating new models of educational theory and practice" (p. 151).

If queer pedagogy unsettles curriculum, I am the embodiment of how it can shake up a faculty—or an identity perception. For at least the year of my own queer gazing, LSHS had to steady itself as it was forced to consider its own queerness. For a community of compulsory heterosexuality that cultivates dispositions of straightness in its resident stakeholders, it is queerer than it knows. Queer is scary because it does indeed "unrest" and "trouble" curriculum (Morris, 1998, p. 285); while straight strives to reach the peaceful center of the known with the comfort of standardization. Shooting for this center is the ultimate straightness discourse within the local school culture, positioning a straight curriculum and the evolution of straight teachers as part of the natural order of things. Straightness is performed and nourished so that it may perpetuate itself, but queer happens. In my own journeying, I return again to Pratt's (1991) re-memorying:

> So I continue to fear the images of God given to me. I have tried to create new spiritual images for myself, my own, as much as any image can be, through poetry...seeking to map my own soul, to know my own fears and desires, and not seek dominion....I try simply to go in search of myself. (p. 212)

Mapping the soul in the search for self disrupts conventional notions of Southernness secured by a straight curriculum.

The mapping of my soul is a working through of tensions I encounter in the interrogation of the paradox of my experience. As the source of my desire—my sexual identity—collides with the fundamentalist discourse that first informed my spirituality, I acknowledge the complexity and contradictions between my identifications and desires rather than deny them. I avow the significance and fountain of spirituality that an upbringing as a fundamentalist Christian has afforded me, yet I am positioned subjectively within its ruptures, and my identification often carries with it a decided (dis)comfort. As I map my soul, I continue the spiritual journey that began within a fundamentalist frame, yet as a queer fundamentalist, my soul map demarcates the violence, narrowness, fear, guilt, and control apparent in fundamentalist thinking.

I bear witness as queer fundamentalist to the anomalous subjectivity of being on "both shores at once" (Anzaldua, 1987, p. 78), yet I do not count myself in antagonistic opposition to fundamentalist Christians or to the religious discourse itself. For, as Anzaldua notes, "it is not enough to stand on the opposite river bank, shouting questions, challenging patriarchal, white conventions. A counterstance locks one into a duel of oppressor and oppressed; locked in mortal combat...both are reduced to a common denominator of violence" (p. 78). This is the way of the radical, narrow fundamentalist; it is not my way, nor that of the fundamentalist Christians who are open to liberatory dialogue. Instead, we might build on a foundation for active love, as hooks (2000a) describes in her discussion with Thich Nhat Hanh on building a community of love. She writes, "Love illuminates matters. When I write provocative social and cultural criticism...I think of that work as love in action. While it may challenge, disturb and at times even frighten or enrage readers, love is always where I begin and end" (2000a). When we begin and end with love, we confront discomfort, fear, and rage with openness, not narrowness; peace, not violence.

The emergence of queerly fundamental Southernness creates spaces for questioning the normalization of straightness within curriculum and holds the expectation that curriculum-shapers at all levels will give account for the mapping out of straightness in both hidden and visible curricula. Queering straight teachers and a straight curriculum offers the hope of knowing fears and desires of the self. The anomalies of spirit and desire that I am witness to as a queer fundamentalist inform curriculum theory by interrupting and reconstructing heterosexual narratives in curriculum. Working queerly fundamental tensions contribute to what Davis (2004) calls, "our human capacity to hold incompatible beliefs, in fact not just to hold them, but to freely combine them into notions that are imagined to be coherent" (pp. 180—181). It is this capacity by which we might commune with one another.

Notes

1   An earlier draft of this chapter appeared as an article in the *Journal of Curriculum and Pedagogy,* Spring 2006.

Chapter 4
"The Price of Restoration": Flannery O'Connor and the South's Biblical Vision

There is something in us, as storytellers and as listeners to stories, that demands the redemptive act, that demands that what falls at least be offered the chance to be restored. The reader of today looks for this motion, and rightly so, but what he has forgotten is the cost of it. His [sic] sense of evil is diluted or lacking altogether, and so he has forgotten the price of restoration. When he reads a novel, he wants either his senses tormented or his spirits raised. He wants to be transported, instantly, either to mock damnation or a mock innocence.

–O'Connor (1969, p. 48)[1]

It is a fearful thing to fall into the hands of the living God...

–Hebrews 10:31

Prologue

Sometimes, I travel incognito. I pass, whether or not I try, as a straight white woman, a conservative Southerner. I think I pass because the lines are blurred; I am indeed a Southern woman, white, raised fundamentalist Protestant. My liberal, intellectual, lesbian identity is harder to detect. Like many Southerners, I am a gabber. I chat with strangers in public places, restaurants, elevators, the line at Wal-mart—to kill time, to be friendly. Mainly, I chat for much the same reason that I write; it is a way, as storyteller and listener, to experience fiction as 'the lie pedagogy needs in order to uncover the truths that make us human" (Doll, 2000, p. *xii*). Perhaps narrative—in the writing and in the telling and in the listening—is itself redemptive. Perhaps it can also be socially and culturally transformative. In any case, I look as "common as an old shoe," as my mother would say, which, of course, I am, but because gay, liberal insurgents are so desperately "othered" by white Southerners, usually as citified Yankees, people rarely suspect me. We swap comments and observations, and I wait for the redemptive act—borne on O'Connor's motion (above) of falling and rising, and then converging. Yet, when I travel undetected, redemptive motion is often difficult to uncover until I write through the encounter later.

Last November I was waiting by my shopping cart in a Walmart grocery aisle while my partner price-shopped for our Thanksgiving turkey. I wait by the cart because she is a relentless comparison shopper, and when I accompany her, I feel like those poor husbands who go shoe shopping with their wives, just wanting to find a place to quietly wait. This day, another spouse, male, craggy face, ballcap, Velcro tennis shoes, and polyester trousers recognized my predicament—if not my domestic status—and approached me to shorten the wait time.

He commenced the chat by commenting on my Alabama Crimson Tide tee-shirt, "We're Not Snobs, We're Just Better Than You." He began, "What's goin' on with the Tide this year? What'd you think about that Alabama-Auburn game?" Alabama had lost, so I told him I was not too happy about it. He struck me as a fellow who wanted to tell, to tell the South, in a manner of speaking, as Hobson (1983) suggests. He did his telling, while I replied in the appropriate places. He was from Birmingham; a daughter still lives there. His son is in Texas, so Baton Rouge is halfway.

Before he had retired, he had been a scout for the Houston Astros. A baseball man. Not a profession I run into every day, I replied, "Is that a fact," more statement than question, for I am easily impressed. After a few minutes, after he felt as though I knew him, or something of him, I suppose, the nature of the chat shifted. He said, "Yeah, I been in baseball for thirty years, but I got out. The Blacks (he lowered his voice as he said *Blacks)* are takin' it over. I mean, they *got* football, what else do they want?" What redemptive actions would there be for me and this fellow? Not much by way of redemption or grace, for I shook my head slowly and uttered a "mnh-mnh," the universal Southern reply that can mean anything from *ain't that a shame* to *I don't believe it*, somewhat in the same way that "bless his heart" allows Southerners to say anything in the world about anybody. *He's so ugly, he'd snag lightening, bless his heart.* In this instance, what it meant, to me, for he would have had no way of knowing, is that I had just been *raced*, presumed to be a secret, lowering-of-the-voice racist because my skin was white and my clothes proclaimed me a probable Southerner. I was disheartened, but not entirely surprised. All this, on a Sunday afternoon, parked in front of the ham hocks at Walmart.

This chapter considers grace as an anomalous aspect of Southernness from which to interrogate the construction of Southern identity and build conversations about progressive transformations of Southern place. I turn a queer gaze upon the South's Biblical vision—the nature and extent of religious beliefs and practices, which Reed (1982) designates as an enduring aspect of Southern culture along with its attachment to local communities (p. 133)—and the complexity, contradictions, and violence embedded in fundamentalist thinking. Within the fissures emerges grace that shatters rather than absolves traditional raced, classed, and gendered notions of Southern identity.

From my own fundamentalist narrative and double consciousness as a queer-raised-fundamentalist, I avow the profound power of fundamentalism and suggest ways to liberate self and the South from its control without disavowing its spiritual discourse. Disturbing fundamentalist thinking in terms of white patriarchal attitudes that constrict Southern identity opens spaces for reconstructing social and cultural consciousness and commitment in the South. To this end, I consider Flannery O'Connor's use of humor and the grotesque to point out fundamental intransigence of traditional forms of Southernness. In her stories, the Misfit functions to disrupt, and with this rift comes grace. I recognize and acknowledge myself as a misfit, exploring ways in which this positioning might disengage me, and others like me, from fundamental narrowness. The Misfit, for example, would have taken exception to the Walmart man's thinking (above) by calling him on prejudiced notions about race and sports, much like my confronting the San Antonio cab driver (which happened since).

Mary Doll (2000) observes, "Fiction is not only necessary for pedagogy, fiction is the lie that pedagogy needs in order to uncover the truths that make us human" (p. xii). I posit Flannery O'Connor's fiction as a pedagogical lie that exposes, through the Biblical vision characteristic of her work, darker truths of humanity—discomfiting, violent, and grotesque. The sacramental truths in her fiction unfold as her characters engage "the terror, mystery, and beauty of the Word made flesh" (Baumgaertner, 1988, p. 22). One truth that makes us human is that we are frail, and, given the choice, we are reluctant to confront our faith, refusing grace because, for the Christian, grace occurs in the shadow of the cross. The price of restoration is that redemption is only possible through death. For the South, this means focusing on the death through which grace, and Southern reconstruction, may occur. The South must lay to rest the Lost Cause—through which there will be neither resurrection nor remission of Southern sins.

Wresting the Angels: Flannery O'Connor and Place

As O'Connor's work may be considered in literary and various cultural criticisms, it may also be woven into interdisciplinary and intersubjective studies of place, primarily in the ways her anagogical perspective informs larger social and cultural contexts. Her pedagogy is found in her fiction, her speeches and essays, and her personal correspondence, in which she discloses individual encounters with grace. O'Connor's stories usually unfold within Southern locales; her characters are usually white Southerners who seek to elude in about equal measure both the devil and the "ragged figure" (WB, 1952, p. 11) of the redeeming Christ. Scholars agree upon O'Connor's affinity for the countrified Southern fundamentalist Protestant's intensity toward religion and fervent belief in sin. As she explores the mystery of the individual within social and cultural contexts, she implicitly establishes the need for a collective, political accounting, thereby advancing a marginalized Southern curriculum of place.[2] I do not seek so much to analyze her work, but her South.

In order to generate further progressive conversation and social political movement through a curriculum of place, I contemplate the anomalies of Southern grace that lie within the tensions of O'Connor's notion of mystery and manners. Both mystery and manners are important elements of her anagogical worldview focused on the intervention of grace in the physical world, or, as she terms it, that "which has to do with the Divine life and our participation in it" (*MM*, p. 72, 111).[3] Because she overtly contextualized her themes within the natural world, a connection exists between these themes and the study of place. So this is a consideration of place, the South, as having sites for moments of grace—which I use here as an outpouring of love, sometimes itself violent and startling. O'Connor noted that, in our search to find it, readers of fiction often misunderstand what grace looks like. "The reader wants his grace warm and binding," she writes, "not dark and disruptive" ("The Catholic Novelist in the South," *CW*, p. 862). Grace that is warm and binding, like the dysfunctional nostalgia that also comforts and conjoins white Southerners, suggests forgiveness, justification of traditional codes and mindsets; whereas disruptive grace upsets false securities and delusory unity.

O'Connor upsets narrow conceptualizations of passive, impotent grace with the violent blows inflicted upon her characters. From the ruptures emerges a rapturous—often violent—grace that illuminates self and self-and-other. Her characters, and, I suggest, perhaps many white Southerners, are "driven—even tormented by the idea that they have been redeemed," often having "to face the frightful idea that God loves them and will go out of his way to save them" (Ragen, 1989, p. 3, 9). Southern rage and guilt not only keep us wallowing in our fallen state, they also keep us at enmity with God (James 4) and unreceptive to love. We refuse transformative grace until it shatters us, and we cling to constricting structures that have sustained the South for 200 years, the Southern code of manners, for instance.

O'Connor believed that these manners of formality and civility have been important to racial relations in the South. It was not the manners, she maintained, that inhibited interpersonal relations;

rather, it was their lack of grounding in love. Unreconstructed manners, for instance, prevented a confrontation of racist remarks while turkey shopping at Walmart. If relations were to improve, she reckoned, the reconstruction of social relations would not be found in the civil rights activism that she witnessed in the mid-1950s, but in the initiation of a new code of manners of mutual charity. She believed that were such a code in place, when charity failed in the day-to-day, as she was certain it would, the code of manners would remain to bolster relations until they were stabilized. The tensions between mystery and manners in Southern place hold a complex interplay of love and rage, violent grace.

How we are faced with, and then accept or reject, our moments of grace informs how we relate to one another and confront raced, classed, gendered, sexualized, and religious social narratives.[4] Doll (2000) explains that, for curriculum theorists, "literary fictions about the South provide effective avenues for exposing social fictions" (p. 7), about race, for example. Southern writers, like O'Connor, "refuse to remain culturally unconscious about racism" (p. 6). Even the Agrarians—as a whole, although some of them tried—could not (Prown, 2001). We are faced, like Nelson, in O'Connor's "The Artificial Nigger," with not seeing the "Other" at all (and for white Southerners, Other is almost always The Black), or, if we see the Other, it is with an unfulfilled yearning for the Other's familial, sexualized nature. In yet another move to represent the Other as "signifier against which white identity is defined" (Prown, p. 73), we might view "them" as redemptive figures, as did Nelson and Mr. Head, in whose misery their white identities were confirmed. At the same time that Southern whites "acknowledge the ghosts" (Doll, 2000, p. 6) that haunt us, we continue to perpetuate what Doll refers to as the constructed "fantasy about aristocracy and landed privilege" (p. 7); these fantasies, in turn, reinforce the Old South codes, manners, of race—and class, gender, sexuality, and religion—that keep Southerners firmly rooted in a nineteenth century false sociocultural ideal and keep us from finding ways to commune with each other, one human to another [5].

A study of the movement of grace within place calls for what Brinkmeyer (1989) terms a "re-centering the self along new lines of awareness" (p. 42), a recursive cycle of radical repositioning—"a self-dispossession" (p. 42)—of the self and self and other that shatters the isolating egocentrism. He writes, "recentering, however, does not mean stasis, for in its ongoing encounters and communications with others, the self continually decenters and recenters itself" (p. 42). This is the connection of O'Connor's work with curriculum, via a *currere* of self. It is a "curriculum that begins with the problem of living a life" (Britzman, 1998, p. 49) by turning the life back upon itself in a movement toward, but not quite achieving, the centering of self.

O'Connor becomes part of the "complicated conversation" (Pinar et al. 1995, p. 848) of curriculum studies in the distortions and breaking moments of sudden grace that she portrays. She crafts freaks and misfits to subvert the pastoral, flowing quietness of a mythic South incapable of sight because of its intransigence. She wrote, "When I am asked why Southern writers write about freaks, I reply it is because we are still able to recognize one" (*MM*, p. 44). The freak that we know exists of and within place; we do too, and so we can recognize him. Sometimes, the freak is us. O'Connor reveals the price of restoration to the freak of self-in-place by the rekindling his or her—and our—diluted sense of evil, allowing both self and place to be considered in light of the grace of Mystery and the mystery of grace.

O'Connor has been included in the curriculum, but she and her anagogical worldview—that of "the Divine life and our participation in it" (*MM*, p. 111)—are noticeably absent in the *study* of curriculum. While curriculum theorists continue to call for the inclusion of spiritual frameworks through which to contextualize curriculum (Pinar, 1995, 2004; Slattery, 1995; Purpel, 1989, 2004; Macdonald, 1995; Huebner, 1999), few have gone so far as to suggest that curriculum studies, particularly those focusing on place and region, might benefit from O'Connor's observations of supernatural grace in the natural world.[6] Within artistic "lines of spiritual motion" (*MM*, p. 113) she sets forth gestures and actions by which humans make contact with Mystery; in rendering the visible world, she thereby suggests an invisible one

(*MM*, p. 80). As curriculum scholars propose to understand curriculum as theological text (Pinar et al. 1995), the comprehensive body of O'Connor's work, including essays/speeches and letters spanning her adult life, offers insight into both her own theology and that which emerges in her fiction. Her insistence on a radical sacramentalism illustrates an interrelated—if particular—view of wholeness that contradicts the modern experience of fragmentation and isolation. (Pinar et al. 1995, p. 660); the lines of spiritual motion that she as an artist creates are analogous to the "processive movement of body, mind, and spirit in the spiral of procreation, death, and resurrection" (Pinar et al. 1995, p. 660) present in a living curriculum.

Although O'Connor demonstrates her regard for the outward form of intense religious feeling in the "backwoods prophets and shouting fundamentalists" (*MM*, p. 207), superimposing O'Connor onto curriculum studies, in this case, of place, is not without its complications. For example, O'Connor's personal correspondence, peppered with pejorative language and racist, classist, and sexist attitudes, is more vexing than her fiction, which deals with racial issues in ways that would suggest moves toward social justice. Neither is her work overtly feminist; it would be counter-intuitive, counterfactual, to propose a feminist treatment of O'Connor, as have Gordon (2000) and Prown (2001), for doing so would deny her the agency as a female writer to maintain, according to Wood (2001), "a deliberate self-chastening, a careful avoidance of the literary and spiritual softness that could have led to the dismissal of her work as conventionally Christian and feminine." My study of O'Connor must take into account the various camps that try to claim her; a curriculum study has room for the interdisciplinary, intersubjective critiques of her work.

Looking critically at O'Connor's work, not in spite of these complications but by openly acknowledging them, might render a more complete consideration of her work. A feminist reading, no matter how seductive that might be, will not do, nor will a "Southern" reading, or a purely theological one. O'Connor is too hard to peg. Prown (2001) tries hard to have O'Connor project her feminine voice over the objective narrator—a masculinist narrator with sexist language—that she worked a lifetime to craft. Prown proposes that O'Connor has "transcended gender" (p. 9ff) to the point that her feminine voice is masculinized for narration. Prown would show that obscure early drafts of *Wise Blood* demonstrate O'Connor's natural inclination toward a gendered voice, one that is therefore resistant to the Agarian New Criticism. Prown argues that original drafts contain developed female characters that were integral to Motes's own spiritual illumination. On the other hand, Wood (2004) points to O'Connor as a proponent of a conservative social agenda. While this is not his primary goal—Wood is a clear admirer of O'Connor's determination to make God's presence known in the natural world, and so affords her work a deeply thoughtful theological treatment—he is devoted at times to reconciling O'Connor's seemingly incongruous professional and personal treatment of racial issues.[7] O'Connor is a sacramentalist who "views the things of this world as vehicles for God's grace" (Baumgaertner, 1988, p. 85), and, as such, her work sometimes does not easily translate into secular applications.

O'Connor proves problematic for me in yet another area. Based on both fictional depiction and personal correspondence—a significant amount is with friends who were lesbians (Wood, 2004; Cash, 2002)—her disposition toward homosexuality is that it is at best "unclean" (*CW*, p. 925) and at worst demonic, evil incarnate (*CW*, p. 1119, 1121). After Francis Marion Tarwater, protagonist of *The Violent Bear It Away*, baptizes and drowns Bishop Rayber, he heads back to the country and his prophetic vocation. He is given a ride in a lavender and cream-colored car by a man wearing a lavender shirt and carrying a lavender handkerchief. The man drugs Tarwater, takes him into the woods, and rapes him. As the man emerges, he looks "furtively about him...His delicate skin had acquired a faint pink tint as if he had refreshed himself on blood" (*CW*, p. 472). The gay-vampire-predator theme is pervasive; O'Connor later explained that the man is the personification of the devil. In order to see evil for the first time, Tarwater must experience evil physically. As Tarwater had shown no regard for Bishop's natural life, he is subjected to the horror of evil by the worst embodiment of a Satanic predator that the author could fashion: an obviously homosexual pedophile. O'Connor reawakens Tarwater's diluted sense of evil so that he might gain spiritual sight, yet she reduces what might have been another complex Misfit—the Man in the Lavender Suit—to a caricature. His lack of dimension exposes O'Connor's own narrowness in this instance.

Dialogic Struggle

Tensions of place and religion displayed in O'Connor's ambivalence toward the South and Southernness at the same time complicate and inform her presence in a curriculum of Southern place. If, as Prown (2001) suggests, O'Connor was ambivalent toward the South and Southerners, as well as toward the Catholic Church, then her ambivalence might be examined in terms of an ambivalence of place. Brinkmeyer (1989) notes,

> She believed that the descent into the self through art, where the artist encountered the multi-voiced self, was also a descent into the writer's homeland; thus, to turn within was also, paradoxically, to turn without. The image of the self, on one level, became for O'Connor the image of the south, and it was this image, teeming with heterogeneous voices, that she as an artist had to engage and give expression to. (p. 34)

The intersections of self and South, within and without, are sites of convergence that might eventually become sites of confrontation; O'Connor's "descent" into her homeland situates her squarely in both place and the study thereof. Engaging self-in-south with social contexts constitutes the autobiographical labor necessary for reconstructing the Southern homeland.

O'Connor believed that the Southern writer wrestles with the social contexts of Southern culture, "like Jacob with the angel, until he [sic] has extracted a blessing" (*MM*, 198). Her own grappling is evident in the Southern voice discernable in her work. She relies heavily, and admittedly, on Southern idiom, stating in an interview, "We carry out history and our beliefs and customs and vices and virtues around in our idiom. You can't say anything significant about the mystery of a personality unless you put that personality in a social context that belongs to it" (*CFO*, p. 40). The struggle precipitates the blessing: if the wrestling is the price of restoration—the struggle of self and South with good and evil in the natural, human, world—then the blessing we extract is illumination. We must subjectivize our sense of evil in order to be receptive to grace. O'Connor's work accesses both the struggle and the blessing.

Brinkmeyer (1989) examines the dialogic nature of O'Connor's work by interrogating the interplay of the author's Catholic sensibilities with the narrator's fundamentalist ones. He draws from Bakhtin's ideas of plurality of consciousnesses and internally persuasive discourse. Brinkmeyer argues that a radical repositioning of self leads to "dialogic interplay" (p. 34) between author and self and author and audience. He states, "Such a dialogic dismantling of the self frees it from the tyranny of its self image" (p. 15). The white South keeps itself prisoner to its own false sentimental racist self-image, partly of guilt and defeat. Brinkmeyer notes that the Southern author is cut off from history and tradition, which serves to "shatter" (p. 7) his or her identity and thus his or her communion with the group. Out of the subjective struggle of the group, which has based its sense of communion on that history and tradition of falsity, a proper shattering would occur; that is, a shattering of the white Southern self. The liberation of self-dispossession will guide the white South toward a new communion of reconstruction.

As he considers O'Connor's artistic struggle to develop her dialogic vision, Brinkmeyer (1989) evokes Bakhtin's plurality of consciousness, a collection rather than a singular, monolithic consciousness. He quotes Bakhtin:

> The very being of man is the deepest communion. To be means to communicate...to be means to be for another, and through the other, for oneself. A persona has no sovereign territory, he is wholly and always on the boundary; looking inside himself, he looks into the eyes of another or with the eyes of another. (p. 14)

Articulation of the artist's plurality of consciousness is critical to the emergent dialogic interplay in O'Connor's work. According to Brinkmeyer, O'Connor's internal struggle, rather than being between conflicting persuasive discourses, is between her internally persuasive discourse and an authoritative discourse, her fundamentalism and Catholicism, respectively (p. 60). From within the ruptures of her own conflicting discourses, O'Connor fashions the Misfit, the embodied dismantling of the self that shatters constricting self-image and social conventions.

Fundamentalist Discourse

The Misfit occupies spaces between sin and redemption and thus presents a complexity of subjectivity that troubles truths about good and evil, right and wrong, salvation and damnation. O'Connor aligned herself with the religious intensity and commitment to the Scriptures of the Southern fundamentalists, apparent in the profoundly fundamentalist narrator in her mature work (Brinkmeyer, 1989, p. 34). Brinkmeyer credits the interplay between her Catholic authorial voice and that of her Protestant narrators as contributing to the "internally persuasive discourse" (p. 60) that runs throughout her work. O'Connor found "painful and touching and grimly comic" (p. 350) the sacramental-less Southern fundamentalist practice of salvation by "wise blood" (p. 350), yet she declared in a 1959 letter to John Hawkes, "I accept the same fundamental doctrines of sin and redemption that they do" (*HB*, p. 350, 518). The doctrine is that one makes his or her choice: *"No man can serve two masters: for either he will hate the one, and love the other; or else he will hold to the one, and despise the other. Ye cannot serve God and mammon"* (Matthew 6:24). Southern stories of epic proportion and mythic dimensions involve no less than good versus evil, Christ or the Devil; the struggle is in trying to decide where we truly stand.

O'Connor's Southern fundamentalist voice works in tension with the deeply embedded and grounding presence of her Catholicism. The privileged narrator voice is, according to Brinkmeyer (1989), "ultimately pressured to reveal its shortcomings and limits. In this invoking and then eventual undercutting of her fundamentalist voice, O'Connor both acknowledges its profound power and liberates herself from its control" (p. 62). This is my purpose in my fundamentalist narrative, and it is the subjective reconstruction the white South awaits—an ethical sense rooted in individual conscience, not in outer laws, such as the Ten Commandments, that may be reduced to their mere representation on a monument. In which case, the lines are often blurred as to whether the struggle over them is for the laws or for the granite on which they are carved, as Judge Roy Moore's courtroom in Alabama attests ("Ten Commandments Judge..." CNN.com. 11/14/2003). As a Misfit who is, among many other complexities, both queer and fundamentalist subject, I acknowledge the profound power of fundamentalist discourse. Like Motes and Tarwater, it continues to influence my being; it is a force in my life. The disruptions of queer desire in tension with my fundamentalist identification position me as Misfit, inhabiting inbetween spaces wherein I see the power as I chip away at its layers of control.

Rendering Justice to the Visible Universe

Dominant social and cultural constricting conceptions of Southern place are apparent in O'Connor's portrayal of the South, particularly its violences and inhibitive codes of manners. One finds in O'Connor not a telling about the South as Shreve McCannon entreated Quentin Compson, but more of a telling the South. How O'Connor does *not* write speaks as much to me as how she does. For instance, she does not write *about* Southern idiom or Southern Protestants, anymore than she writes *as* a white woman or *as* representative of the middle class. By not telling about but observing and bearing witness, O'Connor is able to "render the highest possible justice to the visible universe" (*MM*, p. 80); Conrad's description of the job of the fiction writer to which O'Connor repeatedly referred.[8] The intriguing tensions of the unsaid extend the study of place by disclosing "the terrifying threat of redemption" (Ragen, 1989, p. 202) that is palpable in the South; there

is simultaneously a serendipitous locating of the South from the anagogical and a serendipitous locating of the anagogical from the South
as grace and place inform each other.

In a 1955 interview with Harvey Breit, O'Connor explained the extent to which her work may be considered "Southern." In answer to
Breit's question, "Do you think, too, that a Northerner, for example,
reading and seeing this, would have as much appreciation of the
people in your book, your stories, as a Southerner?," she replied,

> Yes, I think perhaps more, because he [sic] at least wouldn't be distracted by
> the Southern thinking that this was a novel about the South, or a story about
> the South, which it is not...[A] serious novelist is in pursuit of reality. And
> of course when you're a Southerner and in pursuit of reality, the reality you
> come up with is going to have a Southern accent, but that's just an accent;
> it's not the essence of what you're trying to do. (*CFO*, p. 8)

O'Connor wrote about the region in her accent, not to illustrate
the region, but to gain access to the "true country" (*CFO*, p. 110) for
which it is an entrance. "The Georgia writer's true country is not
Georgia....One uses the region in order to suggest what transcends it,
that realm of mystery which is the concern of the prophets" (*CFO*, p.
110). Because they are *not* stories about the South, realities about the
place emerge from the author's strategic use of accent to achieve essence; the violent blow of grace upon her characters is violence inflicted within Southern place, for example.

The anomalous South one finds in O'Connor lies in her explication of grace that is set there. Her focus was less on the South for its
own sake than on grotesquerie or violence; nevertheless, a Southern
accent is embedded, and, as such, contributes to the rendering of the
highest possible justice to the visible—and invisible—South. Her authorial and narrator voices have Southern accents, yet she did not
write in a rage, as Hobson (1983) describes, to "tell about the South."
It is O'Connor's rendering that keeps me honest: I interrogate manifestations of both grace and violence because, in a just rendering of
the Southern portion of the universe, both exist in tension with each
other.

The shock of O'Connor's "angular Christian realism" (Wood, 2004) points out fundamental intransigence characteristic of Southernness. Her oft-cited maxim, "to the hard of hearing you shout, and for the almost-blind you draw large and startling figures," (*MM*, p. 34) is the possible way to get the attention of a place of "mythic dimensions" (p. 202). The South is actually and metaphorically a place not only of mythic dimensions but also of mythic distortions, in its historical, social, and cultural constructs. It is a grotesquerie of freaks and misfits. In "The Fiction Writer and His Region" she writes, "The larger social context...cannot be left out by the Southern writer...the image of the South, in all its complexity, is so powerful in us that it is a force which has to be encountered and engaged" (*MM*, p. 198). As Southerners—and fundamentalist Protestants, as are some of us—we not only *are* loud, large, startling figures—Misfits—we also have to be pummeled with startling figures from time to time to get our attention, so that we might attend to grace. O'Connor's characters, representatives of the Southern idiom that surrounded her, grab the reader and rattle him or her into engaging in larger social contexts.

In O'Connor's stories, the misfit character disrupts the scene in a forced confrontation with evil. Flannery O'Connor transitioned, for me, from being a talented author whose grotesquely humorous, complex stories had significant literary merit to one whose work crossed disciplinary boundaries as I began—subconsciously, at first—reading Hazel Motes as my daddy. Not that Daddy went around committing sins to prove that he did not believe in them; he did. Like Motes, though, Daddy, whether or not he terms it this way, believes fervently in Original Sin. Sin is real, and the devil is real in the world, and the believer is sinful and forever in the devil's clutches. From a lifetime of observing in my father what I believe to be fear and doubt—but what could, in fact, be a number of other demons—I wonder if perhaps he, like Motes, is troubled by "the threat of a savior" (Ragen, 1989, p. 157). Perhaps, like Motes, "he does not fear being one of the lost; he dreads being one of the saved" (p. 157). O'Connor describes Motes' determination to outrun Jesus:

Later he saw Jesus move from tree to tree in the back of his mind, a wild ragged figure motioning him to turn around and come off into the dark where he was not sure of his footing, where he might be walking on the water and not know it and then suddenly know it and drown." (*WB*, p. 11)

Through my transference my father is a prophet-freak, who, states O'Connor, "is disturbing to us because he keeps us from forgetting that we share his state" (*MM*, p. 133). Because I share my father's state, I have my own trees from which the ragged figure moves. I am a Misfit, and I beckon the figure down. The position of Misfit is risky—one is never entirely sure of one's footing. Yet what we must "see" is that there is grace equally in the walking on water and in the sinking. The South is haunted by the ragged figure, always in pursuit along paths of narrowness, tradition, and sameness.

The Force of the Violent

"How may the Southerner take hold of his Tradition? The answer is by violence."
                                                              –Allen Tate (1930)

O'Connor recognized the pervasive violent raging within Southern place, as well as the manners that allowed its people to coexist despite the raging. She countered the violence by employing it to shatter the characters toward the recognition of grace. O'Connor's second novel, *The Violent Bear It Away* took its name from Matthew 11:12: *And from the days of John the Baptist until now the kingdom of heaven suffereth violence, and the violent take it by force* (KJV). In this work, Francis Marion Tarwater took the kingdom of Heaven by force, baptizing and subsequently drowning the retarded Bishop Rayber, a charge given to Tarwater by his great uncle, Mason Tarwater. For O'Connor's early readers and critics, sacramental meanings of God's love were often overpowered by the violent conventions she used to convey her themes, yet the violence was also sacramental. Grace had to be violent in order to compete with evil; violence made the grace as concrete as the evil that her characters confront. In her essays and letters, O'Connor explained the connection between episodes of violence and the ultimate moments of grace that present themselves to her characters and return them to secular and sacred reality. She wrote,

> Our age not only does not have a very sharp eye for the almost imperceptible intrusions of grace, it no longer has much feeling for the nature of the violences which precede and follow them....I have found that violence is strangely capable of returning my characters to reality and preparing them to accept their moment of grace. (*MM*, p. 112)

Martin (1968) points out that Mrs. May's violent death in the story "Greenleaf" (she was gored by a bull) seems to suggest that such violence was necessary to "effect the small insight needed for the rising and converging" (p. 136). Violence, then, may be the harbinger of grace, but *must* it be? *What shall we say then? Shall we continue in sin that grace may abound? God forbid* (Romans 6:1).

Hobson (1983) presents the Southern "rage to explain, the compulsion to tell about the South" (p. 8), as a paradox: the raging compulsion is born at the same time of a marginalizing inferiority complex and a sense of superiority that derives from "[the white Southerner's] heritage of failure and defeat," which he wears as his "badge of honor" (p. 12). Faulkner wrote that the Southern writer, "unconsciously writes into every line and phrase his violent despairs and rages and frustrations or his violent prophesies of still more violent hopes" (in Hobson, p. 3). I propose a connection between violent rage and nostalgia and place: we rage *somewhere*. Some of us assign causality to place in our protestations, "I gotta get *outta* this place!" Place informs and contextualizes violences, even as our violences are contextualized and informed by place. One basis for contextualization is nostalgia, the yearning for place-in-past, which is often an intense homesickness, an irresistible compulsion to return home—in thought or in fact. The yearning is futile, a lost cause, and all that is left is the raging. As Misfit, I confront nostalgia (Chapter 2) by reconfiguring— through narratives of displacement—homeplace as a site that recognizes and honors difference.

Rage muted becomes nostalgia for a place that never was. When she died, O'Connor was working on a third novel called *Why do the Heathen Rage?* The title comes from Psalms 2:1; *Why do the heathen rage, and the people imagine a vain thing?* In verse 11 of that chapter, the psalmist exhorts, "Serve the Lord with fear, and rejoice with trembling." If we are to consider the nature of Southern violence, it is important to see it, as O'Connor might have suggested, as it occurs in the everyday world around us, to put a face on it, to witness the fear and trembling. If, as feminists have contended for at least half a century, the personal is political, then so is the political—and historical—personal. One has only to look around and pay attention in order to see racial, sexist, class, homophobic violence. Still, we can *see* the violences and have no "feeling" (*MM*, p. 112) for their nature. Seeing violences without sensing them does not make them personal. The Misfit through distortions and grotesquerie—through my double consciousness of queer fundamentalist or intellectual blue collar, for example—shocks an unsuspecting South into sight and insight.

In a letter to "A" O'Connor wrote, "You have to suffer as much from the Church as for it" (*HB*, p. 90). Some of us suffer the exile of emotions and the cultivation of a pervasive sense of guilt that is always with us. Others of us—as Misfits—suffer a violent struggling in the darkness in order to feel, or see, whatever it takes to make us know that we *are*. On the other hand, as far as shouting fundamentalist Misfits go, we have in our brand of Protestantism an amplifier of the violence of grace, an ingrained vision of the Hebrew God who rained down love and retribution in equal measure. In a world where, as O'Connor recognized, evil dwells unabated, the price of restoration is engaging it in warfare, and in this, the prophet-freak fundamentalist is also acculturated. However, the same sentence in which O'Connor notes the suffering from and of the Church concludes with her giving meaning to that same suffering, "...you have to cherish the world at the same time that you struggle to endure it" (*HB*, p. 90). For the Christian, at the center of all this suffering, struggling, and enduring should be Christ. If love is not central, then suffering in a struggle to endure is all there can ever be. To cherish the world, we must commune with it in love.

Shattering the Southern Code of Manners

Place, narrowness, and feeling Southern converge within Southern codes of manners by which relations are maintained and social progress thwarted. The Misfit troubles traditional relational manners and calls for transformation. The powerful presence of constricting codes that shape Southern identity is evident in Wood's (2004) *Flannery O'Connor and the Christ-Haunted South*, the scope of which is no less than "the hopeful irony of Southern history." It is a hope with which I am skeptical. He states,

> The South lost the Civil War in defense of an indefensible and evil institution. Yet it proved to be a blessed defeat...the South won the spiritual war by retaining its truest legacy, not the heritage of slavery and segregation and discrimination, but the Bible-centered and Christ-haunted faith that it still bequeaths to the churches and the nations as their last, best, and only true hope. (p. 11)

Wood treats O'Connor's work in light of her sacramentalism. He admires this overriding aspect of her work as he boldly advocates an American society that abides by the conservative, faith-based values that Applebome (1997) believes have diffused into the larger American political and cultural mainstream.

However, I am careful to note that the "Bible-centered," "Christ-haunted" faith that is for conservative Protestants the last, best, only true hope lies not in conservative, fundamental adherence to dogma, but in the possibility for recognizing moments of grace and the subsequent renewal that derive from devotion to the Word, when salvation in the South becomes, not "color-free" (Richardson, 2003, p. 124), but free—in its recognition that it is color *full*. It is liberatory hope, grounded in love, that exacts the price of restoration from us. Neither dogma nor legislation nor popular vote can unlock the Mystery of the humble heart that elevates humanity and so must be pleasing unto God.

Southerners have long maintained social configurations based on intricate codes of manners. Manners allow white Southerners to believe and *feel* that we have good black/white race relations at work, for example—that we get along, *Some of my best friends are black. Why, we go to lunch together*—while remaining oblivious to institutionalized racism in the workplace. Vexed by O'Connor's racist remarks, Wood (2004) points out that O'Connor believed interracial progress in the South would not result from liberal racial experiments, segregation, for example, but from the "slow and careful development of a new set of racial manners" (p. 110). Arguing that the redemptive quality of Southern life lies in its Bible-centeredness and its Christ-hauntedness (p. 123), Wood agrees with O'Connor's contention that manners of formal civility, "gestures that both bind and separate people in deeply informal ways (p. 124), facilitate social intercourse by affording the necessary boundaries. He maintains that manners prevent chaos in civilizations through the bestowal of "order and significance" (p. 124), citing O'Connor: "Traditional manners, however unbalanced, are better than no manners at all" (*MM*, p. 200). Traditional manners of civility, for example, allowed my friend and colleague of twelve years, to reason, "I can still work with you, but our friendship has changed" when I came out as a lesbian to her. Traditional manners form a protective barrier of sameness and privilege, and, as such, are part of constricting Southernness. A new set of manners would come from a common union of progressive motion in the South, from communion.

I am interested in the binding and separating of Southerners (see Wood, above), as well as the significance that manners delegate to those not in on their own development. I do not disagree with Wood—or O'Connor—that learning to coexist in a region with a volatile racial history has produced a code of manners masking the faces of violence and rage. Wood, conservative as he is—as O'Connor was—is no proponent of racism. He simply stops short of condemnation, but then, again, so did O'Connor. For example, Wood (2004) suggests that the failure of Southern institutions—churches, schools, courts—to develop a new code of manners, *rather than any overt racism*, accounts for continued institutionalized racism in the South (p. 110). I would argue that our failure to recognize, develop, and implement such codes is in itself overt racism. My misfit-self troubles traditional codes of manners that mask and soothe by confronting often conflicting positionalities and identifications, such as queerness and fundamentalist Christianity.

Equally important to Wood (2004) is that a code of manners "help prevent the crimes of sentimental self-revelation; they check the uninhibited desire to tell all" (p. 127). When the code not only inhibits over sentimentality but also prohibits the voices that would speak, the order and significance that these manners perpetuate is unfounded. To punctuate his point with Biblical mandate, Wood cites Philippians 2:4: "Look not every man on his own things, but every man also on the things of others," as a "profoundly courteous" (p. 129) gospel call for manners. Rather than a call for manners, this verse is an exhortation for humility and altruism. The same manners that would mask and protect the personal would discourage us from caring for one another, politically, socially, and spiritually.

O'Connor wrote, "It requires considerable grace for two races to live together, particularly when the population is divided about fifty-fifty between them and when they have our particular history. It can't be done without a code of manners based on mutual charity" (*CFO*, p. 103). Southern codes that brutally uphold Southern culture are based on misguided notions of honor and tradition, and are not the same manners that O'Connor refers to as necessary for racial harmony (Wood, 2004, p. 129ff). For example, in "Judgment Day," one of her last stories, O'Connor interrupts the presumed familiarity and kinship that white Southerners often feel toward African Americans. The mistaken notion that positions of white privilege entitle one to behave familiarly—however politely and civilly—toward those outside of that privilege is part of the debilitating code. She wrote,

> When you have a code of manners based on charity, then when the charity fails—as it is going to do constantly—you've got those manners there to pre-

serve each race from small intrusions upon the other...[The South's manners] provide enough social discipline to hold us together and give us an identity. (*CFO*, pp. 102, 104)

In "Judgment Day" (*CS*, 1971), O'Connor's last story, Tanner had his moment of shattering grace when the Black man spoke to him as a human, breaking through Tanner's normative patriarchal mindset toward race and place that had manifest itself in his relating to Coleman. He would have his judgment in a place where racial codes of manners occlude the sight and harden the subject to communing in love with (an)other—in the South.

The complex system of Southern manners contributes to Southern identity, and while in itself is neither the root nor singular conveyance of racism, sexism, heterosexism, or classism, it establishes the protocols by which they continue to be carried out. Manners that have become ritualized codes perpetuating hierarchies and oppression, prejudices and hatred, should not be preserved. Not only did O'Connor confront supposedly Christian manners, she also used the starkness of grotesquerie to denounce empty acts of politeness, rendering justice to the visible means identifying these codes and bearing witness to the futility, the arrogant delusion of self-sufficiency, in adhering to them. Justice to the universe as well as progressive transformation of Southern place begins in the realization of our mutual dependence on each other.

Fundamentalists: Shouting and Otherwise

The Bible Belt influence...gives us a kind of skepticism under God, a refusal to put things in place of the Absolute. It keeps our vision concrete and it forms a sacred heroic background to which we can compare and refer our own actions. (*CFO*, p. 110)

As a queer fundamentalist Christian, I continue the project of claiming my queerness and continue the spiritual journey began within a fundamentalist religious framework. That journey now carries with it an explicit critique of fundamentalism to uncover the danger of narrow thinking that binds the lives of both religious fundamentalists and those progressive thinkers who would nevertheless objectify those who practice it. O'Connor's work is centered in the life of the rural South, a site where "all that is missing [for the Catholic writer] is the practical influence of the visible Catholic Church" (1969, p. 209). It is her Catholic kinship with Protestant fundamentalist "backwoods prophets" (p. 207) that enriches both novelist and the literature of place in which he or she is embedded. She describes the relationship:

> [Catholic writers in the future] will know that what has given the South her identity are those beliefs and qualities which she has absorbed from the Scriptures and from her own history of defeat and violation: a distrust of the abstract, a sense of human dependence on the grace of God, and a knowledge that evil is not simply a problem to be solved, but a mystery to be endured. (p. 209)[9]

Unfortunately, both sides of O'Connor's equation are not in balance, with Southern identity shaped more by its defeat and violation, both real and suspected, than by that which it has absorbed from the Scriptures. The one has subsumed the other until, socially, culturally, and politically, historical defeatism prepossesses spirituality.

Defeated, violated sensibilities have informed the interpretation of Christian scripture, yet as the perfect law of liberty—underscored by Grace—it is enforced with the fervor of the Hebrew warrior-kings against a "sacred heroic background," that is devoid of Grace (*CFO*, p. 110). Southern white fundamentalist Christians appear to identify with the fighting Israelites, in our tenacious struggle to vanquish moral violations imposed by a reprobate society. Treatment of the enslaved, emancipation, civic and social freedoms for people of color and women, integration of educational institutions—historically, Southern fundamentalists have taken political positions on social issues that would maintain a way of life. Yet since the Reagan conservatism of the 1980s, the best defense has proven to be a good offense, as radical conservative groups proactively seek control—their due as God's elect—of socio-cultural-political issues that include content of school curriculum, intellectual and individual freedoms, the right of queers to coexist in the world.

Richardson (2003) accounts for the South in his anthropological discussion of being-in-place, wherein the body organizes experience. The Christian schema, he observes, generally ascribes positive value to that which is ahead and above, negative value to that which is behind and beneath, heaven and hell, for example. Not only do these experiential coordinates valuate place, they also translate into time, the sinful past and glorious eternity, and influence how humans live in the present. He writes,

> And does not this mean that the things of God, the sacred sphere, extend ahead while the things of men and of Satan, the profane sphere, are best put behind our backs? To be sure, circumstances, factual and mythical, distort the model, as in the American South, where the chivalrous past, lost forever in defeat, becomes more sacred than the federally mandated future. Even the Christian schema is not straightforward. (p. 35)

The lost past becomes the present that shapes the future; thus, the sacred and profane become deferred in the perversion.

It is near impossible to tell where the cultural argument ends and the spiritual one begins in the fundamental narrowness of Southern culture and Southern religion. The irreducibility of the two becomes most apparent in political engagements. In Alabama libraries, books with gay references should be destroyed because they are reprehensible in the eyes of God: their very presence might disrupt straightness. Health textbooks in Texas should be revised to advocate sexual abstinence, with only cursory mention of other means of birth control and prevention of sexually transmitted disease. Exposing tenth graders to condoms, sponges, and pills might subvert the purity-ideal of mom and home—not to mention apple pie, if the movie *American Pie* is any indication—and sexual promiscuity is denounced as sin. Southern fundamentalists are prepared to wage war, and have, for as long as there has been Southern fundamentalism, opposed what we perceive as continued violations to white Southern culture.

Trust in the concrete begets the absolutism of seeing only in black and white—clearly right or clearly wrong; dependence upon God's grace generates the misguided thought that we must crusade to earn it; and the knowledge of enduring evil breeds a paranoia of its lurking everywhere about us. We are left susceptible to prophets of the political kind to deliver us from that evil, confirming Doll's prophetic statement, "Whoever controls the accepted notion of God presides over what is socially acceptable" (2000, p. 43). Since the late 1960s, God's people have increasingly formed a conservative voting bloc that supports political agendas most in line with its own notions of Godly society. When a conservative electorate responded that "moral issues" was the chief concern in determining how it would vote (ABC News, November 3, 2004) and voted overwhelmingly (approximately 70% to 30%, on average) to both reelect the radical George W. Bush as president and mandate heterosexual marriage in state constitutions, it reaffirmed a reliance upon God's grace through currying His favors at the polls.

The promise of redemption weighs so heavily upon the South in proportion to our need for it. Ours is an epic warring between sin and salvation; the problem is, we have not yet decided with which side we are aligned. White Southerners are, as Hazel Motes, troubled by the thought of a savior: "He does not fear being one of the lost; he dreads being one of the saved" (Ragen, 1989, p. 157). O'Connor wrote, "The South in other words still believes that man has fallen and that he is only perfectible by God's grace, not by his own unaided efforts" (*HB*, 302). Our unaided efforts are bolstered by what Brinkmeyer (1989) calls our "rational sensibilities" (p. 177); human vision is incomplete and insufficient, failing the self and self and other, and, therefore, God. Our human faith in the perfectibility of fallen man animates the Southern wave of social conservatism of the last half-century. We try to help God along by claiming His intentions of morality and preempting His grace.

In the South, "shouting fundamentalists" (*MM*, p. 207) witness the hand of the living God at work; it is a place where spiritual abstractions are concrete (p. 202), where the mystery is simplified so that "belief might be made believable" (p. 203). Not all fundamentalists shout, and while O'Connor depicts the supernatural in the natural world, she does so with characters who are grotesque, in part due to the violence of their religious practice. Her prophet freaks cry out in the wilderness; O'Connor states that had she not been born Catholic, she would join a Pentecostal Holiness church, among the most charismatic of the fundamentalists (Wood, 2004, p. 30) They truly shout—sometimes in "holy" tongues. Her admiration, it seems, is for those whose beliefs consume them—body, mind, spirit—even if they are ignorant or insensitive to grace (Martin, 1968, p. 46). In a 1959 letter to John Hawkes, O'Connor describes the "wise blood" of the fundamentalist anti-sacramental working toward grace.

> Wise blood has to be these people's means of grace—do it yourself religion...It's full of unconscious pride that lands them in all sorts of ridiculous predicaments. They have nothing to correct their practical heresies and so they work them out dramatically. (*HB,* p. 350)

The profound power of fundamentalism is seen in its identification with the ragged figure of the suffering Christ. Fundamentalists continue to redirect slavery from the body to the mind, from blacks to whites, although all may accept the bonds of Jesus. Slavery was, in this sense, an externalization of white self-self relating.

Fundamentalism is the atonement for the white South's immorality and what drives our legalistic moves to "work out our own salvation with fear and trembling" (Philippians 2:12). We can *achieve* our own salvation, we reason, by working out God's plan for people, including His moral, social, and political plans. If we can but prove to God through our violent faith and "good works" that we are a Godly nation, then he will continue to love us and keep us in his favor. How might we shew these things of man to God? By amending our government's constitution to keep the nation straight, for one, and by proclaiming from civic forums as did Texas, that we are a Christian nation. Aligning textbooks and medical clinics with the Bible would do it, and finding the image of God—rather than a cure of a different sort—in a petrie dish. And what might He shew us in return? Victory over the infidel and continued material prosperity. "Pray or become prey," reads one bumper sticker on one car.

"Demanding the Redemptive Act":
The Grotesque and Southern Identity

O'Connor points out the intransigence of fundamentalist discourse through characters captured in their moments of grace. We are caught, as Hazel Motes and Francis Marion Tarwater in cycles of "stringent religious practice and guilt" (Martin, 1968, p. 121). In clinging to constricting fundamentalism by clinging to the Cross, we engage in continuous attempts to exorcise the same Christ who haunted Motes: a wild, the ragged figure that haunts him, whose gift of redemption is as scary as the devil himself. From the disruptions of the Misfit and the distortions of the grotesque, the South might gain sight; we might recognize that intransigent forms of Southernness submerged in white patriarchal notions of Southern identity are themselves distorted in their narrowness. In "The Grotesque in Southern Fiction" (*MM*, p. 36), O'Connor connects the grotesque with the freak.

> Whenever I'm asked why Southern writers particularly have a penchant for writing about freaks, I say it is because we are still able to recognize one. To be able to recognize a freak, you have to have some conception of the whole man [sic], and in the South the general conception of man is still, in the main, theological." (p. 44)

She suggests that, rather than consider humanity material, or social, the South considers man in light of God and God's relation to him. Southerners are not essentially hyper-intuitive concerning the nature of man, but perceive that God is necessary to wholeness. Southern, fundamentalist Protestant, the Misfit is grotesque in his or her radical convictions and shocks the reader toward the realm of mystery. The Misfit, like O'Connor's writing itself, has a decidedly

Southern accent, which Southerners can recognize because it is familiar.

Di Renzo (1993) refers to O'Connor's grotesque as, "a comic shock
treatment" (p. 5). He notes that the chief technique of grotesque is
degradation, by the Bakhtinian definition, "a lowering of all that is
high, spiritual, ideal, abstract (Bakhtin, 1968, p. 19—20). O'Connor's
grotesque degradation of Lost Cause traditions, such as gender ideals,
ruptures Southern intransigence. For example, the three main characters in "The Life You Save May Be Your Own" are a trio of gro-
tesques: a one-armed man, a toothless old woman, and her daughter
with the mental capacity of a 5 year old. Mr. Shiftlet and the old
woman transgress the manners of interpersonal relationships in
comic exchanges as they barter. She offers a car with a paint job and
her daughter in exchange for a handyman son-in-law. In their final
negotiation, Mr. Shiftlet and the old woman, in a comedic exchange
that is unequivocally Southern, reach a settlement that would set the
moments of grace in motion. That night, rocking on the porch, the old
woman began her bartering at once.

"You want you an innocent woman, don't you?" she asked sym-
pathetically. "You don't want none of this trash."

"No'm, I don't," Mr. Shiftlet said.

"One that can't talk," she continued, "can't sass you back or use
foul language. That's the kind for you to have. Right there," and she
pointed to Lucynell sitting cross-legged in her chair, holding both feet
in her hands (*CS*, p. 151).

Grace would be visited on both the old woman and Mr. Shiftlet in
the person of Lucynell. The embodiment of purity and insusceptible
to their diabolical scheming, Lucynell is lost to her mother, who
seems to accept grace as the girl is driven away by the bridegroom.
Shiftlet rejects grace as he denies his bride and abandons her.[10]

As Martin observes, Lucynell is "congenitally immune" (1968, p.
209) to their calculated bargaining. "[O]ne has the feeling that her hilarious antics mysteriously mock the purposes of both of them and
that her idiocy is a blessed condition far superior to their calculating
devices" (p. 209). In the end, Mr. Shiftlet denies an "angel of Gawd,"

whose innocence embodies grace, as she sleeps, head resting upon the counter at the diner, aptly named the Hot Spot. He willfully rejects his offer of grace in his failure to resist the devil. The comic language and interaction make the degradation of souls more pronounced. Not only is the reader shocked, she is shocked at herself for being shocked, having laughed all the way to the end of the story—right up to the reawakening of a sense of evil, the harbinger of the blow of grace.

I was raised to believe that the devil is alive and at work in the world, every bit as much as Jesus. My daddy and grandmother took every opportunity to point out evil and sin and blame it on Satan, or as she referred to him, "The Ol' Booger Man" (as if the more main- stream nickname "Boogey Man" were not disdainful and descriptive enough). Adultery? Homosexuality? Alcoholism? Rudolf the Red- Nosed Reindeer being broadcast every year on Wednesday night, same time as mid-week Bible study? "That's the Ol' Devil," Daddy would declare. The South has fashioned a world in which there is an ongoing Armageddon, and that only contributes to its grotesque.

"In the cathedral of Flannery O'connor," writes Di Renzo, "the gargoyles have the last laugh" (1993, p. 225). He goes on to delineate these gargoyles, exemplars of the grotesque in her fiction, as "the seemingly deranged Fundamentalists who...assert their faith in a post-Christian South—no matter how ludicrous and obscene it makes them appear..." (p. 4). Perhaps the freak seems deranged due to the ghosts he sees; the grotesquerie of a Christ-haunted South lies in the white Southerner's fear that, "he may have been formed in the image and likeness of God" (*MM*, p. 45). The freak, then, is a distorted figure created to draw our attention, by his obscene assertion of faith, to our "essential displacement" (p. 45) from God's image. In other words, we did not ask for Jesus to redeem us, and God has not done us any favors by creating us in His likeness. In fact it was more of a curse: we are cursed with the awesome realization that we are connected to a God who loves us, and we resent the choice to choose Him. We rage against doing so.

The freak, backwoods prophets, shouting fundamentalists, "good country people" who resist social consciousness. If the South and its narratives are of mythic dimensions, the same might also be said of Southern distortions. The South is conspicuous, misshapen, and glaring; as such, it may show us the "twisted face of good under construction" (Ragen, 1989, p. 26). O'Connor's radical view of spirituality and her use of violent and comic extremes focuses her fiction on the mysteries of human redemption. As Doll (2000) points out, "[O'Connor] introduces hardheaded egocentrics who undergo a conversion experience against their will," often through "hilarious, outrageous, religious" (p. 168) comedic prose. The sudden awefulness out of which grace is ravished upon her characters must be bizarre enough to reveal the nothingness of souls that consumes them as products of place. She "pierces" (Doll, 2000, p. 84) her destined characters with a ludicrous instant of grace that comes upon them violently, for effect, illustrating her notion that salvation comes like a blow to the head and is itself very mystical. They neither ask for it nor expect it; yet they are powerless to refuse it. They are stuck with the awful grace of God.

Sight and Vision

O'Connor portrays her character's deficiencies—their fundamental wrongheadedness (Doll, 2005) in thinking and seeing—as a need for sight. She employs distortion to provide the clarity her characters need for the sight and insight necessary to recognize their own deformities, often describing certain of them, as Doll (2000) points out, "with overly large or distorted eyes, suggestive of their potential for grace, except they are looking through the wrong end of a telescope" (p. 84). In addition to the description of the "unmoored" (*CS*, p. 420) eye of Julian's mother in "Everything That Rises Must Converge," O'Connor describes the eyes of Mary Fortune and her grandfather as, "pale identical eye[s]" (p. 355); when he has killed Mary Fortune, he looked into her face, in which the eyes, "slowly rolling back, appeared to pay him not the slightest attention...[but were] set in a fixed glare that did not take him in" (p. 355). O'Connor describes the eyes of Powell, one of the boys in "A Circle in the Fire" who would be God's agents in initiating the blow by which Mrs. Cope might experience her breakthrough of grace: "One of his eyes had a slight cast to it so that his seemed to be coming from two directions at once as if it had them surrounded" (*CS*, p. 179). Blindness and sightedness, revelation, and violent death are recurrent themes in her work through which the blow of grace occurs.

O'Connor's willful characters, such as Hulga Hopewell in "Good Country People," experience a "shattering" (Brinkmeyer, 1989, p. 179) of the rationalistic self, the "shocking destruction of limited and pretentious visions" (p. 179). A more pointed example for disrupting Southern pretentious visions might be of Mrs. Turpin, in the story "Revelation," who, in her own estimation, is very near to God's own image.

> "If it's one thing I am," Mrs. Turpin said with feeling, "it's grateful. When I think who all I could have been besides myself and what all I got, a little of everything, and a good disposition besides, I just feel like shouting, 'Thank you, Jesus, for making everything the way it is!'..." (*CS*, p. 499)

Openly grateful that she is not like those around her, in whose earshot she offers her public thanksgiving, she draws contempt from "the ugly girl," Mary Grace, who hurls a book aptly entitled *Human Development* at Mrs. Turpin just before uttering one of O'Connor's most delightfully famous lines: "Go back to hell where you came from, you old wart hog" (*CS*, p. 500). The book hits Mrs. Turpin above her left eye. The message is clear: Mrs. Turpin has a need for sight.

God shatters Mrs. Turpin by means of a vision, stripped of pretense, that shows her at the tail-end of a procession into Heaven, following the flawed, unwhole, and impure that she had placed herself above. Her illumination takes place at the hog pen.

> She raised her hands from the side of the pen in a gesture hieratic and profound. A visionary light settled in her eyes. She saw the streak as a vast

swinging bridge extending upward from the earth through a field of living fire. Upon it a vast horde of souls were rumbling toward heaven. There were whole companies of white-trash, clean for the first time in their lives, and bands of black niggers in white robes, and battalions of freaks and lunatics shouting and clapping and leaping like frogs. And bring up the end of the procession was a tribe of people whom she recognized at once as those who, like herself and Claud, had always had a little of everything and the God-given wit to use it right. She leaned forward to observe them closer. They were marching behind the others with great dignity, accountable as they had always been for good order and common sense and respectable behavior. They alone were on key. Yet she could see by their shocked and altered faces that even their virtues were being burned away....(CS, p. 508)

One of the truths that make us human (Doll, 2000, p. *xii*) uncovered in O'Connor's fiction is our humanly "slow participation" (O'Connor, "The Church and the Fiction Writer," *MM*, p. 148) in redemption and our inadequacy in going it alone. Alone, we are open to only enough space that would include ourselves and our visions: one of the requisites for *finding* truth is *seeking* it (Matthew 7:7). Although O'Connor was referring to theological redemption preempted by a mock state of innocence that comes from excessive sentimentality, we may apply the same principle to Southern reconstruction and the excessive sentimentality of white Southern nostalgia. Blindness and shortsightedness are indicative of fundamental wrongheadedness in conventional forms of Southernness—violence, nostalgia, altars of sameness—that the Misfit might point out and anomalous grace might shatter.

The Misfit

This Misfit exists as a loud, large startling figure that shocks other characters, and readers, into sight and insight. The Misfit is an anomalous form of Southernness who works to displace the narrowness of Southern identity. O'Connor prevents her characters from having a too deep connection with place as they do with their own righteousness. Hill (1997) notes: "For O'Connor the world, paradoxically enough, is both redeemed and 'thrown off balance' by the redemptive work of Christ" (p. 552). The Misfit explains this to the grandmother in "A Good Man Is Hard To Find."

> 'If He did what He said, then it's nothing for you to do but throw away everything and follow Him, and if He didn't, then it's nothing for you to do but enjoy the few minutes you got left the best way you can—by killing somebody or burning down his house or doing some other meanness to him. No pleasure but meanness,' he said and his voice had become almost a snarl. (*CW*, p. 152)

The world for The Misfit is off balance because of his "profoundly-felt involvement with Christ's action" (*HB*, p. 437). The world for him is void of humanness; we can either lose ourselves to Christ in following Him, or we subsist with the contemptible nihilism of the isolated self out of communion with humanity. The grandmother is a channel of grace for The Misfit—as he is for her—because through her claiming him as her child, she has illuminated for him humanity. O'Connor explains, "His shooting her is a recoil, a horror at her humanness, but the Grace has worked in him and he pronounces his judgment: she would have been a good woman if *he* had been there every moment of her life" (p. 389). Therein is the paradox of redemption that O'Connor explores in stories ranging from her earliest works to those completed during her final illness; while redemption is made possible by divine action, it requires the essence of humanity. Without The Misfit, there could be no redemption, and that thought terrified him.

When O'Connor declared the South "Christ-haunted," she presented a located people both cursed and blessed by the dead and risen Christ. White Southerners pathologically identify with Christ's suffering—his victimhood—in our service to Him. And in this is found the pathos of redemption: in the service of a suffering Christ, white Southerners violently transgress humanity by murder, hatred, and enslavement—vexed and resentful of the moral obligation of social care and consciousness we have toward one another. It is misguided service by a displaced people, displaced by abjection, what Sibley describes as, "the urge to make separations between...'us' and 'them'…that is, to expel the abject" (1995, p. 8). I am reminded here of Mrs. McIntyre's refusal of moral obligation, in O'Connor's "The Displaced Person," as she interrupts Father Flynn's sacramental discourse to talk to him about "something serious!" *"As far as I'm concerned," she said and glared at him fiercely, "Christ was just another D.P."* (*CS*, p. 229). Mrs. McIntyre, Mr. Shortly, and "the Negro" are locked into a raced-classed-gendered triadic "collusion forever" as they witness the death of the story's Christ figure, Mr. Guizac. White Southerners serve a D.P. *as* D.P.s; grace allows us to be aware of the moral obligation of communion implicit in the relationship. The movement of O'Connor's characters toward their revelation, as they are steeped within Southern place, indicates the movement of grace within place by which humanity, and thus the essence of redemption, is illuminated: The Mystery.

The Price of Restoration

As Southerners, we continue to demand the redemptive act, in our interactions with others within a code of manners, in our practicing of what we believe is a God-pleasing fundamentalism, in our violent raging for restoration. O'Connor speaks to this expectation (see epigram) in the novel reader, "He [sic] wants either his senses tormented or his spirits raised. He wants to be transported, instantly, either to mock damnation or a mock innocence (*MM*, 1969, p. 48). White Southerners yearn for a retreat into comfortable polarity, believing, for example, that one cannot be queer and fundamentalist, nostalgic and progressive. Yet, these are the positionings of the Misfit, who inhabits incompatible positions, occupying and thinking from those positions. There are many risks in working as a Misfit. Pinar writes, "Being on the margins is dangerous but at least you can breathe" (2001, p. 479), and suggests that those who identify ourselves as exiles and Misfits claim the authority of those margins. The self-claiming of exile subjectivity might grant one passage "between and beyond dominant binaries such as insider/outsider, southerner/northerner, victim/survivor" (Pinar, p. 479) or queer/fundamentalist.

My Misfit experience is the kind of "difficult knowledge" (1998, p. 19) that Britzman and others ask us to grapple with. It is difficult work—difficult ideas, difficult subject positions, and difficult theoretical frameworks. Uncovering anomalous forms of Southernness is ethically and politically difficult to work through, yet it is a position of our time in a post-911 world. As Misfit I do not choose an aggressive critique of the South, fundamentalism, or Southern comfort-structures any more than I refuse my queer identity; I occupy both spaces. To grasp firmly to either discourse at the exclusion of the other would begin a "hardening process" (Doll, 2000, p. xix) that runs counter to poststructural thought. Without the nuances of in-betweenesss, a critique of Southernness would be little more than heroic narrative. Instead, currere enables me to understand the experience of being a misfit.

My grotesquerie is neither ready-made nor complete. Grotesque images, according to Bakhtin (1968), "remain ambivalent and contradictory; they are ugly, monstrous, hideous from the point of view of 'classic' aesthetics" (p. 25). I recognize that as a Misfit grotesque of Southern place, I am transgressive, in the words of Di Renzo (1993), "cross[ing] borders, ignor[ing] boundaries, and overspill[ing] margins...play[ing] havoc with our most cherished ideas, celebrating the material world without romanticizing it" (p. 5, 7). As a Misfit, I identify as a Southerner and feel a deep attachment to Southern place, yet constricting notions of Southernness—such as fundamentalism and the manners that guide our relations—negate aspects of my experience, identity, desire, and worldview. Attending to anomalous forms of Southernness—such as a shattering grace and queer Southernness—creates curricular conversation about the possibility of progressive transformation of Southern place through the construction of Southern identity.

Notes

1   Abbreviations of O'Connor Texts:
    CS: The Complete Short Stories

CFO: *Conversations with Flannery O'Connor*
CW: *Flannery O'Connor: Collected Works*
HB: *The Habit of Being: Letters of Flannery O'Connor*
MM: *Mystery and Manners: Occasional Prose*
Three: *Three by Flannery O'Connor*
WB: *Wise Blood*

2   After the reception of *Wise Blood* in 1952, which most critics acknowledged was masterful even as they missed the pervasive Christian themes, O'Connor would write much elucidating what she attempted to accomplish as an artist and Catholic writer. She did stop short, however, of explaining its meaning. In 1961 O'Connor included this statement on meaning-making in a letter to an English professor who identified himself as the "spokesman for three members of our department and some ninety university students" (*HB*, p. 436) who had spent a week debating—wrongly—the correct interpretation of "A Good Man Is Hard to Find":

> The interpretation of your ninety students and three teachers is fantastic and about as far from my intentions as it could get to be. If it were a legitimate interpretation, the story would be little more than a trick and its interest would be simply for abnormal psychology. I am not interested in abnormal psychology…
>
> The meaning of a story should go on expanding for the reader the more he thinks about it, but meaning cannot be captured in an interpretation. If teachers are in the habit of approaching a story as if it were a research problem for which any answer is believable so long as it is not obvious, then I think students will never learn to enjoy fiction. Too much interpretation is certainly worse than too little, and where feeling for a story is absent, theory will not supply.
>
> My tone is not meant to be obnoxious. I am in a state of shock.

I remain conscious throughout this writing that were O'Connor to be alive to read my use of her work to think through Southern studies, she might once more be thrown into a state of shock. My objective is less about interpretation than about finding ways to study the South that include the "shouting fundamentalists" and Southern idiom through which O'Connor contemplated mystery. I do not fix a meaning to her story, but a meaning to her South. Still, I would not wish to incur her rancor.

3   O'Connor explains anagogical vision in the essay, "The Nature and Aim of Fic-
     tion," and in introductory remarks made before reading "A Good Man is Hard
     to Find" in 1962, both collected in *Mystery and Manners (1957)*. Anagogical vision
     would allow the fiction writer "to see different levels of reality in one image or
     situation" (p. 72). Anagogical refers to one kind of means of scripture interpreta-
     tion that has to do with "the Divine life and our participation in it" (p. 72).
     O'Connor believed that gestures or actions on the anagogical level made the
     story work because the gestures could then make "contact with mystery" (p.
     111).

4   See Miller (2005), *Sounds of silence breaking: Women, autobiography, curriculum,* a
     self-complicating work that disrupts unitary, normative concepts of gender, nar-
     rative, and curriculum. Miller works her own tensions of her gendered work and
     non-unitary selves as academic woman, curriculum theorist, and qualitative re-
     searcher.

5   Were conventions of mutual charity in place, Americans, Southern and non-
     Southern alike, might find ground on which to hold conversations on moral is-
     sues, which 21% of American voters indicated was the biggest factor on which
     they based their vote, according to ABC News (November 4, 2004). That was
     higher than war, higher than the economy, higher than terrorism. Moral issues
     might be translated to mean a ban on gay marriage, if the 11 statewide elections
     on which it was on the ballot is any indication, 12, counting the Louisiana
     amendment passed in September 2004. Gay marriage paranoia is not restricted to
     the South. Of the 12 states that voted to ban it, only 5—Louisiana, Georgia, Ken-
     tucky, Mississippi, and Arkansas—are Southern. I would argue that reaction
     against it is part of the social and political conservatism that, as Edgerton and
     Applebome propose, has spread from the South to the rest of the country. Head
     of the ultra conservative Family Research Council, Tony Perkins, former Louisi-
     ana representative, voices support of the Federal Marriage Amendment in an in-
     terweaving of patriotism, children, nostalgia of loss, but mostly of fear.

> ...if we do not amend the U.S. Constitution with a federal marriage amend-
> ment that will protect marriage on the federal level, we will lose marriage
> in this nation.
> "Marriage is about more than tax credits and other financial benefits. It is
> about preserving the best environment for raising children and the safest,

> healthiest living situation for adults. Without strong marriages as our bed-
> rock, our nation will suffer a devastating blow.
> "We must amend the Constitution if we are to stop a tyrannical judiciary
> from redefining marriage to the point of extinction."

While the implication appears to be one of moral values and saving a tradition that we are in danger of "losing," Perkins is sending a message of political control, of conservatism over a liberally-interpreted constitution by liberal, "tyrannical" judges. That he appeals to nostalgia, home, and kids is significant; we will not hesitate to restrict the civil liberties of "Others" if we believe that they are a danger to our homes and kids. Other items on the political agenda of our protectors, such as war expenditures, neglect and abuse of the environment, and corporate tax breaks, will breeze through the back door.

6   Doll (2000) is one exception to this claim. In *Like Letters in Running Water: A My-thopoetics of Curriculum,* Doll includes O'Connor in her discussion of characters who have the potential for grace, yet lack sight or mindset to experience it.

7   In *Flannery O'Connor and the Christ-haunted South,* Chapter 3, "The Problem of the Color Line: Race and Religion in Flannery O'Connor's South," Wood states, Flannery O'Connor was not a racist, either politically or theologically. I maintain, on the contrary, that she was a writer who—thought not without temptation and struggle—offered the one lasting antidote to racism" (p. 94). He concludes the chapter with the "lasting antidote":

> O'Connor agreed that we are all slaves to evil...the scales of the New Tes-
> tament find both the righteous and the unrighteous woefully wanting. Yet
> she also knew that something other than either the shoulder-rubbing soli-
> darity or legally enforced integration was needed for healing the racial
> wounds that continue to suppurate at the core of both the nation and the
> church. She was not resigned, therefore, to the perpetual division of black
> and white into separate, even if equal, spheres...O'Connor gestures at a
> more excellent way, the way of reconciliation between brothers and sisters
> of the same Lord. (p. 119)

In assigning to O'Connor a greater, loftier racial remedy, Wood does not soften, but contextualizes O'Connor's private racist remarks and actions. He acknowledges her frequent and casual use of the word "nigger," as well as her condescending, if amused, attitudes toward the African American and white hired help on her mother's farm. Publicly, O'Connor was critical of Eudora Welty's commentary, published in *The New Yorker* in 1963 following the murder of Medgar Evers, as being self-righteous, inflammatory, and badly written. In 1964, O'Connor refused a request by her friend Maryat Lee to receive James Baldwin in Milledgeville, stating, "No, I can't see James Baldwin in Georgia. It would cause the greatest trouble and disturbance and disunion...I observe the traditions of the society I feed on—it's only fair" (Cash, 2002, p. 152).

8   O'Connor frequently cited Joseph Conrad to support her own views on fiction. Although I cite her use of the phrase "rendering..." from *Mystery and Manners,* it can be found in her letters, essays, and speeches. It originally comes from Conrad's description of art in his preface to *The Nigger of the "Narcissus"* (Conrad, J. [1964], Preface to *The Nigger of the "Narcissus."* In *Joseph Conrad on Fiction.* W.F. Wright (Ed.). Lincoln: University of Nebraska Press). Ragen (1989) explains it this way: The idea of rendering justice to the physical universe supports O'Connor in the belief that in fiction—at least in fiction after Henry James—as much as possible must be shown, rather than told; rendered, rather than reported (p. 17).

9   While the preference for narrative is to maintain this distrust in the abstract, Bible-believers cling in one form or another to the Bible's own abstract narrative. On the other hand, fundamentalist Protestants have sought to make those abstractions as concrete as possible—so that they are fundamental elements of faith. This would help to explain O'Connor's kinship as an artist with the fundamentalists. Both distrust the abstract as a just rendering of the universe.

10 Di Renzo (1993) notes the similarity between O'Connor's marginalized characters and the *Narrenschiffs,* medieval floating madhouses, that, as Foucault explained in *Madness and Civilization,* were created by the sane to "define and insure the marginality of the insane" (in Di Renzo, p. 13). A Southern ship of fools on a passage "between the sacred and the profane, heaven and hell" (p. 15), intended to shock the fools *not on the ship* to attention.

Chapter 5
Conclusion: Cosmopolitanism, Grace, and Communion

The politics of place, and subsequently, a curriculum of place, is bolstered, as we have observed in the South, by the complex workings of Mystery and Manners, which allow diverse people to occupy the same space and maintain our daily lives without completely obliterating each other (mostly). It is not a perfect system, as witnessed by the continued violence that we do to one another; Mystery and Manners alone and unsubstantiated are insufficient, the threadbare remains of a cloak of civility. I conclude by suggesting a reconfiguration of Mystery and Manners as a grace-inspired ethics that manifests itself in acts (in this case pedagogical) of shared humanity, of communion. It is unlikely that one will concede an existence of a shared humanity and act accordingly without first having some understanding of ethics in a world of strangers—that is, ethics in a world of self and other. And for that I turn briefly to Kwame Anthony Appiah's *Cosmopolitanism: Ethics in a World of Strangers* (2006).

Ethics in a world of strangers, or the lack thereof, can be manifest in the unlikeliest of places. For example, a recent episode of ABC's *Primetime Live* entitled, "What Would You Do?" explored whether people are innately racist, driven by prejudice and fear. To find out, ABC equipped cabs with hidden microphones and cameras and hired two actors to play racist cab drivers—a white driver in New Jersey and a black driver in Savannah. The premise was to see people's responses when confronted with hateful racial slurs. The driver, who picked up people of varying ethnicities, genders, and ages, would begin a racist tirade against Blacks, Asians, Hispanics, Jews— whoever was *not* of the same ethnicity as he and his passenger.

Primetime was interested in seeing what people would do when directly confronted with racism: Would they argue with the cabbie or confront him? Would they ask him to stop the car so they could get out? Would they remain silent? Would they join in?

The results of this unscientific study were one sided—as one may or may not expect—after four days of picking up 49 passengers and recording a range of responses, only 7 riders challenged their driver's racist aspersions; most others concurred with the cabbies' remarks and added comments or anecdotes of their own. What struck me was the commentary by the "expert," Carrie Keating, Professor of Psychology at Colgate University. When reporter John Quinones expressed his surprise that these people would voice racist comments to a complete stranger, Keating replied that not only can complete strangers of different races form bonds against "others," but, she says, "Oddly enough, sometimes we're more honest with strangers than we are with people we know well." A simple and commonsensical statement, yet one that holds promise in light of place, cosmopolitanism, preparing future teachers, and communing with one another. To help me make sense of these concepts, I employ my own entanglement with types and stereotypes of Southern place, much as Flannery O'Connor used her geographical attachments as "loud, startling figures" for the "almost-blind" (*MM*, p. 34). She proclaimed the South "Christ-haunted" (p. 44), yet the South is also South-haunted. Southerners are often our own loud, startling figures, and such magnification allows for ease in viewing, while the idea of cosmopolitanism allows for thinking beyond the often closely guarded Southern cultural, social, emotional, and psychological boundaries.

Appiah presents a global view—for lack of a better word—of the idea of a shared humanity, called cosmopolitanism. If I understand it at all, cosmopolitanism can be both a state of being and an action. We have an attitude—a sensibility—that not only are we cohabitants of our world—our small and larger worlds, that is—with others, but we also have a responsibility to care for others. Untill now, when I have thought of cosmopolitanism, I limited my thinking to the stereotype I held: people who are sophisticated, citified, and well traveled. I looked in the dictionary, and that definition is there. Yet, so is this one: "composed of persons, constituents, or elements from all or many parts of the world." This makes sense to me, and it helps take away the classist bias that I have been attributing to the concept.

My own questioning of world citizenship and its bearing on educational policies, theories, and practices that characterize place occurs within a suburban teaching university in the Metro Atlanta area. Kennesaw State University is located in Kennesaw, Georgia, which grew up in the shadow of the mountain for which it is named. In addition to being home to some of Marrietta, Georgia's, most affluent homes, Kennesaw Mountain is also the site of a Civil War battlefield—the June 1864 Battle of Kennesaw Mountain, one of the last before the burning of Atlanta—and one of the last tactical victories for the Confederacy. Pinar suggests a framework for Southern contexts of curriculum studies that move beyond the scope of Southern boundaries. He writes, "As recent studies of 'internationalization' and 'globalization' make clear (see Pinar 2004) curriculum is embedded in national cultures. It is also embedded in regions, and nowhere in the United States is that fact more obvious than in the Deep South" (2004, p. 93). Citizens of Cobb County know their place and their past; the South does not get much deeper than this. As such, I find it a provocative place from which to contextualize the study of curriculum and place.

One interesting context of this place is the concurrent desire for localism and globalism. In an attempt to tap into international markets of students and resources, our university is developing a plan that capitalizes on current and ongoing attempts at globalization and proposes short- and long-term projections. A few weeks ago my department met to discuss a new diversity course being designed for our teacher education program that was specifically a part of this larger vision of globalization. Part of our discussion centered around the concepts of *multiculture, interculture, internationalization, and globalization;* more particularly, how were these concepts different, which was to be the scope of the course, and what does it mean for a university to globalize in the first place? Globalization, based on my perception as well as the comments of colleagues and material distributed by the university's committee, is a geopolitical, economic concept that has very little, or so I have decided, to do with ethics, values, caring, or moral obligation toward others. Self understanding and a greater understanding of others that might be achieved through globalization processes are at least tertiary results, behind financial gain and political alliances. In fact, understanding of other(s) is desirous in that it aids in attaining the other two goals. Or so it seems to me.

Appiah's explanation of cosmopolitanism brings the human consideration into globalism. He writes, "So cosmopolitanism shouldn't be seen as some exalted attainment: it begins with the simple idea that in the human community, as in national communities, we need to develop habits of coexistence: conversation in its older meaning, of living together, association." In other words, it invites communion with one another. Appiah's critics question whether just getting to know the people around the world and around the corner—and engaging them in dialogue—is enough to counter nationalism's egoism and self-obsessed loyalties. One reviewer hopes that it does. I more than hope; I have faith. Sometimes when my teacher education students and I are discussing culture within the contexts of adolescent development, it is easier to identify the problems than to find approaches to dealing with them. I sense the frustration when my students ask, "Well, then, what do we do in situations like that? What can *we* do?" I also sense their skepticism when I answer that one place to start is dialogue, conversation— much like we are engaging in class. They do not want to believe it, or they believe *talking* is insufficient to enact any real change. Educational reform and curriculum development standardizes sameness and allows for differences insofar as they serve accountability measures; self-and-other and self-in-other, central to subjectivity and social reconstruction, complicate not only curricular conversations, but pedagogical ones as well.

A Pedagogical Dilemma

Sexuality and adolescent development. That was the section of the book to be discussed in my EDUC 2202 Adolescent Development class. I began the class by announcing the upcoming lecture on our campus by Matthew Shepard's mother Judy, and I knew I was in trouble when more than one student asked, "Who's Matthew Shepard?" Unbelievable, until I remembered that some of them would have been 12 years old in 1998, the year of his murder. I recounted Matthew's story, which segued into a discussion of gay and lesbian issues that lasted for the remainder of the class period. Most of my students are from Cobb County, Georgia—born and raised here, finishing their education here, hoping to get a teaching job here. It is so important to make them a bit uncomfortable with issues of diversity and culture. Them, all of us—even we liberals who are sometimes smug in our openness.

During this discussion of quite difficult knowledges, there were two comments that made a lasting impression on me. Both made by smart, sweet, hard-working people whom I enjoy working with very much. We had recently viewed a HBO Special, *Middle School Confessions*, which showed a segment on the support organization Long Island Gay and Lesbian Youth Center (LIGALY). My student suggested, in earnest, that rather than have such organizations where youth could go and "make out" while gay and lesbian adults "monitored" their behavior, perhaps there could be organizations for gay youth that were more like Alcoholics Anonymous. A pall fell over the room as I explained that AA is an organization founded for people with a disease that they want to "beat." Gay youth organizations are there for *support*—not treatment—that sexuality is not something most gay people are looking to "beat." I stopped there so the implications of what I was saying might sink in. The other comment followed my own in-class contention that one is either gay, has gay family, gay friends, gay colleagues, gay teachers, gay students, etc, etc. (an idea voiced almost word-for-word by Mrs. Shepard in her speech the next evening). This student acknowledged that perhaps she had led a sheltered life, but she really didn't know any gay people. This time, I replied "Yes, you do," yet I stood mute while every reason in the world went through my head to prevent me from adding, "You're looking at one."

Paula Salvio (2006) suggests a rooted/vernacular/visceral cosmopolitanism that "finds robust expression in terms of practices and processes in everyday life," and I could not help but think how beneficial it might have been in *my* everyday life—not as a quick fix of noncommittal polite tolerance, rather as the means of speaking subjectivity. I might then have robustly expressed my earlier statement this way: that *our* sexuality is not something most gay people are looking to "beat." But, like those taxicab confessions, it is much easier to out oneself publicly to intimate strangers, "particular strangers," Appiah calls them (2006, p. 98), than to distant acquaintances.

While I do not want to over simplify cosmopolitanism—or suggest that social and cultural difficulties are easily solved if everybody just starts talking to everybody else, conversation is inextricably linked to communion. When we share intimate "fellowship" or rapport, we can speak of and from hearts as well as minds. We might then move toward the kind of radical questioning of revolt that Salvio (2006) describes in her analysis of Kelly Oliver's (2004) psychoanalytical work on the colonization of psychic space. The knowing of one another is understood to mean more than a requisite for lucrative financial growth across borders. We admire the activism of "doctors without borders" and "journalists without borders"—what if we were *people* without borders? It is a leap of faith, yes, and it has to start somewhere. It requires a turning loose—of power, privilege, position—with the understanding that the other fellow might cling to his or hers. Naive, you say? Disloyal, you say? Neither, it is rather like Thich Nhat Hanh's explanation of "dependent co-arising" (1987, p. 34), in which we *are* responsible for each other, yet we tend to each other by tending to self by tending to other. It requires an emptying unto fullness, as he might suggest, along with a growing consciousness that understanding is love, and love is understanding.

The interrelatedness of cosmopolitanism and ethics in a world of strangers is a secular framework from which to consider the idea of communion—a means of discussing it apart from religion without severing it from the spiritual. We are obligated to one another, we value each other and each other's practices and beliefs, and there are universal values that transcend boundaries of self and communities. This leaves people poised to then *do* something. We might consider communing.

I am therefore intrigued by Oliver's discussion of forgiveness and Salvio's subsequent comments on the place of forgiveness in a visceral cosmopolitanism. She describes a secular, psychoanalytic forgiveness that "creates for persons who experience oppression and alienation a capacity to compose meaning, to speak of aggressive desires and to articulate harms done within the intersubjective realm of the social" (Salvio, 2006)—oppressed persons that include "educators and students who are subject to the most dire aspects of educational reform" and whose subjectivity is at risk of "alienation and professional melancholia." The dynamic movement of questioning meaning and questioning-for-meaning—Oliver's radical questioning and the central act of secular forgiveness—is synchronous with the regressive, progressive, analytic, synthetical moments of self-formation and social reconstruction. *Currere*, then, is a curricular embodiment of the agency of forgiveness.

How might we relate forgiveness, communion, and cosmopolitanism and situate the relationship into curriculum theory? A place to start, I think, is with Appiah's subtitle: *Ethics in a World of Strangers*. I am reminded of Flannery O'Connor's reference to a Southern "code of manners based on mutual charity" (*CFO*, p. 103) that has sustained social relations for more than two centuries. Manners seem to me to be based on ethics, and in O'Connor's words, "Traditional manners, however unbalanced, are better than no manners at all" (*MM*, p. 200). When we behave mannerly—as my second grade teacher Mrs. Fowler would say—toward one another, one underlying ethic is that of forgiveness, with the presupposition that radical questioning will occur. And what of communion? Communion might be thought of as a means of movement toward agency of forgiveness. Oliver writes, "The agency of forgiveness...is the effect of meaning as it is lived between people;...meaning, or what takes place between us...makes forgiveness possible" (2004, p. 188). *What takes place between us...what is lived between people...*is an intimate sharing of fellowship from whence people transgress, trespass, question, encounter crises, and generally disrupt. And, as we would suggest to our teacher ed students, this is how meaning is made. We rise in our emergent consciousness, each asserting our singularity as "a unique being who means," according to Oliver (p. 189), yet moving toward a convergence of shared humanity engaging one with the other in meaning-making. For, as O'Connor noted in her efforts to render justice to the visible universe, "Everything (and I suggest, everyone) that rises must converge."

Another place for relating these ideas is *place*. Yi-Fu Tuan (1977/2005) describes the nature of a profound attachment to homeland in which religion is inextricably embedded, observing, "Religion could either bind a people to place or free them from it" (p. 152). Understanding curriculum has become for me an abiding desire to delve into the profound attachment held by many Southerners—including myself—to the South as homeland and the religious convictions that bind us to that homeland place. So the ideas of forgiveness and communion are very familiar to me, having been the topics of sermons, Sunday School lessons, Vacation Bible School classes, and songs. (My partner Gladys observes that fundamentalist hymns often sound something like college fight songs, which, in a way, they are. So if you can imagine a stirring plea to be washed in the blood of the lamb, then you have some idea of my point of reference.) I noted earlier that we are speaking of forgiveness and communion in a secular, curricular sense, but I draw alignments so that I might make meaning. The South's unique history and subsequent denial of that history makes it a fitting place to pay attention to the way its inhabitants carry out our obligations to strangers. O'Connor remarked, you will remember, that the South is not so much Christ-centered as it is Christ-haunted; we are haunted precisely *because* we are forgiven and *because* we have the aforementioned obligations. We are terrified to commune. We must therefore expose the nature of our haunting.

So then place is a medium through which to engage curriculum, and individual and collective religious convictions are bound up in place even as they bind to place. In one sentence, Pinar (2004) succinctly links curriculum, place, and fundamentalist Christianity—a triad central to Southern curriculum studies. He writes, "The curriculum tends to function in the South not unlike a secular version of biblical fundamentalism, in which the letter of text is mistaken for its spirit" (p. 241). What I find intriguing is this *spirit* of curriculum, and I am reminded of James Macdonald's (1995) "hermeneutic quest" (p. 173) in which curriculum theory is situated within the meditative hermeneutic cycle. Macdonald explained, "The act of theorizing is an act of faith, a religious act...what defines [both theory and pedagogy] is the spirit and vision that shines through the surface manifestations" (p. 181). The spirit of curriculum is an *inspirited* curriculum, invigorated with the daily practice of making meaning and transgressing social codes. Cosmopolitanism, as the discussion of forgiveness and communion suggests, may be given curricular forum so that we—strangers all—may, as singular and social citizens of the cosmos, come to the realization that we matter to each other.

A Curriculum of Communion

I had been having considerable trouble writing a suitable conclusion, wanting to not only summarize preceding themes and observations, but also to extend the idea of communion beyond the aesthetic and esoteric and propose it as a means of reconstructing dilapidated political and cultural structures in a twenty-first century South, or, in a post-911 world, as so many generally refer to our world around us these days. Like Flannery O'Connor, I face the difficulty of writing for an audience who does not know what grace is and cannot recognize it when it occurs: "The action of grace changes a character. Grace can't be experience in itself…All my stories are about the action of grace on a character who is not very willing to support it…" (*HB*, p. 275). Communion enables the change that takes place from the action of grace on each of us. I propose that grace happens, whether or not we know it for what it is. Some of us are apparently willing to support it, while others would impose a hardened grace based upon a fundamental, narrow judgment of God's desire. Those of us who are open to the action upon us will begin a new communion, one that has been tried in the crucible of grace.

Communion might be a site of convergence for inhabitants of Southern place; it might be our means to rise and converge together. From the Latin *communionem*, which means "a sharing by all or many," communion is the transformative common union by which Southerners might acknowledge one another and engage one another in conversation about progressive social, cultural, and political movement. Communion enables grace: it is what we do with the sight and insight that results from our shattering by grace. In relation to communion and curriculum, I have used terms such as *communion, faith, hope, queer, reconstruction,* and *grace* in my conversation. I have, through the narrative, redefined ways in which they are used, and I have used them and written about them in what might appear to be a whole new language. Yet, I have also sought to maintain common usage of these uncommon words—in part, precisely *because* they are familiar. With acknowledgement to Audre Lorde (1984, p. 110), the Southerners' tools, in this case, can be used to break the earth, harvest the crops, repair the roof, and, when that fails, dismantle the structure and *reconstruct* Southern identity by reconstructing Southern place. The language of fundamentalism, or of home, is a powerful tool.

While curriculum interrogating Southern identity will not transform the South, it can encourage the study and articulation of anomalous aspects of feeling and being Southern. If we are to build progressive conversation and political movement, our labor must be grounded in the knowledge of the complexity of Southern identity and identification. A curriculum of anomalous forms of Southernness might engender a sense of oneness, of communion. And although anomalies such as extremism—white supremacy, racist and homo-phobic hate crimes, for example—might also surface, they surface to be confronted. Curricular communion is disruptive, after all, and from it we expect discomfort; it only reinforces our strength to love.

Throughout the research I have considered what it means to feel Southern by investigating aspects of place inundated by white, patri-archal conventions of Southern identity. I have found that the textures of place are not woven together in silky smoothness that delights the touch, but they are rather like rough-hewn, itchy, ubiquitous burlap, used for everything from potato sacks to rugs. Each chapter has dis-placed Southern place and conventional traits of Southern identity with new conceptions of nostalgia, homeplace, queerness, and grace that further complicate the conversation of a curriculum of place.

Grace that resists absolution of traditional raced, classed, and gendered components of Southern identity might shatter Southern selfness toward blinding vision; revelatory grace wipes away pre-tence and opens us to what we may have in common. As a misfit in-timately familiar with feeling outside communion, mine is a search for sites of communion: with self, self and other, that, by extension, embodies the convergence of separation, guilt, and defeat within white Southern identity. I continue to struggle with my place in this place.

"The South," writes Mary Aswell Doll, "knows it is haunted" (2000, p. 6). The problem is that although it may realize it is haunted, the South either does not know how or has deliberately avoided mourning the deaths of those whose ghosts continue to haunt it or engaging them in conversation. Instead, it piously focuses on the dead but risen—murdered but alive—body of Christ. In any case, too much remains unconfronted, and the dead return to haunt the living, "because they have not been granted a proper burial" (Salvio, 2001, p. 98). The South, both literal and symbolic place, could be a site of con-vergence, where its people communicate in common union, account-ing for the past for the sake of the future. Being haunted—being "spooked"—precludes the separation necessary to mourn. One mourns what is past. Both whites and blacks may mourn the past. No reconstruction of the South—whether social, cultural, political, or individual—can occur without mourning for sins, for loss, for a dead past (Freud, 1917/1989; Butler, 1997; Salvio, 2001). And yet, are we to be static, stagnant, in this mourning? Miles Richardson (2001) contends, "In return for death we give presence" (p. 269); our singularity is contextualized, and we may therefore recognize it in other. Mourning is therefore a process of communion, the "gift of hope" (Richardson, 2001, p. 269) by which we are transformed.

Christians partaking in communion memorialize a death in acts of remembrance and contemplate the resurrection; this is the basis for faith, "the substance of things hoped for, the evidence of things not seen" (Hebrews 11:1). Communion is a common sharing of mourning in the search for hope. In remembrance of bodies lynched, for example, there might be a radicalized communion in which forgiveness is sought, reparation paid. Spiritual and social reparation, ultimately, is the price of Southern restoration, and it is one that some white Southerners are loathe to pay. Neither a political nor economic issue, reconstructive reparation includes but transcends formal declarations of apology and monetary restitution. Instead, it is rather like the man who watches the clock while the preacher commences his second hour of sermon; if his heart were right with God, he would not be concerned with the time.

The white wave of resistance to calls for racial reparations is merely an outward display of what is really in the Heart of Dixie. Peter Applebome (1997) states, "Southerners have forever been trying to summarize what exactly it is that they're so hellbent on preserving and which Southern virtues are in danger of being plowed over along with the South's sins" (p. 350), and cautions, "We would all be worse off if in our admirable rush to extinguish forever the South's ancient sins, we end up burying its enduring virtues as well" (p. 353). Communion-centered reconstruction complicates conversation beyond a preservation of virtues, veiled in nostalgia, or the perpetuation of guilt, from sins veiled by that same nostalgia. In "The Regional Writer," O'Connor responds to Walker Percy's answer when he was asked how the South produces so many good writers: "Because we lost the war" (*MM*, p. 59). O'Connor explains.

> What he was saying was that we have had our Fall....We have gone into the modern world with an inburnt knowledge of human limitations and with a sense of mystery which could not have developed in our first state of innocence—as it has not sufficiently developed in the rest of the country. The South, in other words still believes that man has fallen and that he is only perfectible by God's grace, not by his own unaided efforts. (*MM*, p. 59; *HB*, p. 302)

Reconstruction—life after the Fall—will occur with the acknowledgement of the uncomfortable knowledges of human limitations and the mourning for sins committed.

There is an old joke, one of the few I can remember, in which the Mississippi River is about to flood and engulf the area with its mighty waters. One fellow, a faithful Christian, prays for God to deliver him from harm. The local emergency authorities evacuate by sending around a jeep, then a boat, and then a helicopter as the floodwaters get deeper. Each time, the fellow refuses the ride, assuring the authorities that God will save him...After he drowns, he wakes up at the Pearly Gates and asks St. Peter why God had not heard his prayer. "He sent you a jeep, a boat, and a helicopter," replied St. Peter. "What else were you waiting for?"

White Southerners wallow in The Fall, The Lost Cause, and Lost War, just as surely as the fellow in the story sat up on his rooftop and watched the floodwaters rise. We crusade for Him, legislate for Him, judge for Him—do everything in the world except commune with Him. *God is love; and he that dwelleth in love dwelleth in God, and God in him* (I John 4:18). While the white Southerner waits for God's perfection in a strategy to avoid taking responsibility and making reparations, the tides of self-righteousness, defensiveness, social intolerance, and hatred continue to rise. O'Connor suggested that a centering of life on redemption allowed the artist to "see" by the light of faith, sharpening his or her perception of grotesquerie and perversion as they exist in the world, in place (*CFO*, p. 110). When we have hearts of common union, social and cultural distortions of modern life will be rendered unacceptable as we look "into the eyes of another...with the eyes of another" (Bakhtin in Brinkmeyer, 1989, p. 14). When we subsist in a living love toward each other, we begin the transformative journey of common union with each other, and we rejoice in the Mystery: communion with self, with each other, and with God.

Curricular Communion

This book constitutes a storying of Southern identity, and identity is a story whose narrative is never complete, is always becoming, is always complex. The research is my investigative witnessing, the intellectual ethic of studying the space of telling. *Tell about the South,* entreated Shreve McCannon to Quentin Compson, *What's it like there. What do they do there. Why do they live there. Why do they live at all* (Faulkner, 1936/1972, p. 142). Faulkner recognized the Southern urge toward self-examination, what Fred Hobson (1983, p. 1) calls the "Southern rage to explain." Coupled with Leigh Gilmore's (1994a, 1994b, 2001) "autobiographic demand," critical life narrative that presents a narrative dilemma of dividing and doubling the writer, I struggle to tell both self and South, as each has been inbricated in the other.

It is sometimes difficult to distinguish between my story and that of the place, and I have attempted, as Salvio (2001) describes, to "navigate through the delicate tensions that are inherent in the narrative structure of auto/biography—the tension between telling stories and sustaining family loyalties, articulating family secrets and properly mourning a traumatized past" (p. 114). Often the stories have been *about* and inseparable *from* the loyalties, secrets, and mourning— with the tension located in the telling, rather than between the act of telling and the feeling of emotion. The raging, then, has sometimes been not only in the telling about the South, but also in the feeling Southern. My idea of communion arises from the desire for a disruptive navigation of Southern past-in-place and the self entangled therein by which to conceptualize new meanings of Southernness.

This analysis of identity with/in Southern place has strengthened my belief in the need and capacity for people—in this case people who inhabit the South—to engage in complicated conversation that leads to *communion*. I conclude by offering communion as a ritual metaphor for a Southern curriculum of place. The idea of communion as metaphor for Southern place is fitting in that it is a site of *convergence*, a site where more is required of us than tolerance or manners or informed awareness toward each other. Communion requires investment of the spirit, occasionally the suspension of disbelief; grace is an act of God that exacts something from us—not in return but as a result, whether we commune with the dead, the sacrificed, the enslaved, the suffering, and so forth. Curricular grace is the shattering awareness that the possibility exists for a loving self-in-community and community-in-self. Grace is the challenge to transform—through the act of communion—self and place toward the possible. Communion is pedagogical action that we take toward and for one another once social fictions are revealed. It is the intellectual process by which we begin personal and social transformation and initiate progressive reconstruction in the South.

Reconstruction is a deeply rooted, deeply contested term, engendering massive resistance throughout the South's history. I acknowledge its historical, political, social, economic, and cultural complexity, and I remain self-conscious about using the term. I realize that in the course of the narrative I conflate Reconstruction with what historians have named *Redemption*, and *Restoration*, chronological and political periods when all pretense of constructing any sort of racially equal and just South was abandoned and blatantly countered. This research has reconfigured the term based on communion—curricular reconstruction based on curricular communion.

What I am *doing* is a Southern reconstruction. Are Southerners ready to take on this new definition; will we reclaim a reconstruction to mean something other than a place set firmly in a past—even a past veiled by nostalgia? The answer must be yes—*if* we can first embrace the idea of communion by which is engendered a bond between self and other. In this situated presence of selves-in-place we recognize that we are, according to Richardson, "each unique in the presence of one another" (2003, p. 221) and thus offer each other "our gift of being" (2001, p. 265). This is the Mystery of the bonds of communion, borne out of a state of self-love in relation to other, that constitutes and creates the reconstructed South. My curriculum of place-through-self transforms the notion of communion as it is traditionally conceived—in spiritual and ecclesiastical terms—into a curricular idea of union and disruption, of ethics and solidarity with others, of love and discomfort.

Curricular communion is significant to curriculum studies in that it offers a way to actively engage in the complicated conversation of curriculum in the twenty-first century. As communion is a most intimate component of worship, so too is curricular communion a convergence of feelings and events, a focused collection of hearts and minds. It embodies a powerful, active, community-building love between what Thich Nhat Hanh, in an interview with bell hooks, calls "self and no-self." He states, "Anything you do for yourself you do for the society at the same time. And anything you do for society you do for yourself also." hooks goes on to note, "This is the love we seek in the new millennium, which is the love experienced in community, beyond self" (hooks, 2000a, interview). Communion extends the conversation beyond the self so that curriculum, like love, may be experienced transformatively.

Notes

1   I Corinthians 11:18—19: [18]For first of all, when ye come together in the church, I hear that there be divisions among you; and I partly believe it. [19]For there must be also heresies among you, that they which are approved may be made manifest among you.

Bibliography

Abbott, S. (1998). *Womenfolks: Growing up down South*. New York: Mariner Books.

ABC News. (2006). Ethical dilemma, Pt. 2/Taxi driver experiment. *Primetime Live*. March 23, 2006.

Adams, P.C., Hoelscher, S., & Till, K.E. (Eds.). (2001). Place in context. In P.C. Adams, S. Hoelscher, & K.E. Till (Eds.). *Textures of place: Exploring humanistic geographies*. (pp. xiii-xxxiii). Minneapolis: University of Minnesota Press.

Allen, L. (Meeropol, A). (1937). Strange Fruit. As performed by Billie Holiday.

Allison, D. (1989). *Trash*. New York: Firebrand Books.

———. (1992). *Bastard out of Carolina*. New York: Penguin Books.

———. (1994). *Skin: Talking about sex, class, & literature*. New York: Firebrand Books.

———. (1995). *Two or three things I know for sure*. New York: Penguin Books.

———. Interview. (1999, May 26). *Borders.com*. Retrieved March 22, 02, from http://www.nbc.talkcity.com/transcripts/borders/5-26-1999.

Anzaldua, G. (1987). *Borderlands La Frontera: The new mestiza*. San Francisco: Aunt Lute Books.

Appiah, K.A. (2006). *Cosmopolitanism: Ethics in a world of strangers*. New York: W.W. Norton & Company.

Applebome, P. (1997). *Dixie Rising: How the South is shaping American values, politics, and culture*. New York: Harcourt Brace.

Asher, N. (2001). In contemplation: A curriculum for healing. *Paper Presented at Bergamo 2001: JCT Conference on Curriculum Theory and Classroom*.

———. (2002). (En)gendering a hybrid consciousness. *Journal of Curriculum Theorizing, 18*(4), 81–92.

———. (2003). Engaging difference: Towards a pedagogy of interbeing. *Teaching Education, 14*(3), 235–247.

Ashley, K., Gilmore, L., & Peters, G. (Eds.). (1994). *Autobiography & postmodernism*. Boston: University of Massachusetts Press.

Associated Press. (2004). Marriage wording to change in Texas books. ABCNews.com, 11/05/2004. Retrieved from http://abcnews.go.com/US/print?id=2307000.

———. (2004). Swaggart apologizes for talk of killing gays. MSNBC.com, 9/23/2004. Retrieved from http://msnbc.msn.com/id/6074380/print/1/displaymode/1098/

———. (2005). Democrats voted out of church because of their politics, members say. *USA Today.* Retrieved on May 10, 2005 from http://www.usa-today.com/news/nation/2005-05-07-church-politics_x.htm.

———. (2005). Political pastor blames "misunderstanding." He tries to welcome back ousted members. *MSNBC.com.* Retrieved on May 10, 2005, from http://www.msnbc.msn.com/id/7769149.

Ayers, E. (1992). *The promise of the new South: Life after Reconstruction.* Oxford: Oxford University Press.

———. (1996). *All over the map: Rethinking American regions.* Baltimore: Johns Hopkins University Press.

———. (2004). Reconstruction: The second Civil War. *The American Experience.* Transcript. PBS. WGBH Boston: WGBH Educational Foundation.

Bakhtin, Mikail. (1968). *Rabelais and his world.* Cambridge: MIT Press.

Balmer, R. (2000). *Mine eyes have seen the glory: A journey into the evangelical subculture in America* (3rd ed.). New York: Oxford University Press.

Baumgaertner, J. (1988). *Flannery O'Connor: A proper scaring.* Chicago: Cornerstone Press.

Bergson, H. (1990/1959). *Matiere et memoire.* Paris: Quadrige/PUF.

Berlant, L. (Ed.). (2000). *Intimacy.* Chicago: University of Chicago Press.

Blight, D. (2004). Reconstruction: The second Civil War. *The American Experience.* Transcript. PBS. WGBH Boston: WGBH Educational Foundation.

Boldt, G.M., & Salvio, P.M. (2006). *Love's return: Psychoanalytic essays on childhood, teaching, and learning.* New York: Routledge.

Bouchard, D. (Ed.). (1977). *Michel Foucalt: Language, counter-memory, practice.* Ithaca, NY: Cornell University Press.

Bowman, D. (2000). The last acceptable prejudice. Salon.com, 8/16/2000. Retrieved from http://archive.salon.com/sex/feature/2000/08/16/byrne_fone/index.html.

Boym, S. (2001). *The future of nostalgia.* New York: Basic Books.

Brink, J., & Mencher, J. (Eds.). (1997). *Mixed blessings: Gender and religious fundamentalism cross culturally.* New York: Routledge.

Brinkmeyer, Jr., R. (1989). *The art and vision of Flannery O'Connor.* Baton Rouge: Louisiana State University Press.

Britzman, D. (1997). The tangles of implication. *Qualitative Studies in Education, 10*(1), 31—37.

———. (1998). *Lost subjects/contested objects: Toward a psychoanalytic inquiry of learning.* Albany: SUNY Press.

Brownmiller, S. (1984). *Femininity.* New York: Linden Press, Simon and Schuster.

Butler, J. (1997). *The psychic life of power: Theories of subjection.* Stanford, CA: Stanford University Press.

Carter, J. (2005). *Our endangered values: America's moral crisis.* New York: Simon & Schuster.

Cartledge, T.W. (2005, May 11). Pastor resigns after conflict over politics. *Biblical recorder.* Retrieved June 2, 2005, from http://www.biblicalrecorder.org/cgi--bin/pf.pl.

Cash, J. (2002). *Flannery O'Connor: A life.* Knoxville: University of Tennessee Press.

Cash, W.J. (1941). *The mind of the South.* New York: Alfred Knopf.

Cvetkovich, A. (2003). *An archive of feelings: Trauma, sexuality, and lesbian public culture.* Durham: Duke University Press.

Darder, A., Baltodano, M., & Torres, R. (Eds.) (2002). *The critical pedagogy reader.* New York: Routledge.

Davis, B. (2004). *Inventions of teaching: A genealogy.* Mahway, NJ: Lawrence Erlbaum.

de Lauretis, T. (1990). Eccentric subjects: Feminist theory and historical consciousness. *Feminist Studies, 16*(1), 115—149.

Deleuze, G. (1989). Qu'est-ce qu'un dispositif? In *Michel Foucalt: Philosophe.* Paris: Seuil.

———. (1988). *Bergsonism.* Translated by H. Tomlinson and B. Habberjam. New York: Zone Books.

Deleuze, G., & Guattari, F. (1980). *A thousand plateaus: Capitalism and schizophrenia* (B. Massumi, Trans.).

Detwiler, F. (1999). *Standing on the premises of God: The Christian Right's fight to redefine America's public schools.* New York: New York University Press.

DeVane, S. (2005, May 9). Church removes members for political views, deacon says. *Biblical recorder.* Retrieved June 2, 2005, from http://www.biblicalrecorder.org/content/news/2005/5_9_2005/ne090505achurch.shtml.

Dews, C., & Law, C. (Eds.). (2001). *Out in the South.* Philadelphia: Temple University Press.

Di Renzo, A. (1993). *American gargoyles: Flannery O'Connor and the medieval grotesque.* Carbondale, IL: Southern Illinois University Press.

Doll, Jr., W. (2002). Ghosts and the curriculum. In W.E. Doll, Jr. & N. Gough (Eds.), *Curriculum visions* (pp. 23-69). New York: Peter Lang.

Doll, M. A. (1995). *To the lighthouse and back: Writings on teaching and living.* New York: Peter Lang.

―――. (1998). Queering the gaze. In W. Pinar (Ed.), *Queer theory in education.* Mahwah, NJ: Lawrence Erlbaum Associates.

―――. (2000). *Like letters in running water: A mythopoetics of curriculum.* Mahwah, NJ: Lawrence Erlbaum.

―――. (2005). Personal correspondence, 2/21/2005.

Doll, M., Wear, D., & Whitaker, M. (2006). *Triple takes on curricular worlds.* Albany, NY: SUNY Press.

Dunbar, A. (Ed.). (2004). *Where we stand: Voices of Southern dissent.* Montgomery: NewSouth Books.

Edgerton, J. (2004). The Southernization of American Politics. In A. Dunbar (Ed.). *Where we stand: Voices of Southern dissent.* (pp. 197-223). Montgomery, AL: New South Books.

Edgerton, S. H. (1991). Particularities of 'Otherness': Autobiography, Maya Angelou, and me. In J. Kincheloe & W. Pinar (Eds.), *Curriculum as social psychoanalysis: The significance of place* (pp. 77—97). Albany: SUNY Press.

―――. (1996). *Translating the curriculum: Multiculturalism into cultural studies.* New York: Routledge.

Ellsberg, R. (Ed.). (2003). *Flannery O'Connor: Spiritual writings.* Maryknoll, NY: Orbis Books.

Ellsworth, E. (1989/1994). Why doesn't this feel empowering? Working through the repressive myths of critical pedagogy. In Stone, L. (Ed.), *The Education feminist reader* (pp. 300—327). New York: Routledge.

―――. (1997). *Teaching positions: Difference, pedagogy, and the power of address.* New York: Teachers College Press.

Faulkner, W. (1954). *The Faulkner reader.* New York: Random House.

―――. (1936/1972). *Absalom, Absalom!* New York: Vintage Books.

Faust, D.G. (1996). *Mothers of invention: Women of the slaveholding South in the American Civil War.* New York: Vintage Books.

―――. (2004). Reconstruction: The second Civil War. *The American Experience.* Transcript. PBS. WGBH Boston: WGBH Educational Foundation.

Fernandes, L. (2003). *Transforming feminist practice: Non-violence, social justice and the possibilities of a spiritualized feminism.* San Francisco: Aunt Lute Books.

Fine, M. (1994). Working the hyphens: Reinventing self and other in qualitative research. In N. Denzen & Y. Lincoln (Eds.). *Handbook of Qualitative Research.* Thousand Oaks: Sage Publications.

Fraser, Jr., W.J., Saunders, Jr., R.F., & Wakelyn, J.L. (Eds.). (1985). *The web of Southern social relations: Women, family, and education.* Athens, GA: University of Georgia Press.

Freire, P. (1970). *Pedagogy of the oppressed.* New York: Herder and Herder.

———. (1993/1917). *Pedagogy of hope: Reliving pedagogy of the oppressed.* New York: Continuum.

Freud, S. (1989). Mourning and melancholia. P. Gay (Ed.), *The Freud reader.* New York: Norton.

Gaines, E.J. (1972). *The autobiography of Miss Jane Pittman.* New York: Bantam.

Garber, L. (Ed.). (1994). *Tilting the tower: Lesbians teaching queer subjects.* New York: Routledge.

Gilmore, L. (1994a). Policing truth: Confession, gender, and autobiographical authority. In K. Ashley, L. Gilmore, & G. Peters (Eds.). *Autobiography and postmodernism.* Amherst: University of Massachusetts Press.

———. (1994b). *Autobiographics: A feminist theory of women's self-representation.* New York: Cornell University Press.

———. (2001). *The limits of autobiography: Trauma and testimony.* Ithaca: Cornell University Press.

Gordon, S. (2000). *Flannery O'Connor: The obedient imagination.* Athens, GA: University of Georgia Press.

Gourdine, A. (2003). *The difference place makes: Gender, sexuality, and diaspora identity.* Columbus: Ohio State University Press.

Gray, R. (2002). Inventing communities, imagining places: Some thoughts on Southern self-fashioning. In S. Jones & S. Monteith (Eds.), *South to a new place: Region, literature, culture* (pp. xiii—xxiii). Baton Rouge: LSU Press.

Green, M. (1988). *The dialectic of freedom.* New York: Teachers College Press.

Gross, R.M. (1996). *Feminism & religion: An introduction.* Boston: Beacon Press.

Hackney, S. (2004). Identity politics, Southern style. In A. Dunbar (Ed.), *Where we stand: Voices of Southern dissent* (pp. 181—196). Montgomery: New South Books.

Hagood, M.J. (1996/1939). *Mothers of the South: Portraiture of the white tenant farm woman.* Charlottesville: University Press of Virginia.

Hale, G.E. (1998). *The Making of Whiteness: The culture of segregation in the South, 1890-1940.* New York: Vintage Books.

Hamilton, E. (1930). *The Greek way.* New York: W.W. Norton & Company.

Harbeck, K. (Ed.). (1992). *Coming out of the classroom closet: Gay and lesbian students, teachers and curricula.* New York: Harrington Park Press.

Harris, J. (2001). God gave U.S. 'What we deserve,' Falwell says. Washingtonpost.com, 9/14/2001. Retrieved from http://www.washingtonpost-.com/ac2/wpdyn?pagename=article&node=&contentId=A28620-2001Sep14.

Hart, A. (2004, March 27). Hoop skirts, pearl-handled revolvers and a mirror to see clearly with. *Savannah Morning News,* p. 8D.

Hawley, J. (Ed.). (1994). *Fundamentalism & gender.* New York: Oxford University Press.

Haynes, C. (1998). *Divine destiny: Gender and race in nineteenth-century Protestantism.* Jackson: University Press of Mississippi.

Heriot, M. J. (1994). *Blessed assurance: Beliefs, actions, and the experience of Salvation in a Carolina Baptist church.* Knoxville: University of Tennessee *Press.*

Heyrman, C.L. (1997). *Southern cross: The beginnings of the Bible Belt.* New York: Alfred A. Knopf.

Hill, S. (1998). Fundamentalism in recent Southern culture: Has it done what the Civil Rights Movement couldn't do? *The Journal of Southern Religion.* Retrieved October 29, 2001, from http://jrs.as.Wvu.edu/essay.htm.

———. (1999). *Southern churches in crisis revisited.* Tuscaloosa: University of Alabama Press.

———. (Ed.) (1997). *Encyclopedia of religion in the South.* Macon, GA: Mercer Press.

Hobson, F. (1983). *Tell about the South: The Southern rage to explain.* Baton Rouge: LSU Press.

———. (1999). *But now I see: The white Southern racial conversion narrative.* Baton Rouge: LSU Press.

Honig, B. (1994). Difference, dilemmas, and the politics of home. *Social Research* 61(3), 563-598.

hooks, b. (1990). *Yearning: Race, gender, and cultural politics.* Boston: South End Press.

———. (1994). *Teaching to transgress: Education as the practice of freedom.* New York: Routledge.

———. (2000a, January). On building a community of love. Shambhala Sun Online. Retrieved April 9, 2003, from http://www.shambhalasun.com.

———. (2000b). *Where we stand: Class matters.* New York: Routledge.

———. (2001). *Salvation: Black people and love.* New York: Perennial.

———. (2002). *Communion: The female search for love.* New York: HarperCollins.

Huebner, D., Hillis, V. & Pinar, W. (Eds.). (1999). *The lure of the transcendent: Collected essays by Dwayne E. Huebner.* Mahwah, NJ: Lawrence Erlbaum.

Hughes, R. (1996). *Reviving the ancient faith: The story of Churches of Christ in America.* Grand Rapids: William B. Eerdman Publishing Company.

Hunsberger, B. (1995). Religion and prejudice: The role of religious fundamentalism, quest, and right-wing authoritarianism. *Journal of Social Issues, 51,* 113—129.

Hwu, W. (1998). Curriculum, transcendence, and Zen/Taoism: Critical ontology of the self. In W. Pinar (Ed.), *Curriculum: Toward New Identities* (pp. 263—294). New York: Garland Publishing.

Jennings, W. (1979). Theme from *The Dukes of Hazard* (Good Ol' Boys).

Kemp, S., & Squires, J. (Eds.). (1997). *Feminisms.* Oxford: Oxford University Press.

Kesson, K. (2001). Contemplative spirituality, currere, and social transformation: Finding our 'way.' *Journal of Curriculum Theorizing. 17*(4), 67—88.

Khayatt, M. (1992). *Lesbian teachers: An invisible presence.* Albany, NY: SUNY.

Kimmel, M.S. (1996). *Manhood in America: A cultural history.* New York: Free Press.

Kincheloe, J. (1991). Willie Morris and the Southern curriculum: Emancipating the Southern Ghosts. In J. Kincheloe & W. Pinar (Eds.), *Curriculum as social psychoanalysis: The significance of place* (pp. 123—154). Albany: SUNY Press.

Kincheloe, J., & Pinar, W. (Eds.). (1991). *Curriculum as social psychoanalysis: The significance of place.* Albany: SUNY Press.

Kincheloe, J., Pinar, W., & Slattery, P. (1994). A last dying chord? Toward cultural and educational renewal in the South. *Curriculum Inquiry, 24*(4), 407—437.

King, F. (1995). *The Florence King Reader.* New York: St. Martin's Press.

Klein, M. (1996, January). *The sex lies of the religious right: How conservatives distort the facts of life.* Retrieved October 29, 2001, from The Playboy Forum Web Site: http://www.radical-sex.com.

Lather, P. (1996). *Methodology as subversive repetition: Practices toward a feminist double science.* Paper presented at AERA, New York City.

Lawrence, T. (2004). Paint me a Birmingham. *Strong.* Dreamworks Nashville.

Lorde, A. (1984). *Sister outsider: Essays & speeches* . Freedom, CA: The Crossings Press.

Luhman. (1998). Queering/quering pedagogy? Or, pedagogy is a pretty queer thing. In Pinar. W. (Ed.). Queer theory in education (pp. 141–156). Mahwah, NJ: Lawrence Erlbaum.

Lugg, C. (2000a). *For God and country: Conservatism and American school policy.* New York: Peter Lang.

———. (2000b). Reading, writing, and reconstructionism: The Christian Right and the politics of public education. *Educational Policy, 14,* 622. Retrieved November 8, 2001, from http://ftviewer.epnet.com.

Macdonald, B.J. (Ed.). (1995). *Theory as a prayerful act: The collected essays of James B. Macdonald.* New York: Peter Lang.

Martin, B., & Mohanty, C. (1986). Feminist politics: What's home got to do with it? Bloomington: Indiana University Press.

Martin, C. (1968). *The true country: Themes in the fiction of Flannery O'Connor.* Nashville: Vanderbilt University Press.

Martin, R. (2002). *Unmasking the Devil: Dramas of sin and grace in the world of Flannery O'Connor.* Ypsilanti, MI: Sapientia Press.

Martin, W. (1997). *With God on our side: The rise of the Religious Right in America.* New York: Broadway.

Martusewicz, R.A. (1997). Say me to me. In S. Todd (Ed.), *Learning desire: Perspectives on pedagogy, culture, and the unsaid* (pp. 97–113). New York: Routledge.

McConnell, M.W. (1998). Commentary, in Encounters in law, philosophy, religion, and education. In J.T. Sears & J.C. Carper (Eds.), *Curriculum, religion, and public education: conversations for an enlarging public square.* New York: Teachers College Press.

McCullers, C. (1979/1946). *The member of the wedding.* New York: Bantam Books.

McLaren, P. (2000). *Che Guevara, Paulo Freire, and the pedagogy of revolution.* Lanham, MD: Rowman & Littlefield.

McPherson, T. (2003). *Reconstructing Dixie: Race, gender, and nostalgia in the imagined South.* Durham, NC: Duke University Press.

Mead, F.S., & Hill, S.S. (Eds.). (2001). *Handbook of denominations in the United States* (11th ed.). Nashville: Abingdon Press.

Mencken, H.L. (1958). The Sahara of the Bozart. In J.T. Farrell (Ed.), *Prejudices: A selection.* New York: Random House.

Merriam-Webster's 11ᵗʰ Collegiate Dictionary and Thesaurus. Version 3.0. 2003.

Miller, A. (1953). *The Crucible.* New York: Penguin Books.

Miller, D.W. (2000, June). Striving to understand the religious right. *Chronicle of Higher Education, 56*(43), A17−A18.

Miller, N. (2002, June 11). We love homosexuals, James Merritt tells SBC. *BP News.* Retrieved June 12, 2002, from BP News Web Site: http://www.bpnews.net.

———. (2005, May 10). N.C. pastor's primary desire is peace & unity for congregation. BP news. Retrieved June 2, 2005, from http://www.bpnews.net-/printerfriendly.asp?ID=20766.

Mintz, B., & Rothblum, E. (Eds.). (1997). *Lesbians in academia: Degrees of freedom.* New York: Routledge.

Mitchell, M. (1936, 1999). *Gone with the wind.* New York: Warner Books.

Molick, C. (2001). *Quotes: Homophobia and sexism.* Retrieved October 29, 2001, from http://www.bible.org/quotes/phobia.

More gays, lesbians marry on eve of court hearing. CNN.com, 2/17/2004. Retrieved from http://www.cnn.com/2004/US/West/02/16/samesex.marriage/index.html.

Morris, M. (1998). Unresting the curriculum: Queer projects, queer imaginings. In Pinar. W. (Ed.). Queer theory in education (pp. 275−286). Mahwah, NJ: Lawrence Erlbaum.

———. (1999). Toward a ludic pedagogy: An uncertain occasion. In Pinar, W. (Ed.), *Contemporary curriculum discourses* (pp. 412−424). New York: Peter Lang.

Moss, D. (2001). On hating in the first person plural: thinking psychoanalytically about racism, homophobia, and misogyny. *Journal of the American Psychoanalytic Association. 49*(4): 1315−34.

Munro, P. (1998). Engendering curriculum history. In W. Pinar (Ed.), *Curriculum: Toward new identities* (pp. 263−294). New York: Garland Publishing.

———. (1998). *Subject to fiction: Women teachers' life history narratives and the cultural politics of resistance.* Philadelphia: Open University Press.

National Education Association. (2001). *The Religious Right.* Retrieved October 29, 2001, from National Education Association Web Site: http://www.nea.org/pub-liced/paycheck.

National Gay and Lesbian Task Force. (2003). *Know thy enemy: A compendium of recent quotes about the Supreme Court sodomy ruling and the same-sex marriage backlash* (July 30, 2003 ed.).

New International Version Study Bible. (1985). Grand Rapids: Zondervan.

Nhat Hanh, T. (1987). *Being peace.* Berkeley, CA: Parallex Press.

———. (1995). *Living Buddah, living Christ.* New York: Riverhead Books.

————. (1998). *Teachings on love*. Berkeley, CA: Parallex Press.

Nicholson, L. (Ed.). (1990). *Feminism/Postmodernism*. New York: Routledge.

No Child Left Behind: A Desktop Reference. (2001). Jessup, MD: Education Publications Center, U.S. Department of Education.

Noddings, N. (1999). Moral education as a form of life. In J.T. Sears & J.C. Carper (Eds.), *Curriculum, religion, and public education: Conversations for an enlarging public square* (pp. 120–126). New York: Teachers College Press.

O'Connor, F. (1969). *Mystery and manners: Occasional prose*. S. Fitzgerald and R. Fitzgerald (Eds.). New York: Farrar, Straus & Giroux.

————. (1971). *The complete stories*. New York: Farrar, Straus, and Giroux.

————. (1979). *The Habit of being: Letters*. S. Fitzgerald (Ed.). New York: Farrar, Straus & Giroux.

————. (1987). *Conversations with Flannery O'Connor*. R. Magee (Ed.). Jackson: University of Mississippi Press.

————. (1988). *Collected works*. New York: Library of America.

Oliver, K. (2004). *The colonization of psychic space: A psychoanalytic social theory of oppression*. Minneapolis: University of Minnesota Press.

Opfer, D. (2000). Paranoid politics, extremism, and the Religious Right: A case of mistaken identity? In S. Talburt & S. Steinberg (Eds.), *Thinking Queer: Sexuality, Culture, and Education* (pp. 85-103). New York: Peter Lang.

Percy, W. (1987). *The thanatos syndrome*. New York: Farrar, Straus, and Giroux.

Phillips, K. (2006). *American theocracy: The peril and politics of radical religion, oil, and borrowed money in the 21st century*. New York: Viking.

Pinar, W. (1991). *Curriculum as social psychoanalysis: The significance of place*. Albany: SUNY Press.

————. (1994). *Autobiography, politics and sexuality: Essays in curriculum theory, 1972-1992*. New York: Peter Lang.

————. (Ed.). (1998). *Queer theory in education*. Mahwah, NJ: Lawrence Erlbaum Associates.

————. (2001). *The gender of racial politics and violence in America*. New York: Peter Lang.

————. (2004). *What is curriculum theory?* Mahway, NJ: Lawrence Erlbaum.

Pinar, W., Reynolds, W., Slattery, P., & Taubman, P. (1995). *Understanding curriculum*. New York: Peter Lang.

Pitt, A. (2003). The play of the personal: Psychoanalytic narratives of feminist education. New York: Peter Lang.

Political Research Associates, the Policy Institute of the National Gay and Lesbian Task Force, and Equal Partners in Faith. (October 1998). *Calculated compassion: How the ex-gay movement serves the Right's attack on democracy* [Brochure].

Pollak, J. (1994). Lesbian/gay role models in the classroom: Where are they when you need them? In L. Garber (Ed.), *Tilting the tower: Lesbians teaching queer subjects.* (pp. 131—134). New York: Routledge.

Powell, K.M. (2002). Writing the geography of the Blue Ridge Mountains: How displacement recorded the land. *Biography: An Interdisciplinary Quarterly,* Winter, 25(1), 73—94.

Pratt, M.B. (1984). Identity: Skin, blood, heart. In E. Bulkin, M.B. Pratt, and B. Smith (Ed.), *Yours in struggle: Three feminist perspectives on anti-semitism and racism.* New York: Long Haul Press.

———. (1985). *We say we love each other.* San Franscisco: Spinsters Ink.

———. (1990). *Crime against nature.* Ithaca, NY: Firebrand Books.

———. (1991). *Rebellion: Essays 1980-1991.* Ithaca, NY: Firebrand Books.

———. (1999). *Walking back up Depot Street: Poems.* Pittsburg: University of Pittsburg Press.

Probyn, E. (1996). *Outside belongings.* New York: Routledge Publishing.

Prown, K.H. (2001). *Revising Flannery O'Connor: Southern literacy culture and the problem of female authorship.* Charlottesville: University Press of Virginia.

Putman, C. (1965). Green, green grass of home. Retrieved from http://www.nashville-songwritersfoundation.com.

Ragen, B.A. (1989). *A wreck on the road to Damascus: Innocence, guilt, and conversion in Flannery O'Connor.* Chicago: Loyola University Press.

Reaves, J. (2000, June 13). *Are Southern Baptists flirting with a schism?* Retrieved October 29, 2001, from http://www.time.com.

Reed, B. (Ed.). (2002). *Nothing sacred: Women respond to religious fundamentalism and terror.* New York: Nation Books.

Reed, J.S. (1982). *One South: An ethnic approach to regional culture.* Baton Rouge: Louisiana State University Press.

———. (1983). *Southerners: The social psychology of sectionalism.* Chapel Hill: University of North Carolina Press.

———. (2003). *Minding the South.* Columbia, MO: University of Missouri Press.

Richardson, M. (2001). The gift of presence: The act of leaving artifacts at shrines, memorials, and other tragedies. In P. C. Adams, S. Hoelscher, & K.E. Till (Eds.). *Textures of place: Exploring humanistic geographies.* (pp. 257—272). Minneapolis: University of Minnesota Press.

————. (2003). *Being-in-Christ and putting death in its place: An anthropologist's account of Christian performance in Spanish America and the American South.* Baton Rouge: Louisiana State University Press.

Ritivoi, A.D. (2002). *Yesterday's self: Nostalgia and the immigrant identity.* New York: Rowman & Littlefield.

Roberts, D. (2002). The South of the mind. In S. Jones & S. Monteith (Eds.), *South to a new place: Region, literature, culture* (pp. 363—373). Baton Rouge: LSU Press.

Rodgers, J. (1929). Waitin' for a train. Copyright, Peer International.

Rodriguez, N. (1998). (Queer) youth as political and pedagogical. In W. Pinar (Ed.), *Queer theory in education* (pp. 173—185). Mahwah, NJ: Lawrence Erlbaum.

Rubin, Jr., L. (Ed.). (1979). *The literary South.* New York: John Wiley & Sons.

Ruttenberg, D. (2004, Spring). Striking a balance: Carol Lee Flinders on spirituality, politics, and the spaces in between. *Bitch: Feminist Response to Pop Culture, 24,* 51.

Saliers, E. (1990). Southland in the springtime. *Nomads Indians Saints.* Epic Records.

Salvio, P. (2001). Loss, memory, and the work of learning: Lessons from the teaching life of Anne Sexton. In D. Holdstein & D. Bleich (Eds.), *Personal effects: The social character of scholarly writing* (pp. 93—117). Logan, UT: Utah State University Press.

————. (2006). "The opposite direction": Radical questioning and the work of forgiveness. Paper presented at the American Association for the Advancement of Curriculum Studies, Berkeley, California, April 2006.

Schubert, W.H. (1986). *Curriculum: Perspective, paradigm, and possibility.* NY: Macmillan.

————. (2004). Foreword: Reflections on the place of curriculum. In D.M. Callejo Perez, S.M. Fain, & J.J. Slater (Eds.), *Pedagogy of place: Seeing space as cultural education.* New York: Peter Lang.

Scott, A.F. (1984). *Making the invisible woman visible.* Urbana: University of Illinois Press.

————. (1995). *The Southern lady: From pedestal to politics 1830-1930.* Charlottesville: University Press of Virginia.

Sears, J. T. (1991). *Growing up gay in the South: Race, gender, and the journeys of the spirit.* New York: Harrington Park Press.

———. (1998). Crossing boundaries and becoming the other. In J.T. Sears. & J. C. Carper (Eds.), *Curriculum, religion, and public education: Conversations for an enlarging public square* (pp. 38—58). New York: Teachers College Press.

Sedgwick, E.K. (2003). *Touching feeling: Affect, pedagogy, performativity.* Durham: Duke University Press.

Segrest, M. (1985). *My mama's dead squirrel: Lesbian essays on Southern culture.* Ithaca, NY: Firebrand Books.

———. (1994). *Memoir of a race traitor.* Boston: South End Press.

Sewall, G.T. (1998). Religion and the textbooks. In J.T. Sears & J.C. Carper (Eds.), *Curriculum, religion, and public education: conversations for an enlarging public square* (pp. 73—84). New York: Teachers College Press.

Sibley, D. (1995). *Geographies of exclusion.* New York: Routledge.

Slattery, P. (1995). *Curriculum development in the postmodern era.* New York: Garland.

Slattery, P., & Daigle, K. (1994). Curriculum as a place of turmoil: Deconstructing the anguish in Walker Percy's Feliciana and Ernest Gaines' Pointe Coupee. *Curriculum Inquiry, 24*(4), 407—437.

Smith, S. (Ed.). (1998). *Women, autobiography, theory: A reader.* Madison: University of Wisconsin Press.

Smith, S., & Watson, J. (2001). *Reading autobiography: A guide for interpreting life narratives.* Minneapolis: University of Minnesota Press.

Southern Baptists to vote against women. (2000, June 13). Retrieved October 29, 2001, from http://www.cnn.com.

St. Pierre, E. (1995). *Arts of existence: The construction of subjectivity in older, white, Southern women.* Unpublished dissertation. Columbus: The Ohio State University.

———. (2000). Nomadic inquiry in the smooth spaces of the field: A preface. In E. St. Pierre & W. Pillow (Eds.), *Working the ruins: Feminist poststructural theory and methods in education* (pp. 258—283). New York: Routledge.

———. (2001). Coming to theory: Finding Foucalt and Deleuze. In K. Weiler (Ed.), *Feminist engagements: Reading, resisting, and revisioning male theorists in education and cultural studies* (pp. 141—163). New York: Routledge.

Stone, L. (Ed.). (1994). *The education feminism reader.* New York: Routledge.

Strike, K.A. (1998). Dialogue, religion, and tolerance: How to talk to people who are wrong about (almost) anything. In J.T. Sears & J.C. Carper (Eds.), *Curriculum, religion, and public education: Conversations for an enlarging public square* (pp. 59—69). New York: Teachers College Press.

Sumara, D., & Davis, B. (1999). Interrupting heteronormativity: Toward a queer curriculum theory. *Curriculum Inquiry, 29*(2), 191—208.

Swomley, J. (1996, January 11). Promises we don't want kept. *The Humanist.* Retrieved November 2, 2001, from http://ask.elibrary.com.

Talburt, S. (2000). *Subject to identity: Knowledge, sexuality, and academic practices in higher education.* Albany: SUNY Press.

———. (2005). Responding to the present: Public/private practices and global identities. *Journal of Curriculum Theorizing,* 21(2), 3-8.

Talburt, S., & Steinberg, S. (Eds.). (2000). *Thinking queer: Sexuality, culture, and education.* New York: Peter Lang.

Teilhard de Chardin, P. (1960). The Divine milieu: An essay on the interior life. Translated by B. Wall. New York: Perennial.

Till, K.E. (2001). Reimagining national identity: "Chapters of Life" at the German Historical Museum in Berlin. In P.C. Adams, S. Hoelscher, & K.E. Till (Eds.). *Textures of place: Exploring humanistic geographies.* (pp. 273—299). Minneapolis: University of Minnesota Press.

Tong, R. P. (1998, 1989). *Feminist thought: A more comprehensive introduction* (2nd ed.). Boulder, CO: Westview Press.

Tuan, Yi-Fu. (1977/2005). *Space and place: The perspective of experience.* Minneapolis: University of Minnesota Press.

Tuana, N., & Tong, R.P. (Eds.). (1995). *Feminism & philosophy: Essential readings in theory, reinterpretation, and application.* Boulder, CO: Westview Press.

Tumulty, K. (2002, October 14). Jesus and the FDA. *Time.* 26.

Unger, M. M. (Ed.). (1988). *The new Unger's Bible dictionary* (Rev. ed.). Chicago: Moody Press.

Wallis, J. (2005). *God's politics: Why the right gets it wrong and the left doesn't get it.* San Francisco: Harper.

Walker, A. (1989). Everyday Use. In *Adventures in American literature* (Pegasus Edition). Dallas: Harcourt Brace Jovanovich.

Weedon, C. (1999). *Feminism, theory, and the politics of difference.* Malden, MA: Blackwell Publishers.

Weiler, K. (1991). Freire and a feminist pedagogy of difference. *Harvard Educational Review, 61,* 449-474.

Welty, E. (1978). *The eye of the story: Selected essays and reviews*: NY: Random House.

Wexler, P. (1996). *Holy sparks: Social theory, education, and religion.* New York: St. Martin's Press.

Whitlock, R.U. (2003). Some measure of healing: Dorothy Allison as theorist. *Journal of Curriculum Theorizing.* 19, 73-86.

———. (2006). South to a queer place. *Journal of Poverty. 10*(2).

———. (2006). Season of lilacs: Nostalgia of place and homeplace(s) of difference. *Taboo: The Journal of Culture and Education.* Fall-Winter 2005.

———. (2006). Queerly fundamental: Surviving straightness in a rural southern high school. Journal of Curriculum and Pedagogy. Spring 2006.

Williams, T. (1974, 1947). *A streetcar named desire.* New York: Signet.

Williamson, J. (1986). *A rage for order: Black-white relations in the American South since emancipation.* New York: Oxford University Press.

Windham, K. T. (1969). *13 Alabama ghosts and Jeffrey.* Tuscaloosa, AL: University of Alabama.

Wood, R.C. (2001). The failure of the aesthetic and moral intelligence in recent criticism of Flannery O'Connor. Retrieved from http://www3.baylor.edu/~Ralph_Wood/oconnor/OConnorsFeministCritics.pdf on 3/19/2004.

———. (2004). *Flannery O'Connor and the Christ-haunted South.* Grand Rapids: William B. Eerdmans Publishing Company.

Woog, D. (1995). *School's out: The impact of gay and lesbian issues on America's schools.* Boston: Alyson Publications.

Index

OMPLICATED

A BOOK SERIES OF CURRICULUM STUDIES

This series employs research completed in various
disciplines to construct textbooks that will enable
public school teachers to reoccupy a vacated public
domain—not simply as "consumers" of knowledge,
but as active participants in a "complicated
conversation" that they themselves will lead. In
drawing promiscuously but critically from various
academic disciplines and from popular culture, this
series will attempt to create a conceptual montage for
the teacher who understands that positionality as
aspiring to reconstruct a "public" space. *Complicated
Conversation* works to resuscitate the progressive
project—an educational project in which self-
realization and democratization are inevitably
intertwined; its task as the new century begins is
nothing less than the intellectual formation of a public
sphere in education.

The series editor is:

Dr. William F. Pinar
Department of Curriculum Studies
2125 Main Mall
Faculty of Education
University of British Columbia
Vancouver, British Columbia V6T 1Z4
CANADA

To order other books in this series, please contact our Customer
Service Department:

(800) 770-LANG (within the U.S.)
(212) 647-7706 (outside the U.S.)
(212) 647-7707 FAX

Or browse online by series:

www.peterlang.com